T3-BID-984

THE

MEMBERSHIP

MANUAL

An Encyclopedia of Parliamentary Rules
used at
Business Meetings of Democratic Organizations

by

PROFESSOR JAMES A. McMONAGLE
Wayne State University
Detroit, Michigan

PROFESSOR EMIL R. PFISTER
Central Michigan University
Mt. Pleasant, Michigan

VANTAGE PRESS

NEW YORK   WASHINGTON   HOLLYWOOD

JF
515
. M22

FIRST EDITION

*All rights reserved. No part of this
publication may be reproduced in any form without
prior written consent of the authors.*

Copyright, 1970, by James A. McMonagle and Emil R. Pfister

Published by Vantage Press, Inc.
120 West 31st Street, New York, N.Y. 10001

Manufactured in the United States of America

PREFACE

The uniqueness of *The Membership Manual* lies in its arrangement. When it comes to a question of parliamentary procedure people want to be able to find what they want easily. Rules must be looked up quickly if they are to be effective. The person who has the rule at his fingertips instantly and who has it in language that can be understood is the person who will be most effective. This book satisfies both of these needs.

HOW TO USE THE MEMBERSHIP MANUAL

There are two methods which may be used in finding the right rule when it is needed. Both are effective.

1. The book contains a simple alphabetical index. All of the items are numbered to correspond to the numbers of the items in the body of the book. Also, page numbers are given. Thus, by simply checking the index it is an easy matter to find any item in the book.

2. It is not necessary to use the index. Since the entire book is arranged alphabetically, any item can be found quickly in the same manner that one would use in looking up a word in the dictionary. When there is any doubt as to which word to look up in the title of an item, use either word since the item is repeated. For example, if it is desired to learn about absentee voting, it may be found under the heading "ABSENTEE VOTING" and it also may be found under "VOTING, ABSENTEE."

3. The Manual is indexed for even quicker reference. Place thumb on the desired letter on the back page of the Manual. Flip pages until that letter appears under your thumb. You are now at the beginning of the desired alphabetical letter.

PARLIAMENTARY LAW CHART

TYPE OF MOTION	Must it be SECONDED?	Is it DEBATABLE?	Can it be AMENDED?	Can it be TABLED?	Can it INTERRUPT a speaker?	In order if other question is PENDING?	Does it require a 2/3 VOTE?	Can it be RECONSIDERED?
Adjourn	Yes	No	No	No	No	Yes	No	No
Adjourn, to Fix the Time to Which to	Yes	No	Yes	No	No	Yes	No	Yes
Adopt Committee Report	Yes	Yes	Yes	Yes	No	No	No	Yes
Amend	Yes	1	Yes	2	No	Yes	No	Yes
Amend an Amendment	Yes	1	No	2	No	Yes	No	Yes
Appeal	Yes	3	No	4	Yes	Yes	No	Yes
As if in Committee of the Whole	Yes	Yes	No	Yes	No	Yes	No	No
Blank, Create a	Yes	No	No	No	No	Yes	No	No
Call for Orders of the Day	No	No	No	No	Yes	14	No	No
Committee of the Whole	Yes	Yes	No	Yes	No	Yes	No	No
Consider by Paragraphs	Yes	No	Yes	2	No	Yes	No	No
Division of Assembly	No	No	No	No	Yes	No	No	No
Division of Question	5	No	Yes	No	No	Yes	No	No
Excused from Duty, Ask to Be	No	No	No	No	No	No	No	No
Expunge	Yes	Yes	Yes	Yes	No	No	6	No
Extend Debate	Yes	No	Yes	2	No	Yes	Yes	Yes
Informal Consideration	Yes	Yes	No	Yes	No	Yes	No	7
Limit Debate	Yes	No	Yes	2	No	Yes	Yes	Yes
Main, or Original	Yes	Yes	Yes	Yes	No	No	No	Yes
Modify a Motion, Leave to	No	No	No	No	No	Yes	No	No
Nomination	No	Yes	No	No	No	No	No	No
Nomination, Method of	Yes	No	Yes	No	No	No	No	No
Nominations, to Close	Yes	No	Yes	No	No	No	Yes	No
Nominations, to Reopen	Yes	No	Yes	No	No	No	No	7
Objections to Consideration	No	No	No	No	Yes	Yes	Yes	7
Order, Question of	No	No	No	No	Yes	Yes	No	No
Parliamentary Inquiry	No	No	No	No	Yes	Yes	No	No
Polls, to Close	Yes	No	Yes	No	No	No	Yes	No
Polls, to Reopen	Yes	No	Yes	No	No	No	No	7
Postpone Definitely	Yes	Yes	Yes	2	No	Yes	No	Yes
Postpone Indefinitely	Yes	Yes	No	2	No	Yes	No	8
Previous Question	Yes	No	No	2	No	Yes	Yes	Yes
Privilege, to Raise Question of	No	No	No	15	Yes	Yes	No	No
Ratify	Yes	Yes	Yes	Yes	No	No	No	Yes
Read Document, Leave to	No	No	No	No	No	Yes	No	No
Recess	Yes	No	Yes	No	No	Yes	No	No
Reconsider	Yes	9	No	4	Yes	Yes	No	No
Reconsider and Enter in Minutes	Yes	9	No	4	No	Yes	No	No
Reconsider, Call up Motions to	No	9	No	4	No	No	No	No
Refer to Committee	Yes	Yes	Yes	2	No	Yes	No	Yes
Renew	10	10	10	10	10	10	10	10

(concluded on next page)

PARLIAMENTARY LAW CHART

TYPE OF MOTION	Must it be SECONDED?	Is it DEBATABLE?	Can it be AMENDED?	Can it be TABLED?	Can it INTERRUPT a speaker?	In order if other question is PENDING?	Does it require a 2/3 VOTE?	Can it be RECONSIDERED?
Request Information	No	No	No	No	Yes	Yes	No	No
Request That Document Be Read	No	No	No	No	Yes	Yes	No	No
Resignation	Yes	Yes	Yes	Yes	No	No	No	No
Rescind	Yes	Yes	Yes	Yes	No	No	11	7
Special Order, to Make	Yes	Yes	Yes	Yes	No	Yes	Yes	Yes
Substitute Motion	Yes	Yes	12	Yes	No	Yes	No	Yes
Suspend Rules	Yes	No	No	No	No	13	Yes	No
Table, Lay on	Yes	No	No	No	No	Yes	No	No
Table, Take from	Yes	No	No	No	No	No	No	No
Voting, Method of	Yes	No	Yes	No	No	Yes	No	No
Withdraw a Motion, Leave to	No	No	No	No	No	Yes	No	No

EXPLANATION OF NUMBERS IN CHART

1.—Debatable only if the Motion is debatable.

2.—Only with Motion to which it applies.

3.—No, if it refers to disorderly conduct; to the proper order of business; to an undebatable Motion; or if it arises when a Division of the Assembly is taking place. Otherwise, Yes.

4.—Yes, but it takes the Motion to which it refers to the Table with it.

5.—No, if the subjects in the Motion have no relation one to another. Otherwise, Yes.

6.—It requires a majority of the entire membership.

7.—An affirmative vote cannot be reconsidered.

8.—A negative vote cannot be reconsidered.

9.—Only when called up and then only if the Motion to be reconsidered is debatable.

10.—The Motion it is proposed to renew is covered by the rules governing that type of Motion.

11.—Yes, if no notice has been given in advance. Otherwise, No.

12.—Because a Substitute Motion is really an Amendment, only one Amendment to it may be pending at the same time.

13.—Yes, if connected with the pending Question. Otherwise, No.

14.—Yes, if a Special Order has been set for that hour. Otherwise, No.

15.—Yes, if it becomes pending before the Assembly. Otherwise, No.

INDEX

–D–

–E–

–J–

–L–

–M–

–P–

–Q–

–R–

–S–

$-$T$-$

–U–

–V–

THE
MEMBERSHIP
MANUAL

1. ABSENTEE VOTING. An absent member of a strictly deliberative body cannot vote. This is especially true in governmental bodies, the state legislatures and the United States Congress. In such organizations as these, the members must be present when the vote is called for. Many organizations, such as national societies however, have a membership which is so scattered that it is virtually impossible to get them all together at any one time.

When it is desirable to secure as nearly a total vote as possible, two methods of absentee voting are available. These are by mail and by proxy. Voting by mail is allowed in governmental elections but proxy voting is prohibited. However, absentee voting must be provided for in the rules.

Absentee voting by mail is used in societies which are widely scattered and in organizations which seldom or never meet. It may be used also if a member must be absent but wishes to express his opinion on an issue which is to be decided.

Proxy voting is permitted only if provision for it is made in the rules of the society and if the proxy is given in writing. In this case a member may give his proxy to another member who then votes for both on all issues or on such issues as are specified in the proxy. In proxy voting, it should be noted that governmental law is above the rules of the club, society or organization. Thus if the laws of the State allow members to appoint proxies the only recourse for such a secret lodge or society is not to incorporate.

2. ACCEPT, ADOPT, AGREE TO, DISTINCTION AMONG. When a committee report has been presented to the organization it is said to have been "received" and must be disposed of in one of several ways depending upon its content. In some instances, the motion for the disposal of the report is made by the reporting member of the

27

committee and in other cases the motion should come from some other member of the assembly.

1. When the report contains only information of facts for the assembly, it is only proper for another member to move to "accept" the report. Actually such a motion is not necessary but is usually used to indicate approval of the report of the work of the committee and has the effect of endorsing its contents. If the assembly does not approve the report, the motion to "accept" should be defeated since its passage makes the organization responsible for it.

2. If the committee has made a recommendation but has not placed it in the form of a motion, the proper form is to move to "adopt" the recommendation. This may be made by the reporting member of the committee or by any other member of the assembly.

3. If the recommendation is in the form of a motion or a resolution or resolutions, the proper form is to move to "adopt" and again may be made by anyone but is usually made by the reporting member. A word of warning is important here. If the motion to "adopt" is passed in this instance or in the case of (2) above, it means that the assembly agrees to carry out the recommendation contained in the motion. Therefore, if the assembly does not wish to take the action recommended in the motion or resolution presented by the committee, the motion to "adopt" must be defeated. The parent body need not adopt an entire committee report. It may eliminate parts or adopt with reservations but it may not add to a committee report since then it is not the report of the committee.

The motion to "adopt" is the same as to "agree to." Thus the motion to "accept" a report applies if no action is involved but the assembly accepts responsibility, whereas the motion to "adopt" means to agree to the report and to carry out its recommendations. Frequently these two motions "to accept" and "to adopt" are used interchangeably, however, the above distinction is preferable.

3. ACCEPT A REPORT, MOTION TO. This is actually an unnecessary motion but is usually offered in courtesy to the committee which has reported. It is usually made by someone other than a member of the committee and indicates approval of the report or of the work done. If either the work or the report is not acceptable, the motion "to accept" should be defeated since its passage makes the organization responsible for it.

4. ADJOURN, ANNOUNCING VOTE ON MOTION TO. When the business for which a meeting has been called is completed or when, for any other reason, it is desired to close the meeting, someone moves "to adjourn." If no time has been set for another meeting, this motion has the same status as any main motion and may be amended and debated. When the vote on this motion is equal or nearly equal, the chairman says, "The ayes seem to have it; the ayes have it, the motion is adopted and we stand adjourned without day (sine die)." If the vote is obviously in the affirmative, the expression, "The ayes seem to have it," should be omitted. If a time has been set for another meeting, the chair declares the meeting "adjourned to three o'clock in the afternoon on January 27th," or whatever date has been set.

Preferably before taking a vote on the motion "to adjourn" and certainly before declaring the adjournment, the chair should be certain that all necessary announcements are made and notices given.

5. ADJOURN, EFFECT OF, ON UNFINISHED BUSINESS. The effect of an adjournment upon unfinished business is as follows, unless the organization has adopted rules of its own to the contrary:

1. If the adjournment does not end the session (see SESSION AND MEETING, DISTINCTION BETWEEN) the interrupted business becomes the first in order at the next meeting after the reading of the minutes. It is treated exactly the same as if no adjournment had taken place because an adjourned meeting which does not end a session is legally the continuation of the previous meeting of which it is an adjournment.

2. If an organization has regular sessions as often as quarterly, when the last meeting of a session is adjourned and thus the adjournment closes the session (such as the last meeting of a session of Congress), the same situation as (1) pertains. That is, the interrupted business is taken up at the first meeting of the next session exactly where it was broken off by the adjournment. The exception to this rule is in elected bodies where either all or part of the membership is elected for a definite term. In this case, the unfinished business which was interrupted by the adjournment, becomes dead with the expiration of the term for which all or part of the organization was elected. For example, if a piece of business is interrupted by adjournment of a last meeting of a session and if there is an election of membership in the interval between that session and the next session, then the interrupted business does not hold over and must be introduced as new business

just as though it had not previously been brought up. Thus members of an organization who have been defeated for re-election but who are continuing to meet while finishing their term cannot force their successors to consider a piece of business, because they cannot postpone it nor make it a special order of business if either an election or a change of membership intervenes.

3. If the organization does not meet as often as quarterly and business is interrupted by adjournment which closes the session, the interrupted business is also dead at the end of the session. As in the case of elected bodies as stated above, the interrupted business may be introduced at the next session just as though it had never been considered before.

6. ADJOURN, IN ORDER WHEN NO QUORUM IS PRESENT. If an organization has the power to compel its members to attend meetings and a quorum (see QUORUM) is not present at the time the meeting is supposed to convene, the proper procedure is to wait a few minutes before calling the meeting to order. After the meeting has been opened, if a quorum is still not present, the organization may order a "call of the house" (see CALL OF THE HOUSE) and thus force the absentees into the meeting. Or if it pleases, the organization may provide for an adjourned meeting and then adjourn.

If the organization does not have the power to compel attendance, it has no recourse but to adjourn if a quorum is not present.

Only three motions may be made when a quorum is not present. They are: the motion to fix the time of the next meeting, the motion to fix the time to which to adjourn and the motion to adjourn. No other business may be conducted.

7. ADJOURN, MOTION TO. There are two forms of the motion to adjourn. The *unqualified form* calls for immediate adjournment whereas the *qualified form* sets a future time for adjournment or sets a time for a future meeting.

If it is desired to adjourn immediately and without referring to any future meeting, the unqualified form is used as follows: "I move we adjourn." If this motion is passed, the meeting is adjourned when so declared by the chairman.

If it is desired to adjourn at a given future time, the qualified form is used as follows: "I move that we adjourn at three o'clock." Or if the desire is to adjourn immediately and also to fix the time for reconvening, the qualified form is used as follows: "I move that we adjourn to meet on January twenty-seventh at one o'clock in the afternoon."

When unqualified, the motion to adjourn is always privileged. However, if no arrangement has been made for a future meeting, the effect would be to dissolve the organization. Therefore, if no future meeting has been arranged, the unqualified motion to adjourn yields to the motion "to fix the time of the next meeting." When it is qualified, the motion to adjourn is not privileged and therefore has the same status as any other main motion.

The privileged motion to adjourn takes precedence over all other motions except the motion "to fix the time of the next meeting" to which it yields. Subsidiary motions may not apply to it including the motion to amend and it is not debatable. It cannot be reconsidered but it may be withdrawn. It can be repeated after intervening business even though that business may be only progress in debate. This privilege is liable to abuse however, if a member continues to repeat it merely to obstruct business. Therefore, the chair should refuse to entertain the motion when it is consistently repeated by the same member unless he has reason to believe the motion is sincere.

Like most other motions, the mover must obtain the floor, unless by general consent the motion is entertained without the formality. The motion to adjourn cannot be made during a vote or while verifying a vote, but when the vote is by ballot, it is in order before the result is announced or even before the ballots are counted. In this case, the result of the vote should be announced as soon as business is resumed at the next meeting. No appeal, or question of order, or inquiry may be entertained after the motion to adjourn has been made unless it is a matter that requires a decision before adjournment. This is for the purpose of preventing members from raising questions merely to stall off adjournment.

Before putting the motion to adjourn, the chair should be certain that no important business has been omitted. Even though this motion is undebatable when privileged, this does not prevent calling attention to business that must be settled before adjournment. Even after the vote is taken, a meeting is not adjourned until the chair declares adjournment.

8. ADJOURN, MOTION TO FIX TIME AT WHICH TO. This motion is for the purpose of setting the time for future adjournment. The proper form is to say; "I move we adjourn at ten o'clock in the evening." Its effect is not to adjourn the meeting now but to set a time when the meeting will adjourn. Then when the time arrives, (ten o'clock in the evening, for example) the presiding officer simply declares the meeting adjourned without the necessity of another motion. The motion to fix the time at which to adjourn is a simple main motion without any privilege whatever. It is debatable, requires a simple majority vote, can be amended and have other secondary motions applied to it.

9. ADJOURN, MOTION TO FIX TIME TO WHICH TO. Because of the fact that if an organization adjourns without providing for a future meeting it is automatically dissolved, the motion "to fix the time to which to adjourn" is of prime importance. Therefore, this motion is privileged and outranks all other motions and may be made even after the motion to adjourn has been passed provided the chairman has not declared the meeting adjourned. This motion is undebatable but amendments changing the time are in order. If it is made when no other motion is pending and when the society has already made provisions for a future meeting, it is a main motion, is debatable and may be amended.

If there is no fixed place for meetings or if it is desired to change the meeting place, the motion "to fix the time to which to adjourn" may include the place of meeting. This may also be amended.

This motion is sometimes confused with the motion "to fix the time *at* which to adjourn." (see **ADJOURN, MOTION TO FIX TIME AT WHICH TO.**) The motion "to fix the time to which *to* adjourn" is for the purpose of arranging for a continuation of the same meeting at a later time. The proper form of making the motion is; "I move that when we adjourn, we adjourn to meet on January 27th at one o'clock in the afternoon." The first method of making this motion does not adjourn the present meeting but merely fixes the time for the next meeting. The latter statement of the motion does both. It adjourns the present meeting and at the same time also fixes the time for the next meeting.

10. ADJOURN, NOT IN ORDER DURING VOTE The motion to adjourn enjoys a very high rank in the precedence of motions. For this reason, it is sometimes misused to disrupt business or prevent the conducting of business. The chairman has the right to refuse to recognize the motion if it is proposed for this purpose. The motion to adjourn is never in order (except in case of emergency or disaster) while

32

a vote is being taken. If a vote is taken and a division of the house is called for, the motion to adjourn is out of order until the vote has been retaken since this is still a part of the process of taking the original vote. When the vote is by ballot, it is in order to adjourn before the ballots have been counted and the result announced, if the actual voting is completed.

11. ADJOURN, NOT USED IN COMMITTEE OF THE WHOLE. (SEE also RISE) When the "Committee of the Whole" has completed its business it does not adjourn, it rises and is then ready to report. The proper motion is "to rise and report." This motion is equivalent to adjournment without day in a regular meeting because it means that the committee does not expect to meet again.

12. ADJOURN, SINE DIE. There is no such motion "to adjourn sine die." Sine die is a Latin term meaning without day and refers to the effect of adjournment on the future status of the society. If the simple, unqualified motion to adjourn is passed and if the organization has made no provision for a future meeting, then it is said to have "adjourned sine die" and the effect is to dissolve the organization since a society which adjourns without any provision for another meeting has actually adjourned itself out of existence, but if provision has been made for a future meeting to be held, its effect is merely to close the session.

13. ADJOURN, WHEN NOT PRIVILEGED. The simple or unqualified motion to adjourn is a privileged motion. It takes precedence over all other motions except the motion "to fix the time to which to adjourn" or the motion "to fix the time of the next meeting" (which is the same thing) to which it yields. If the motion to adjourn is qualified in any way, such as adjourning "at a certain time" or "to a certain time" or when, if it is passed, it will dissolve the organization because no provision has been made for a future meeting, it is no longer privileged and is handled the same as any main motion (see **MAIN MOTIONS**). In this case, it is debatable, amendable and subsidiary motions may apply to it.

14. ADOPT, AGREE TO, ACCEPT, DISTINCTION AMONG. When a committee report has been presented to the organization, it is said to have been "received" and must be disposed of in one of several ways depending upon its content. In some instances, the motion for the disposal of the report is made by the reporting member of the committee and in other cases the motion should come from some other member of the assembly.

1. When the report contains only information or facts for the assembly, it is only proper for another member to move to "accept" the report. Actually such a motion is not necessary but is usually used to indicate approval of the report or the work of the committee and has the effect of endorsing its contents. If the assembly does not approve the report, the motion to "accept" should be defeated since its passage makes the organization responsible for it.

2. If the committee has made a recommendation but has not placed it in the form of a motion, the proper form is to move to "adopt" the recommendation. This motion may be made by the reporting member of the committee or by any other member of the assembly.

3. If the recommendation is in the form of a motion or a resolution or resolutions, the proper form is to move to "adopt" and again may be made by anyone but is usually made by the reporting member. A word of warning is important here. If the motion to "adopt" is passed in this instance or in the case of (2) above, it means that the assembly agrees to carry out the recommendation contained in the motion. Therefore, if the assembly does not wish to take the action recommended in the motion or resolution presented by the committee, the motion to "adopt" must be defeated.

4. The motion to "adopt" is the same as to "agree to." Thus the motion to "accept" a report applies if no action is involved but the assembly accepts responsibility, whereas the motion to "adopt" means to agreee to the report and to carry out its recommendations. Frequently these two motions, "to accept" and "to adopt," are used interchangeably, however the above distinction is preferable.

15. ADOPT A REPORT, MOTION TO. Adoption of a committee report by the organization indicates that the assembly not only accepts as its own and assumes responsibility for the report, but also agrees to carry out any action recommended in the report. Thus if the committee recommends that the organization sell its clubhouse and the report is adopted, it means that the assembly has agreed to sell. The adoption of a recommendation of action by a committee is the same as the passage of a main motion to do the same act.

16. AGENDA. An agenda is a list of items of business to be brought before an assembly for consideration at a specific meeting. This should not be confused with order of business which is the over-all procedure of a meeting, beginning with calling the meeting to order and ending with adjournment.

17. AMEND BY FILLING BLANKS. Amendments proposed for the purpose of filling blanks are not treated in exactly the same manner as ordinary amendments since different members of the assembly may propose several names or numbers to fill the blank. Of course, no one member may propose more than one name or number unless by general consent. Any number of names or numbers may be proposed without a second. For example, suppose the motion is before the assembly to authorize the refreshment committee to spend "blank" amount of money. Several members may propose varying amounts of money — ten dollars, fifteen dollars, twenty dollars, twenty-five dollars. All these amounts are proposed as suggestions not as amendments. In this case, the presiding officer would start the vote with the highest amount (twenty five dollars). If this amount did not receive a majority vote, he would then proceed to twenty dollars and so on down until he reached an amount that was approved by the majority. Thus he would arrive at the highest amount that would be approved by the majority of the assembly. On the other hand, suppose the club decided to sell the clubhouse and the "blank" to be filled was to determine the asking price. Several amounts are suggested. The chair would start the vote on the lowest amount to determine how many would be willing to sell for that price and would continue to vote on each successively higher amount until he reached the amount for which the majority would be willing to sell. Thus in the case of filling the blanks with numbers, the vote is started at one end of the scale (either the lowest or highest depending on which is least likely to receive a majority) and proceeds on up or down until a majority is reached. It is a good general rule to start with the largest sum and proceed downward.

In the case of filling the blank with a date, it is wise to start with the most distant and proceed toward the present.

When the blank is to be filled with a time, the chair usually starts with the longest. For example, suppose a contractor is to be allowed a "blank" amount of time to do a job. The question is, what is the maximum time to be allowed. Suggestions are made — two years, one year, six months. The chair starts with two years. If a majority is not willing to allow that much time, the chair proceeds to the next suggested time until he gets a majority vote.

If the blank is to be filled with a name, the chair calls for a vote on each name in the order suggested until one name receives a majority vote. If the blank is to be filled with several names, say three, and only three names are proposed, it does not require a vote. The three proposed names are automatically inserted. But if the blank is to be filled with three names and five are suggested, the chair calls for a vote on each name successively in the order suggested until three have received a majority. If the number of names to be inserted is not specifically stated, all names that receive a majority are inserted in the blank.

The purpose of making a motion which includes blanks is to make it possible to offer several suggestions for filling the blanks without the formality of offering separate amendments. Also, if the amendment process is used, only two (an amendment and an amendment to the amendment) are possible. Whereas, in filling blanks, any number of suggestions may be offered and each considered in turn until one receives majority support. For example, suppose the motion is made to sell the clubhouse. In debate the question arises; "What shall be the asking price?" Someone moves to amend the motion by adding the words, "for $5,000." Then someone else moves to amend the amendment by substituting $7,500 for $5,000. In this case, no further suggestions can be added and the club must consider only two amounts. On the other hand, if a blank is created and the original motion is made "to sell the clubhouse for 'blank' amount," then any number of suggestions may be made as to the amount to fill the blank, "$5,000," "$7,500," "$10,000," "$12,000." Since the least likely asking price is $5,000, the chairman would start with this amount. If it received a majority vote, that would be the amount inserted to fill the blank. But if it did not receive a majority, the chairman would then proceed to the next higher amount until he arrived at an amount that did get a majority vote and that amount would fill the blank.

A good basic rule for the chairman to follow is always to begin with the item least likely to be adopted and to proceed until one item receives a majority vote. That item is then used to fill the blank.

Ordinarily, blanks should be filled before the main motion or resolution is voted upon, but if it is obvious that the main motion is opposed by a large majority, the previous question may be called for before the blank is filled. This would force a vote on the main motion before the blank had been filled. Thus, if the motion is made to sell the clubhouse for "blank" amount and the motion is obviously unpopular and the previous question is passed, a vote is immediately taken on selling the clubhouse. Usually this would be defeated and that would end the matter. But if the motion *should* be passed to "sell the clubhouse for 'blank' amount," then it would be necessary to fill the blank in the manner described above.

18. AMEND BY INSERTING OR ADDING, OR BY STRIKING OUT, AN ENTIRE PARAGRAPH. When it is desired to amend a motion or a resolution by inserting or striking out an entire paragraph or substituting one paragraph for another, it is important to prepare the new paragraph in its best possible form before proposing it so that it will appear at its best and will require as few changes as possible. Since this is an amendment to a main motion or resolution, it cannot be made while another amendment is pending. Once a paragraph has been inserted into a motion or resolution it cannot be changed except by adding to it. Furthermore, once it has been inserted by amendment, a paragraph cannot be struck out except in conjunction with other paragraphs so it is essentially a new amendment. This is to prevent an opposed minority from immediately moving to strike it out as soon as a paragraph has been inserted and thus delaying action on the main motion or quibbling over an already settled issue.

Likewise, once an amendment to strike out a paragraph has been passed, the paragraph cannot be reinstated and an amendment to do so is out of order unless it has been changed to such an extent that it has virtually become a new question.

If the motion to insert a paragraph is lost, it does not prevent another amendment to insert a part of the paragraph or the same paragraph provided it is reworded so it is essentially different or the objectionable parts are corrected.

Also if the motion to strike out a paragraph is lost, it is still in order to amend by striking out parts of the paragraph. Thus, even though an assembly may refuse to strike out an entire paragraph, it still may strike out parts of it by means of another amendment.

19. AMEND BY INSERTING OR ADDING WORDS. It is possible to amend a motion or a resolution by inserting words or by adding words. If the words come within a sentence or a paragraph, the expression "to insert" is used. When the proposed words are to be placed at the end of a sentence, paragraph or motion, the term "to add" is used.

When such an amendment is made and seconded in the proper manner, those who favor it should make certain that the proposed words say exactly what is wanted. This should be done by an amendment to the amendment and before the amendment has been voted on because, once a vote is taken, it is much more difficult to make further alteration. For example, if the amendment is passed, it becomes impossible to eliminate the same words except by eliminating only a part of them or by eliminating all of them along with other words from the original motion. In the same way, if the amendment is rejected, it becomes impossible to propose the same words again unless they are included with other words or are substituted for other words in the original motion and then only if this presents an essentially new motion to the assembly.

The proper form of this amendment is: "I move to amend the motion by inserting the words 'X Y Z' after the word 'C' so the motion will read 'A B C X Y Z D E'."

20. AMEND BY STRIKING OUT AND INSERTING WORDS. The amendment to strike out and insert words is sometimes called "amendment by substitution" and is a combination of the amendment "to strike out words" and the amendment "to insert or add words." It will be noticed that this amendment has two parts, "to strike out" and "to insert." Therefore, if second degree amendments are to be applied to it, those affecting the strike out part should be considered first and then those applying to the insert part. After this, the question is put on the amendment "to strike out and insert."

Once passed, the inserted words cannot be struck out nor the stricken words reinserted unless they are so changed as to make a new question. If lost, it does not preclude the amendment to strike out the same words nor the amendment to insert the same words. Nor does it prevent another amendment "to strike out and insert," provided either the words to be struck out or inserted are enough different so that the motions are not identical. If the words to be struck out are separated, an amendment may be offered to strike as much of the motion as is necessary to include all the words to be struck out and to insert the desired revision including the words to be inserted. If it is desired to insert words in a different place from those struck out, then the inserted words must be materially the same as those struck out. On the other hand, if the words to be inserted are to occupy the same place as the eliminated words, they may, in fact, should, differ from the words struck out, but they must be germane to the rest of the motion. The amendment to strike out words in one place and to insert different words in a different place is not in order. Either the words must be the same and the place changed or the place must be the same and the words changed. If it is desired to make several changes in a motion, it is better to reword the whole motion and offer it as a "substitute motion."

21. AMEND BY STRIKING OUT WORDS. An amendment made for the purpose of deleting words from a motion can be applied only to consecutive words as they appear in the original motion. If it is desired to strike out words which are separated by other words, it is necessary to use separate amendments for each group of words or else to amend by substituting a whole new clause or sentence for the one containing the words. For example, if the motion "That we have a *pot-luck* picnic with a *formal* program on Friday afternoon" is before the organization and it is desired to strike out the underlined words, it requires one amendment to eliminate the word "pot-luck" and another amendment for the word "formal." Or it can be amended by substituting the words "a picnic with a program" for the words "a pot-luck picnic with a formal program." Both the underlined words above cannot be eliminated by one amendment to strike out because they are separated by the words "picnic with a."

The amendment to strike out words, if it is of the first degree, may be amended only by striking out words. The effect of such an amendment to the amendment is to leave the words in the original motion. For instance, in the motion above, "That we have a *pot-luck picnic with a* formal program on Friday afternoon," suppose the amendment is made to strike out the underlined words "pot-luck picnic with a." If this were passed, the motion as amended would read, "That we have a formal program on Friday afternoon." But suppose an amendment to the amendment to strike out the words "picnic with a" were applied to the amendment. Then if the amendment to the amendment were passed and the amendment as amended were passed, the effect would be to return the words "picnic with a" to the original motion so it would read, "That we have a picnic with a formal program." Thus only the word "pot-luck" would have been deleted.

If the amendment to strike out certain words is passed, the words thus eliminated cannot be reinstated unless the wording is so changed as to make it different motion. On the other hand, if the amendment to strike out certain words fails, it does not prevent the following amendments from being made concerning the same words:

1. to strike out the same words and insert other words.
2. to strike out part of the same words.
3. to strike out part of the words and insert other words.
4. to strike out these words along with others.
5. to strike out these words with others and insert words.

22. AMEND BY SUBSTITUTING ONE MOTION FOR ANOTHER.

The motion to substitute one motion for another motion is, in reality, a method of amending. However, because of the peculiar nature of this type of amendment, it is handled in a different manner from an ordinary amendment. The chair should entertain second degree amendments to the original motion and after the motion has been perfected by its supporters, the chair should call for second degree amendments to the substitute motion. When this is done and both motions have been perfected, the organization is ready to vote on the amendment to substitute one motion for the other. If the substitution is adopted, it is still necessary to vote on the main motion as amended because it has only been voted to substitute not to adopt. If the amendment to substitute is lost, the society has only decided that particular substitution shall not be made, therefore, the original motion must still be voted on. When a substitute motion is offered by a committee, it is handled in the same manner.

23. AMEND BY SUBSTITUTING ONE PARAGRAPH FOR ANOTHER.

There are three methods of amending a motion or resolution when the change affects an entire paragraph. An amendment may be made "to strike out" a paragraph, or to "add or insert" a paragraph or "to substitute one paragraph for another." This last is a combination of the first two. Since the debate, if any, will resolve itself around the question of which paragraph to include in the main motion, the chair should first entertain second degree amendments to the original paragraph and after it has been perfected by its supporters, the chair should call for second degree amendments to the proposed paragraph. When this is done and both paragraphs have been perfected, the organization is then ready to vote on the amendment to substitute one paragraph for the other.

Sometimes the substitution includes the entire motion or

40

resolution. It is then called a "substitute motion." In this case and if the substitution is adopted, it is still necessary to vote on the main motion as amended because it has only been voted to substitute not to adopt. When one paragraph has been substituted for another, it cannot be amended except by adding to it. Also the eliminated paragraph cannot be reinserted unless it has been changed enough to make it a new paragraph.

If the amendment to substitute is lost, the organization has only decided that particular paragraph shall not replace the one specified, therefore, it is in order to offer it as a substitution for some other paragraph, or it may be inserted without replacing any paragraph. Also the retained paragraph may be amended in any way desired including the amendment "to strike out." No amendment is in order that presents a question that has already been decided.

It is not correct parliamentary language to speak of substituting one word or part of a paragraph for another. The word "substitute" is applied only to an entire paragraph. However, when a motion or resolution is being considered by sections, it is in order to "substitute" one section for another. One cannot move to substitute one entire resolution or report for another until all sections have been considered and the entire resolution or report has been opened for amendment by the chair.

When a motion or resolution is referred to a committee and at the time of referral has first and second degree amendments pending, they may report it back with a substitute motion or resolution which they recommend. In this case, the chair should first take up the pending amendments, then the substitute motion recommended by the committee which is handled exactly the same as any other amendment to substitute.

24. AMEND, MOTION TO. The purpose of the motion to amend is to make the main motion more satisfactory to the society. Some motions cannot be amended, (see **AMENDED, MOTIONS THAT CANNOT BE**) but the motion to amend can be applied to all others and can itself be amended, however, an amendment to an amendment cannot be amended. The motion to amend takes precedence over the motion to postpone indefinitely as well as the motion to which it is applied and it yields to all other secondary motions and to all incidental and privileged motions. It requires a majority vote even when the motion to which it is applied requires a two-thirds vote. The motion to amend is debatable. An amendment must be germane to the motion. Only one amendment to a main motion may be pending at a time, but as many amendments as desired may be used if each is disposed of before the next is made. The same rule applies to an amendment of an amendment. The proper form is; "I move to amend the motion (or amendment) by —— (state the amendment)."

25. AMENDED, MOTIONS THAT CANNOT BE. The motion to amend cannot be applied to any of the following motions:

1. to adjourn (except when it is qualified or when made in an assembly with no provisions for a future meeting.)
2. call for the orders of the day.
3. questions of order and appeal.
4. to object to consideration of a question.
5. call for a division of the assembly or house.
6. to grant leave to withdraw a motion.
7. to grant leave to speak after indecorum.
8. a request of any kind.
9. to take up a question out of its proper order.
10. to suspend the rules.
11. to lay on the table.
12. to take from the table.
13. to reconsider.
14. the previous question.
15. to postpone indefinitely.
16. to amend an amendment.
17. to fill a blank.
18. a nomination.
19. a point of order.
20. to ask leave to speak out of order.
21. for the reading of papers.
22. raising a question of privilege.
23. to accept a report.
24. to close nominations.
25. to enter in the minutes.
26. to go into executive session.
27. to place on file.
28. to receive.

26. AMENDMENT, IMPROPER. An amendment is improper and out of order and may not be made when:

1. It is not germane to the subject to be amended.

2. It changes the affirmative to the negative or the reverse. For example, if the motion is made "That we sell our clubhouse," the amendment to insert the words "do not" before the word "sell" would be out of order because it reverses the motion and changes the affirmative to the negative. Likewise if the motion was that "We do not sell our clubhouse," the amendment to strike out the words "do not" would not be in order because it changes the motion from the negative to the affirmative.

3. It is the same as another motion already decided at the same session. Suppose the motion has been passed "that we sell the property adjacent to the clubhouse." Then later in the same session, it is moved "that we sell our clubhouse." An amendment to add the words "and the property adjacent to" would be out of order. This would be just as true if the motion to sell the adjacent property had failed earlier because it had been considered at the same session.

4. It changes one form of an amendment to another form. If an amendment is made to "strike out," an amendment to the amendment cannot be made "to strike out and insert" since this is a different form of amendment.

5. It substitutes one form of amendment for another form.

6. It strikes out the word "resolved" in a resolution.

7. It changes the meaning of the main motion in such a way as to leave no reasonable motion before the group.

8. It is frivolous or absurd.

27. AMENDMENT, MOTIONS THAT ARE NOT SUBJECT TO. All original main motions are subject to amendment. All other motions may be amended except the following:

1. to adjourn (except when qualified or when no provision has been made for a future meeting).

2. call for the orders of the day.

3. questions of order and appeal.

4. objection to consideration of a question.

5. call for a division of the house.

6. to grant leave to withdraw a motion.

7. to grant leave to speak after indecorum.

8. a request of any kind.

9. to take up a question out of its proper order.
10. to suspend the rules.
11. to lay on the table.
12. to take from the table.
13. to reconsider.
14. the previous question.
15. to postpone indefinitely.
16. to amend an amendment.
17. to fill a blank.
18. a nomination.

28. AMENDMENT MUST BE GERMANE TO THE SUBJECT TO BE AMENDED. The word germane is defined as "related to, akin to, or relevant to." An amendment must be germane to the motion which it is intended to amend. That is, it must be "related to, akin to, or relevant to," the subject to which it is applied. Also an amendment of the second degree, that is, an amendment to an amendment, must be germane not only to the amendment to which it is applied but, also, through it, to the main motion. An amendment which changes the main motion in such a way that it becomes a new motion is not germane nor can a new motion be introduced under the guise of an amendment. On the other hand, an amendment may conflict completely with the spirit of the main motion to which it is applied and still be germane. For example, a motion "to thank" an individual may be amended by substituting the word "condemn" for the word "thank" because it is related to the main motion and therefore is germane.

Following are examples of amendments that are germane and not germane:

1. An amendment adding the words "and ping pong paddles" to the motion "to purchase a ping pong table" is germane but it would not be germane to add an amendment "to hire a ping pong coach."

2. If the motion "to pay the expenses of the president to the national convention" were pending, it would be germane to amend by inserting the words "and vice-president" after the word "president." It would not be germane to move an amendment "to thank the national committee for the invitation to attend."

3. A motion "to purchase a typewriter for the secretary" could be amended by adding "and a typewriter table" and this in turn could be amended by an amendment of the second degree "to include a chair

44

for the table." But the main motion could not be amended by adding a motion "to increase his salary."

4. A motion to thank two members for their work on a certain project could be amended by adding the name of a third member provided it was for the same project, but the third name could not be added if he were to be thanked for a different project.

29. AMENDMENT OF ANYTHING ADOPTED AS A MAIN MOTION. Certain matters such as the constitution, by-laws, standing rules and rules of order may be amended after they have been adopted because they are permanent instruments of the society. The method of amending documents of this sort should be prescribed in the document itself. On the other hand, an ordinary piece of business, once it is adopted, may not be amended. For example, if the motion has been passed "to have a picnic on July fourth at ten o'clock in the morning in X park," it is not possible to change the motion in any way. The time to make such changes is at the time the motion was pending and not after it has been adopted.

The motion to amend the constitution, by-laws, standing rules or rules of order is a main motion not a secondary one and therefore is treated in every way as such.

30. AMENDMENT OF CONSTITUTION, BY-LAWS AND RULES OF ORDER. Every constitution, set of by-laws and rules of order and standing rules should contain an article providing a method by which they may be amended. If they do not contain such an article, they may be amended at any regular (but not special) meeting of the society by a majority vote of the *entire* membership. If a copy of the proposed amendment was submitted in writing at the immediately preceding meeting, then they may be amended by a two-thirds vote of *those voting* if a quorum is present. The above is the basic parliamentary rule for amending these documents. Beyond this rule, each organization may and should set up its own rules.

In an organization which meets as infrequently as once a year, such as a national society which meets only in annual national conventions, provision should be made for notifying members by mail of a proposed amendment to the constitution, by-laws or standing rules instead of notice being required at the previous meeting in order to make it unnecessary to wait a whole year to modify or amend the document.

In a society which meets frequently but which also holds monthly, quarterly or annual meetings devoted especially to business, it is best to allow amendments to be made *only* at these less frequent meetings rather than at any ordinary meeting. However, an organization that holds frequent regular meetings and does not hold extra monthly, quarterly or annual meetings, should make provision to amend at the ordinary regular meetings.

In specifying that previous notice of a proposed amendment be given or that the amendment be previously submitted, the expression "*the* previous meeting" should be used and not "*a* previous meeting" since the latter would permit delay of consideration of adoption and members who may have attended for the express purpose of being present when the amendment was considered could be defeated. This would also defeat the object of giving previous notice which is to give opportunity to those especially interested to attend.

The expression "a two-thirds vote *of the members*" should never be used since even in small societies it is almost impossible to secure one hundred percent attendance and in large societies, full attendance is so rare that an amendment could never be accomplished. On the other hand, a majority vote of the full membership is possible as is also a two-thirds vote of those voting. If it is desired to require a larger majority than two-thirds of those voting, the rule may be made to require passage by a vote of "two-thirds of those present." The assumption is that with previous notice being given, all persons really interested in the fate of the amendment, will attend the meeting at which it is to be considered.

Frequently it is not required to give previous notice in writing, in which case, oral notice is sufficient. Also frequently, written notice is not required to contain the exact amendment but only a general statement of its content. In fact, unless the rules of the society specify that the exact amendment be submitted, a general statement of content is always sufficient.

The previous appointment of a committee to revise the constitution, by-laws or standing rules and ordered to report at a given meeting constitutes sufficient notice unless the method of amending stated in the rules specifically requires that the complete amendment be submitted in writing. On the other hand, if such requirement is made, one of two procedures would have to be followed. Either the committee would have to prepare the revision, submit it in writing and then wait until the next meeting to consider its adoption or they would have to prepare the revision, submit it to the membership by mail and then consider it at the next meeting. Which of these procedures would be followed would depend upon the statement of the method of amending contained in the instrument to be amended. A society should exercise great care in amending a document as important as its constitution, by-laws or standing rules. Whatever rules are provided for amending should be followed explicitly.

As soon as an amendment to the constitution, by-laws or standing rules has been adopted it goes into effect immediately unless the motion to adopt contains a provision to the contrary or unless a motion to that effect has been previously adopted. If the motion to adopt does not contain a provision setting a time for the amendment to go into effect and it is desired to do so, it may be accomplished by an amendment to the motion to adopt. Such amendment has the same status as any amendment to a main motion and requires only a majority vote.

When a proposed amendment to the constitution, by-laws or standing rules is being considered, it may be amended by a majority vote. It is not required that an organization adopt a proposed amendment just as it stands, however there are certain restrictions which limit the extent to which a proposed amendment may be changed. It is not proper to extend the proposed amendment beyond the limits stated therein. The reason for this is to prevent the proposal of a very slight change, which might not attract attention, from being extended (by a majority vote) to a serious modification that would be undesirable. For example, suppose the membership in the organization were limited to one hundred persons by the constitution and an amendment were proposed to increase the membership to one hundred twenty persons. An amendment to this proposal would be in order to change the number to one hundred fifteen or to one hundred ten or to any number *between* one hundred and one hundred twenty. It would not be in order to amend the proposal by changing the number to two hundred fifty or to any number *over* the proposed one hundred twenty. Nor would it be proper to amend the proposal to any number under or *less than* the original one hundred as stated in the constitution.

Also it is not in order to amend a proposed change of a constitution, by-law or standing rule by adding to it any matter with which it is not concerned. To illustrate this, suppose the constitution provided for a membership of forty married couples and an amendment was pending to change this number to fifty married couples. This proposal could be amended to change the number to anything *between*

47

forty and fifty, but could not be amended to include single persons since this would be including a matter outside the intent of the proposed amendment.

When a committee is appointed to revise a set of rules such as the constitution, by-laws or standing rules, the report of the committee is not handled in the same manner as an ordinary amendment of the rules. In the first place, the appointment of such a committee is sufficient notice that they will submit a new set of rules to take the place of the old. Furthermore, the adoption of the new set of rules should be handled in the same manner as was used in adopting the original rules. That is, the procedure is the same as if the rules were being adopted for the first time. They may be changed by both first and second degree amendments. However, since the old rules are not pending, no amendment may be made to change or perfect them.

The constitution or by-laws may be changed even though that change may affect the status of an officer already serving, even to the extent of eliminating the office. For example, if the constitution provided for a corresponding secretary and a member were serving in that capacity, it would be possible to amend the constitution and eliminate the office. Or if the by-laws provided for a salary of $2,000 to be paid to the executive secretary and a member was doing the job and receiving the salary, the by-laws could be amended to cut or increase the salary. Of course, it is also possible in making amendments of this sort, to include the provision that the change will not go into effect until the end of the term of office of the present incumbent. This parliamentary rule is based on the assumption that there exists a contract between the officer and the society which can be changed or terminated by either party if due consideration is given to the other party. For example, an executive secretary whose salary has been cut and who has resigned as a result, would have no right to refuse to perform his duties up to the time the resignation had become effective or until his successor had been secured. On the other hand, the society would have no right to compel him to continue beyond a reasonable amount of time.

The article which deals with the method of amending the constitution, by-laws or standing rules of a society should be very carefully written. The word amend covers all proposals for change in such documents and it is undesirable to use any substitute words such as "add to," "annul," "repeal," "strike out," etc.

31. AMENDMENT OF FIRST AND SECOND DEGREE. An amendment of a motion is an amendment of the *first* degree. An amendment of an amendment is an amendment of the *second* degree. An amendment of an amendment of an amendment is an amendment of the *third* degree and is too complicated so is never permitted. It is never in order to propose more than one amendment of the same degree at one time. In other words, if an amendment of the first degree is before the organization, another first degree amendment may not be offered until the first has been disposed of. The same is true of amendments of the second degree.

The motion "to amend" takes precedence over the motion "to postpone indefinitely" and yields to all other secondary or subsidiary motions. It also yields to all privileged and incidental motions except the motion "to divide the question." It can be applied to all motions *except* the following:

1. to adjourn (except when qualified or when made in an assembly which has no provision for a future meeting.)
2. to call for the orders of the day.
3. questions of order and appeal.
4. objection to consideration of a question.
5. call for a division of the house.
6. to grant leave to withdraw a motion.
7. to grant leave to speak after indecorum.
8. a request of any kind.
9. to take up a question out of its proper order.
10. to suspend the rules.
11. to lay on the table.
12. to take from the table.
13. to reconsider.
14. call for the previous question.
15. to postpone indefinitely.
16. to amend an amendment.
17. to fill a blank.
18. nominations.

An amendment is debatable if the motion to which it applies is debatable, otherwise it is not. It requires only a majority vote regardless of the vote required on the main motion. On the other hand, an amendment to a constitution, by-laws or any other previously adopted rule of an organization, requires a two-thirds vote. An amendment to such an amendment, however, requires only a majority.

Amendments must be disposed of in the reverse order in which they are proposed. That is:

1. if a motion is on the floor, and
2. if an amendment to the motion is offered, and
3. if an amendment to the amendment is offered, they must be handled in the following order:
   a. the amendment to the amendment,
   b. the amendment (as amended, if it was),
   c. the main motion (as amended, if it was).

Amendments may be made in the following ways:

1. by substitution—that is, by substituting a whole new motion for the original motion.
2. by striking out—that is, by striking out or deleting words, phrases, sentences or even whole paragraphs.
3. by inserting—that is, by inserting words, phrases, sentences or paragraphs.
4. by striking out and inserting—that is, by striking out words, phrases, sentences or paragraphs and inserting in their place other words, phrases, sentences or paragraphs.

The proper form for offering an amendment is:

1. "I move to amend by substituting (such a motion) for (the pending motion)."
2. "I move to amend by striking out (such a word, etc.)."
3. "I move to amend by inserting the word (or phrase, etc.) after the word . . . ."
4. "I move to amend by striking out (such a word, etc.) and inserting the word (or phrase, sentence or paragraph)."

32. AMENDMENT OF PROPOSITIONS CONTAINING SEVERAL PARAGRAPHS . In parliamentary procedure, the word paragraph is used not only to mean paragraph in the ordinary sense, but also to indicate sections, resolutions, articles or any other normal subdivision of a proposition. Thus if a resolutions committee were to recommend several resolutions for consideration and each of these resolutions were acted upon separately one at a time, the assembly would be said to be considering them "by paragraph."

When a committee makes a recommendation for the adoption of a report containing several paragraphs, such as a series of resolutions, a constitution, a set of by-laws, a set of standing rules or any other matter of this sort, the procedure is as follows:

1. The reporting member of the committee (usually the chairman) reads the entire recommendation and moves its adoption. If he should fail to make such a motion, the chair may call for it and the motion to adopt may be made by any member of the assembly. The chair may even assume that the motion has been made and state the question as though it had. However, this last procedure, although it is legal, is dangerous because it may result in confusion. It is better to have the motion to adopt clearly stated and seconded.

2. After the motion to adopt has been made, seconded and stated (restated by the chair), the recommendation is submitted in writing to the secretary who then reads the first paragraph. This paragraph is then debated and, if desired, it is amended in the same manner as any main motion. When the debate is complete and all proposed amendments acted upon, the paragraph is *not* adopted but the secretary moves on to the next paragraph and it is considered in the same manner.

3. When all paragraphs have been considered in this manner, the secretary then reads the entire proposal *as amended* and another opportunity is given to make any other amendments desired including adding paragraphs or deleting them. Then the vote is taken on the original motion to adopt and if passed, the document is adopted.

33. AMENDMENT OF REPORTS OF COMMITTEES OR BOARDS.

When the report of a committee includes a recommendation for action, it should be accompanied by a motion to adopt the report. When this is done, the motion to adopt becomes an ordinary main motion and may be treated as such. This being the case, the recommendation may be amended in the same manner as any other regular motion. It should be pointed out, however, that if the matter was referred to the committee in the first place, objection to consideration of the motion to adopt may not be made since the matter was previously considered at the time it was referred. Also it should be made clear that any amendments which are applied or attached to the recommendation are acts of the assembly and are not a part of the committee's recommendation. The assembly has no right to change the report of the committee in any way, although it does have the right to alter what it adopts. Thus if the Picnic Committee recommends that the society hold a picnic on July fourth at three o'clock in the afternoon and this recommendation is amended to change the time to one o'clock in the afternoon, the minutes should clearly indicate that the recommendation of the committee was three o'clock because the recommendation of the committee cannot be altered by the society. Since the time was changed to one o'clock by the society, this should be indicated as an act of the society not as the recommendation of the committee. The committee's report should be recorded exactly as it was made and any alterations in it made by the assembly should be indicated as such.

34. AMENDMENT OF RESOLUTIONS. The process of amending a resolution is not basically different from that of amending an ordinary motion since a resolution is merely a somewhat different form of a main motion. When the motion to adopt a resolution has been properly made, seconded and stated (stated by the chair), it is ready for debate. If a member wishes to amend it, he rises, obtains the floor and states his amendment. The chair then calls for a second and if seconded, declares the amendment open for debate which must be confined to the amendment. When debate is completed, the chair proceeds to a vote on the amendment and declares it passed or failed as the case may be. He then calls for further discussion on the resolution as amended (if the amendment passed) or on the resolution (if the amendment failed). A resolution, like any main motion, may be amended any number of times as long as the amendments are proposed and considered one at a time. An amendment to a resolution must be germane to the resolution. An amendment may not be made to strike out the word "resolved" from a resolution. An amendment to an amendment of a resolution is in order since it is an amendment of the second degree.

35. AMENDMENT OF STANDING RULES. Standing rules deal with the business of the organization. They are the rules which govern the ordinary operation or activity but which are not of such importance that they should be included in the constitution or by-laws. They should be easily adapted to the immediate needs of the moment and should serve as a general guide for procedure. Standing rules may be adopted without previous notice and by a two-thirds vote. They do not interfere with the freedom of operation of the society because a majority vote will suspend them. Of course, it goes without saying that the standing rules must not be in conflict with the constitution, by-laws or rules of order.

36. ANNOUNCING THE RESULT OF A VOTE. When a motion has been properly made, seconded, stated, debated and voted on, it becomes the duty of the chair to announce the result of the vote. When a voice vote is used, the chair says; "Will those in favor of the motion to . . . . make it known by saying 'aye.' Those opposed 'no.' The ayes (or nos) have it and the motion is carried (or lost)," depending on which side has the majority. If the vote is close and the chair cannot decide which side has won, it is wise for him to change the method of voting. He should say, "The chair is in doubt. All those in favor of the motion to . . . . make it known by raising the right hand. Those opposed raise their right hand. The ayes (or nos) have it and the motion is carried (or lost)." The chair has the right to ask the secretary to assist him in the count and to consult with him to determine the accuracy of the count. If the vote is a tie and he wishes to vote in the affirmative, he announces that it is a tie vote, announces his vote for the affirmative and declares the motion passed.

37. ANNUAL REPORTS OF BOARDS AND THEIR AMENDMENT. If a society has a board of directors or similar committee, it is usual to provide for an annual report. Usually this comes at the end of the fiscal or calendar year or at the end of the term of office of the board. The report contains a brief account of what has been done during the year and makes recommendations for the future. It is common practice for the society to adopt the report and publish it in its annual proceedings. In case any changes in, or amendment of, the report are made by the society, these changes should be indicated as such and the report should be preceded by a note to that effect. The minutes should read as follows:

"The Board of Directors submitted its annual report which, after discussion and amendment, was adopted as follows, the words in parentheses having been struck out and those underlined (or in italics) having been inserted before the report was adopted."

The society has no right to change the report of the board. It may refuse to adopt the report or allow it to be printed, but it cannot make it appear that the report contained anything different from what has been reported by the board. By the use of parentheses and underlining or some other similar device, it can be indicated exactly what was reported by the board and what was adopted by the society.

38. ANNUL, MOTION TO. The purpose of the motion to annul, repeal or rescind is to undo an act already taken. This can be done if no action has been taken to carry out the act and no commitments have been made. However, if any action has been taken, the motion to annul, repeal or rescind is out of order. It is a special main motion and therefore cannot interrupt anything that is on the floor. It is not in order during the same meeting at which the action to which it is applied was passed and it may be applied only to business that has been passed since it is obvious that it is impossible to repeal something that is not in effect. Since it is a main motion, it requires a second, is debatable and may have applied to it any motion that would apply to any other main motion.

If no previous notice of intent to make the motion to annul, repeal or rescind is given, the motion requires a two-thirds vote to pass. However, if proper notice has been given either at the previous meeting or in the notice of meeting, then it requires only a majority vote. This notice may interrupt business, but may not interrupt a speaker who has the floor.

39. APPEAL FROM DECISION IN ASSIGNING THE FLOOR. If there is dissatisfaction or objection to the way the chairman is assigning the floor to members for motions or debate, any two members may appeal. One makes the appeal and the other seconds it. Such an appeal is handled in the same way as any appeal from the decision of the chair. If the chair himself is in doubt as to who should be given the floor, he may put it up to a vote of the assembly. The member receiving the most votes is given the floor.

40. APPEAL FROM THE DECISION OF THE CHAIR. It is the responsibility of the presiding officer to make rulings on all matters of decorum, parliamentary procedure, germaneness of motion and debate, violations of the constitution, by—laws, standing rules and rules of order. In all such cases, when a member violates any of these rules, he is declared "out of order." If a member, who has been declared out of order by the chair, does not agree with the decision, he may "appeal from the decision of the chair" unless there is already another appeal pending at the time, in which case, the second appeal must wait until the first appeal has been decided. Appeal must be made at the time the chair made the decision or ruling. If a member does not appeal immediately, that is, if any business or debate takes place before the appeal is made, it is too late to appeal.

Any appeal from the decision of the chair may interrupt speaker, requires a second and may not be amended. However, an appeal yields to orders of the day, lay on the table, question of privilege and adjourn. Appeals may be made without the maker being recognized by the chair. If the appeal is on a matter of indecorum, it is not debatable. In all other cases it is debatable. Whether debatable or not, the chairman may state his reasons for the decision without leaving the chair. The procedure in appeal is as follows:

1. the chair makes a decision.
2. the member, without waiting to be recognized, says; "Mr. Chairman, I appeal from the decision of the chair."
3. The appeal is seconded.
4. the chair says; "Appeal from the decision of the chair on (states the matter) has been made and seconded. All those in favor of the decision of the chair make it known by (state the method of voting such as raising the right hand). Those opposed. The ayes have it and the decision of the chair is sustained." (Or, "The nos have it and the decision of the chair is overruled.")

A majority vote in the negative supports the appeal and overrides the chair. A tie vote or a majority vote in the affirmative will support the chair and override the appeal. The vote on an appeal may be reconsidered, but an appeal may not be renewed.

If a motion is on the floor at the time an appeal is made, the motion may or may not adhere to the appeal depending on whether or not the decision of the chair affects the status of the main motion. For example, if a matter is on the floor and a member is declared out of order because his remarks are not germane, the status of the motion is not at stake and it does not adhere to the appeal. On the other hand, if a member makes a motion and he is declared out of order because his motion is in violation of the constitution, then the fate of the motion is affected by the decision and will adhere to the appeal. If the main motion does not adhere to the appeal, the consideration of the main motion is continued as soon as the appeal is decided.

41. ARCHIVIST, DUTIES OF. In the archives of a society are kept the legal documents, historical documents and documents relating to activities, rights, agreements and laws. The archivist is the custodian of the archives. It is his duty to protect and keep these records and to be responsible for making them available to members.

42. ASSEMBLY, HOW ORGANIZED AND BUSINESS CONDUCTED

IN. When a group of persons wish to call a meeting of people who are not organized in a society, several preliminary preparations should be made:

1. they should agree on a date, time and place of meeting.
2. they should decide who is to be invited to attend.
3. they should arrange for one of them to call the meeting to order.
4. they should arrange for someone to nominate a chairman and who should be nominated.
5. they should arrange for someone to explain the purpose of the meeting.
6. Sometimes it is a good policy to have a set of resolutions prepared and ready to submit to the meeting.

When the time of the meeting arrives and it is felt that most of those who are going to attend have arrived, the person previously chosen to call the meeting to order steps to the fromt, gets attention and says, "The meeting will please come to order. The chair will entertain nominations for a chairman of this meeting." At this time the person previously selected to nominate the chairman does so by nominating the person previously agreed upon. Frequently the person who called the meeting to order makes the nomination. In this case he says; "The meeting will please come to order. I move that Mr. X be elected as chairman." If this motion is seconded, he calls for a vote and if passed, Mr. X takes the chair. This is frequently the safer method especially in large groups because there is less chance of a popular, but incompetent person being made chairman.

As soon as the newly elected chairman takes over, which he does as soon as he is elected, he calls for nominations for a secretary. If several names are placed in nomination, the chairman calls for a vote on the first name heard. If this person receives a majority he is declared elected. If not, the chairman proceeds to the second name and so on until one does receive a majority. The secretary should sit at the front of the room near the chairman.

The chairman should stand while conducting business although he may sit down during debate if he wishes. It is unnecessary to second a nomination though it is not illegal and may be done if a member wishes. A nomination is not debatable, but this does not prevent the person making a nomination from saying a few words in favor of his candidate.

Usually a chairman and secretary are the only officers needed in an assembly of this sort, but if others are wanted they may be elected in the same manner as the secretary.

43. ASSEMBLY OR HOUSE, DIVISION OF THE. When a vote has been taken and the result announced, if a member questions the announced result, he may call for a division of the assembly or house. This means that the vote must be retaken. The person calling for a division does not need to be recognized by the chair. He merely says; "I doubt the vote" or merely calls out, "Division." This call must be made, however, before any other business has been announced. It does not require a second, is not debatable or amendable and may not be reconsidered. It is not voted on, but is decided by the chair who must proceed immediately to retake the vote.

If the original vote was by voice or by a show of hands, another method such as rising must be used for the second vote. Where there is any doubt about the outcome of a vote, any member has the right to insist on a division. However, the chair should not allow this privilege to be misused. If the decision of the first vote was perfectly clear, the chair should refuse to entertain a call for a division. He may do this by stating that a division is unnecessary. If the member still insists, he must do so by appealing from the decision of the chair which will probably die for want of a second or if it does get a second, will certainly lose when the appeal is voted on. If a member wishes for a roll call vote or a vote by ballot he may move to that effect. This requires a second and a majority vote.

Originally a division of the house meant exactly that. All those in favor of the proposition moved to the right side of the hall and those opposed to the left and each side was counted. This practice was still followed in Canada.

44. ASSEMBLY, RIGHT OF, TO EJECT PERSONS. Every organization, society or assembly has the right to determine who may and who may not attend its meetings. This determination may be made in the constitution, by-laws or standing rules of the society. Or it may be made by a vote of the assembly. Thus either by a rule or by a vote, the society may decide to eject a person or persons. When this decision is made it is the responsibility of the presiding officer to carry out the decision and he may use whatever force necessary to see that it is done.

If the society has a sergeant-at-arms, he may be called on by the presiding officer to eject the unwelcome person and he may request whatever assistance is necessary to carry out the order. If there is no sergeant-at-arms, the chairman may appoint members to do the evicting.

Force may be used to eject a party, but care should be exercised because if the members should be unnecessarily forceful, they may be liable for damages. This liability applies only to the ejecting person and does not apply to the presiding officer nor to the society because they did not exceed their legal rights in ordering the ejection.

45. ASSEMBLY, RIGHT OF, TO PUNISH MEMBERS. It is the inherent right of any assembly, organization or society to make its own rules and laws provided these laws do not conflict with the laws of the nation, state or municipality within which the organization operates. The society also has the right to enforce its laws upon its members and to punish any member for disobedience of the law. The most extreme penalty that may be used is expulsion from membership.

If the society deems it necessary for its own protection to publish or give public notice that the person is no longer a member, it may do so. The society does not have the right to go beyond what is necessary for its protection however. For example, the society may make a public statement that the party is no longer a member, but it may not publish the charges of which he was found guilty and for which he was expelled. The publication of these charges is grounds for libel.

46. ASSEMBLY, TRIAL BY MEMBERS OF. Every assembly, society or organization has the right to require its members to live within the legal and moral code set up by the society. Therefore the organization has the right to investigate the character and actions of its members. The society can request its members to testify and can punish them by expulsion if they refuse. When a charge is brought against the character of a member, it is usually referred to an investigating or disciplinary committee. Some organizations have a regular standing committee on discipline which reports any cases brought to its attention.

When a case is brought to the attention of a committee, whether standing or special, it investigates and reports. The committee report, while it need not go into complete detail, should make a recommendation of action and should contain resolutions to cover the case so it is unnecessary to make any additional resolutions from the floor. When it is recommended that a member be expelled from the society, the committee usually offers two resolutions. One fixes the time to which to adjourn and the second instructs the secretary to order the accused to appear before the assembly at the adjourned meeting to show cause why he should not be expelled.

As soon as charges have been preferred and the member notified to appear for trial, he is technically under arrest. He is deprived of all his rights as a member of the society until the trial is completed. A member should not be tried at the same meeting that he is accused unless he wishes it or unless the charge is something he has done at the meeting.

The secretary should notify the member in writing to appear at the appointed time and should include with this notice a copy of the charges against him. If the member fails to appear, it is usually sufficient reason for immediate expulsion.

If the member appears at the appointed time, he is given a form of trial with the membership of the society sitting in judgment. The committee again reports and frequently this is the only evidence necessary. However the committee may offer additional evidence if it wishes. The accused member has the right to make any explanation he wishes and introduce evidence and witnesses. Both parties have the right to cross-examine opposing witnesses and refute opposing testimony. If the accused wishes, he may be represented by counsel as long as the counsel is a member in good standing of the organization.

When all the evidence for both sides has been presented, the accused member should leave the room and the membership should consider the evidence and finally vote on the proposed punishment. The vote should be by ballot unless the evidence, one way or the other, is so overwhelming that the decision is reached by general consent. Expulsion should require a two-thirds vote with no less than a quorum voting including the members of the investigating committee.

There is considerable difference between a trial in a court of law and one in a society, organization or assembly. In a court of law concrete evidence is necessary to convict. Common knowledge is not enough. In a society where the greatest punishment is expulsion, common knowledge or moral conviction is sufficient for a verdict of guilty.

Sometimes, if the nature of the accusation is very delicate or it appears that the trial will be long and complicated, the accused appears before a committee instead of before the whole assembly. When this is done, the committee hears the evidence and reports its recommendations to the society. The committee offers resolutions to cover the punishment and the society acts on these resolutions. When the report of the committee is submitted, the accused is permitted to reply and then leaves the room while the society votes. All members of the society, except the accused are permitted to vote.

47. ASSEMBLY, WORD TO BE REPLACED BY THE NAME OF THE BODY. The term "assembly" is a general term used to designate any deliberative body. Whenever the group has a name, that name should replace the word assembly when motions are made or other reference is made to the body. It is better to say, "I move that this Club . . . ." rather than, I move that this assembly . . . ."

48. ASSEMBLIES, RIGHTS OF. The following are the inherent rights of any legal society, club or organization:
1. right to makes its own rules and laws provided they do not conflict with any higher society of which it is a part nor with the laws of any governmental body under whose jurisdiction or within whose territory it operates.
2. right to enforce its rules and laws.
3. right to punish members, the most extreme penalty being expulsion from the society.
4. right to protect itself by publishing the fact that an expelled person is no longer a member of the society but not the right to publish the reasons for his expulsion.
5. right to incorporate in accordance with the laws of the state in which it operates.
6. right to determine who shall be present at meetings.
7. right to forcibly eject undesirable persons using sufficient force to effect his removal but no more.
8. right to assistance by the police in ejecting undesirable persons or in maintaining order.
9. right to impeach any of its officers and to remove them from office.

49. AUDITOR AND AUDITING COMMITTEE. Some organizations, because the accuracy of the financial report is so important, have a certified public accountant audit their books periodically, usually at the end of the fiscal year. Other groups, whose financial accuracy is not so important, appoint an auditing committee to check the accuracy of the books. In either case, the duty of the auditor or the auditing committee is to check the financial accounts and to certify as to their correctness.

If the report of the auditor or auditing committee is accepted, it is the same as approving the report of the treasurer and relieves him of any further responsibility except in case of fraud.

50. AUDITOR'S REPORT, FORM OF. Financial reports are for the information of the members of the society. Too much detail in the way of specific receipts and disbursements only serve to confuse and do not enlighten. It is the duty of the auditor or auditing committee to go into these details but the report to the membership need not contain them. The amount of such detail to be included in the auditor's report must be determined by the society itself.

At the end of the regular financial report of the treasurer, the auditing committee merely makes the following statement:

Examined and found correct

George Smith
Harry Brown
    Auditing Committee

51. BALLOT, BLANKS NOT COUNTED IN. A blank piece of paper or printed ballot which has not been filled out or checked should not be counted as a ballot and does not figure in the total number of votes cast. Such blanks are simply ignored and discarded as waste. Also a blank piece of paper which is folded with an otherwise proper ballot does not cause the ballot to be rejected. Often persons who do not wish to reveal the fact will turn in a blank piece of paper in place of a ballot. This procedure is not illegal, the blank is simply ignored.

52. BALLOT, FORM OF REPORT ON VOTE BY. When the tellers have counted the ballots and compiled the results, they must report. This report should contain, in tabulated form, all important information. Blank ballots are not counted and do not affect the number necessary for election. On the other hand, illegal ballots are included in the total number of votes cast and therefore do affect the number necessary for election. For example, if 100 votes are cast and there are two candidates, the number necessary for election is 51. In this case, if there were two blank ballots, the number necessary for election would be reduced to 50 or one over one-half of 98. However, if 100 votes are cast and 10 are marked but are illegal and two are blank the number necessary for election would still be 50 or one over one-half of 98.

In the above example, the Teller's report would be as follows:

Number of votes cast 98
Number necessary for election 50
Number cast for Mr. X 61
Number cast for Mr. Y 27

Illegal votes

One ballot containing two for Mr. X
folded together 1
One ballot for Mr. Z, not a
member of the society 1
Number cast for Mr. A who is ineligible 8

Notice this report includes the ten illegal ballots but does not mention the two blank ballots.

53. BALLOT, IRREGULAR. Irregularities on ballots such as misspellings, errors in grammar or punctuation, or putting a check mark in place of an X should be ignored as long as the meaning is clear. In the case of elections, the candidate for whom it was intended should be credited with the vote even though his name is misspelled or the directions on the ballot are not followed exactly.

If there is real doubt concerning the intent of the ballot, the tellers may invalidate it or they may submit it to the assembly for instructions. In any case, the tellers should report all irregularities.

54. BALLOT, NOMINATING OR INFORMAL. In electing officers, many organizations, especially small ones, do not go thru the formality of nominating candidates. Instead, ballots are passed out and the members write the name of one person for each office to be filled. If the same name receives a majority of votes for the same office, he is declared elected. On the other hand, if several names receive votes for the same office and no one name receives a majority, all the names are considered nominated and a second vote is taken on these names. If, on this second ballot, a name receives a majority, he is declared elected. If not, a motion is passed to eliminate all but the two names receiving the most votes and a third vote is taken. Obviously one of these two will receive a majority and thus will be elected. On rare occasions a tie will occur, in which case the decision is made by lot unless the society decides to solve the problem in some other manner.

55. BALLOT, OUT OF ORDER FOR SECRETARY TO CAST, IF RULES REQUIRE VOTE BY. When the rules of an organization require that a vote be taken by ballot, it is out of order to move that the secretary or anyone elso cast an unanimous ballot because opposition to this motion would reveal how the person had voted or intended to vote on the motion requiring the ballot vote. This would destroy the secrecy of the ballot vote.

56. BALLOT, RULE OF ELECTION BY, CANNOT BE SUSPENDED. If an organization has a rule that elections must be by ballot, this rule cannot be suspended even by an unanimous vote because any person voting against such a suspension of the rule would thus expose his vote in the election and this would be a violation of his rights. A rule requiring secret ballot in elections is a protection of the minority and this protection cannot be violated. Also, if elections are to be by secret ballot, it cannot be moved that the secretary cast an unanimous ballot bacause any person voting against such a motion would reveal his opposition to the candidate and thus nullify the value of the secret ballot.

57. BALLOT, VOTING BY. Voting by ballot is the most secret method of voting and this is its main attribute. It is the most time-consuming and therefore should be used in the ordinary society only when secrecy is desired.

When the vote is by ballot, the chair should allow a reasonable amount of time and then should ask if all have voted. If no one objects, he should instruct the tellers to collect the ballots. Tellers are usually appointed on the spot by the chairman. Sometimes, in larger groups, the motion is made to close the polls. The chair should not entertain such a motion until he is certain that all have voted who wish to do so. This motion requires a two-thirds vote. If it is desired to reopen the polls, it may be done by a motion to that effect which requires only a majority vote. Neither the motion to close the polls nor the motion to reopen them is debatable.

Because of its secrecy, voting by ballot is used whenever there is a possibility that members might hesitate to express their preference publicly. Most organizations use it in elections and in taking in and expelling members.

If two ballots are folded together and both are marked, both should be rejected and counted as one fraudulent vote but if a blank piece of paper is folded with an otherwise legal ballot, the ballot is considered legal. Persons not wishing to cast a vote and not wishing to reveal the fact may turn in a blank piece of paper. Such blanks are merely discarded and are not counted as fraudulent ballots. Misspellings and other slight errors do not invalidate a ballot as long as the meaning is clear.

When the rules of an organization require that a vote be taken by ballot, it is out of order to make any motion which cannot be opposed by members without exposing their views on the pending motion. For example, if the rules require that the vote on motion "X" be by secret ballot and the result of such vote is not unanimous, it cannot be moved that an unanimous ballot be cast bacause opposition to this motion would reveal that the member had not voted in favor of motion "X."

Secret ballot may be required by the passage of a motion to this effect. Such a motion requires a majority vote.

58. BLANKS, FILLING. Amendments proposed for the purpose of filling blanks are not treated in exactly the same manner as ordinary amendments since different members of the assembly may propose several names or numbers to fill the blank. Of course, no one member may propose more than one number or name unless by general consent. Any number of names or numbers may be proposed without a second.

For example, suppose the motion is before the assembly to authorize the refreshment committee to spend "blank" amount of money. Several members propose varying amounts of money — ten dollars, fifteen dollars, twenty dollars, twenty-five dollars. All these amounts are proposed as suggestions not as amendments. In this case, the presiding officer would start the vote with the highest amount (twenty-five dollars). If this amount did not receive a majority vote, he would then proceed to twenty dollars and so on down until he reached an amount that was approved by the majority. Thus he would arrive at the highest amount that would be approved by the majority of the assembly. On the other hand, suppose the club decided to sell the clubhouse and the "blank" to be filled was to determine the asking price. Several amounts are suggested. The chair would start the vote on the lowest anount to determine how many would be willing to sell for that price and would continue to vote on each successively higher amount until he reached the amount for which the majority would be willing to sell. Thus in the case of filling the blanks with numbers, the vote is started at one end of the scale (either the lowest or the highest depending upon which is least likely to receive a majority) and proceeds on up or down until a majority is reached. It is a good general rule to start with the largest sum and proceed downward.

In the case of filling the blank with a date, it is wise to start with the most distant and proceed toward the present.

When the blank is to be filled with a time, the chair usually starts with the longest. For example, suppose a contractor is to be allowed a "blank" amount of time to do a job. The question is, what is the maximum time to be allowed? Suggestions are made — two years, one year, six months. The chair starts with two years. If a majority are not willing to allow that much time, the chair proceeds to the next suggested time until he gets a majority vote.

If the blank is to be filled with a name, the chair calls for a vote on each name in the order suggested until one name receives a majority vote. If the blank is to be filled with several names, say three, and only three names are proposed, it does not require a vote. The three proposed names are automatically inserted. But if the blank is to be filled with three names and five are suggested, the chair calls for a vote on each successively in the order suggested until three have received a majority. If the number of names to be inserted is not specifically stated, all names that receive a majority are inserted in the blank.

The purpose of making a motion which includes blanks is to make it possible to offer several suggestions for filling the blanks without the formality of offering separate amendments. Also, if the amendment process if used, only two (an amendment and an amendment to the amendment) are possible. Whereas, in filling blanks, any number of suggestions may be offered and each considered in turn until one receives majority support. For example, suppose the motion is made to sell the clubhouse. In debate the question arises, "What shall be the asking price?" Someone moves to amend the motion by adding the words, "for $5,000." Then someone else moves to amend the amendment "by substituting $7,500 for $5,000." In this case no further suggestions can be added and the club must consider only the two amounts. On the other hand, if a blank is created and the original motion is made "to sell the clubhouse for 'blank' amount," then any number of suggestions may be made as to the amount to fill the blank . . . . "$5,000," "$7,500," "$10,000," "$12,000." Since the least likely asking price is $5,000, the chairman would start with this amount. If it received a majority vote, that would be the amount inserted to fill the blank. But if it did not receive a majority, the chairman would then proceed to the next higher amount until he arrived at an amount that did get a majority vote and that amount would fill the blank.

A good basic rule for the chairman to follow is always to begin with the item least likely to be adopted and to proceed until one item receives a majority vote. This item is then used to fill the blank.

Ordinarily, blanks should be filled before the main motion or resolution is voted upon, but if it is obvious that the main motion is opposed by a large majority, the previous question may be called before the blank is filled. This would force a vote on the main motion before its blank had been filled. Thus, if the motion is made to sell the clubhouse for "blank" amount and the motion is obviously unpopular and the previous question is passed, a vote is immediately taken on selling the clubhouse. Usually this would be defeated and that would end the matter. But if the motion *should* be passed, then it would be necessary to fill the blank after the motion to which it applied had been passed. This is still a perfectly legal procedure since the blank may be filled either before or after the motion to which it is applied is passed.

59. BLANKS FOR "WRITE–IN" CANDIDATES. When elections are held by secret ballot and printed ballots, with the names of the nominees on them, are used, it is necessary to provide space for "write-in-candidates." Unless it is prohibited by the rules of the organization, members may vote for any eligible person whether or not he has been officially nominated.

60. BLANKS NOT COUNTED IN BALLOTING. A blank piece of paper or a printed ballot which has not been filled out or checked should not be counted as a ballot and does not figure in the total number of votes cast. Such blanks are simply ignored and discarded as waste. Also a blank piece of paper which is folded with an otherwise proper ballot does not cause the ballot to be rejected. Often persons who do not wish to vote, and who do not wish to reveal the fact, will turn in a blank piece of paper in place of a ballot. This procedure is not illegal, the blank is simply ignored.

61. BOARDS, ANNUAL REPORTS OF, AND THEIR AMENDMENT. If a society has a board of directors or similar committee, it is usual to provide for an annual report. Usually this comes at the end of the fiscal or calendar year or at the end of the term of office of the board. The report contains a brief account of what has been done during the year and makes recommendations for the future. It is common practice for the society to adopt the report and publish it in its annual proceedings. In case any changes in or amendments of the report are made by the society, these changes should be indicated as such and the report should be preceded by a note to that effect. The minutes should read as follows:

"The Board of Directors submitted its annual report which, after discussion and amendment, was adopted as follows, the words in parentheses having been struck out and those underlined (or in italics) having been inserted before the report was adopted."

The society has no right to change the report of the board. It may refuse to adopt the report or allow it to be printed but it cannot make it appear that the report contained anything different from what has been reported by the board. By the use of parentheses and underlining or some other similar device, it can be indicated exactly what was reported by the board and what was adopted by the society.

62. BOARDS CANNOT DECIDE UPON QUORUM. In regard to what constitutes a quorum, boards, executive committees, etc. are on the same basis as ordinary committees. Since their power is delegated to them by the parent body, the number that must be present at a meeting in order to conduct business, which is called a quorum, is determined by the parent body unless this power is specifically delegated to the board.

63. BOARD OF MANAGERS. There are several names by which an executive board may be designated. Among them are the following:
1. Board of Managers.
2. Board of Directors.
3. Board of Trustees.
4. Governing Board.
5. Board of Governors.
6. Executive Committee.
7. Executive Board.
8. Administrative Board.

All such boards are small deliberative groups which represent a larger parent organization and they derive all their power and authority from the parent society. They do not have any inherent power of their own. The authority of the board may be stated in the constitution or in the by-laws or be given to it by vote of the society. Such things as duties, time of meeting, officers and procedure are determined by the parent organization. The by-laws and other rules governing the board are adopted by the one parent society unless the board is authorized to adopt it own.

The purpose of such a board is to represent the parent body, to conducted the business of the society between meetings and to carry on such other business as is assigned to it. In societies which meet infrequently, such as quarterly or annually, a board is vitally important.

64. BOARDS, REPORTS OF, IN THE ORDER OF BUSINESS. Most societies adopt a regular order of business. While this is fairly standard, some societies vary it to suit their needs. At any rate, whatever the order of business may be, the reports of boards come at the same time and are treated in the same manner as the reports of standing committees.

65. BOARDS, RULES OF PROCEDURE IN. In large boards it is necessary to apply the rules of parliamentary procedure the same as in any ordinary society. However, most boards are small, usually not numbering more than a dozen or so. In these boards, the same rules apply as are used in ordinary committees. It is not necessary to be recognized by the chair before speaking. There is usually no need for a second to motions and the chairman does not need to relinquish the chair in order to speak or make a motion. There is no limit to the number of speeches. In other words, as air of informality prevails since the more formal rules of procedure would hamper rather than help the conducting of business is so small a group.

66. BUSINESS, HOW CONDUCTED. The following are some of the simple but necessary principles to be observed in conducting business in an orderly and efficient manner:

1. *Obtaining the floor.* A member desiring to speak on any matter before the assembly should rise in his place and address the presiding officer by his title, such as "Mr. Chairman," "Mr. President," "Mr. Moderator," then wait to be recognized by the chair before he continues to speak. The chair recognizes him by name or, if he is an officer, by title. When the member has been recognized by the chair, he then has the floor and may discuss any motion that has been made, seconded and stated by the chair or he may himself offer a motion.

2. *Recognizing members.* In case two or more members address the presiding officer simultaneously, the chair must use his judgment as to which should be permitted to speak. He should keep in mind such questions as the following:

    A. Has either previously spoken on the question before the house? If so, the floor should be given to the one who has not already spoken.

    B. Is there any special reason why one or the other should be given the preference?

    C. Ordinary consideration, tact and courtesy on the part of the chairman should always prevail.

3. *Making a motion.* If a member desires to have a matter considered by the assembly, he should always present it in the form of a resolution or a motion. If the subject is complicated, it is best to bring it up in the form of a written resolution a copy of which should be handed to the secretary. Usually a resolution is unnecessary and a

simple motion is enough. Simple motions are not presented in written form. In making such a motion, the speaker should say, "I move that such and such an action be taken" or "I desire to offer a motion to the effect that such and such a thing be done." The expressions, "I move you" and "I make a motion" are incorrect.

4. *Stating a motion.* Stating a motion is the action of the chairman in getting a motion before the assembly. The following procedure is correct form:

> A. When a motion has been presented by a member, the chairman repeats the motion and then asks, "Is there a second?"
>
> B. A second may be offered by any member without rising and addressing the chair.
>
> C. When the motion has been seconded, the chairman should say, "It has been moved and seconded that such and such an action be taken. Is there any discussion?" This opens the matter for debate.

5. *Discussing the motion.* No subject should be discussed before the assembly until it has been presented in the form of a motion or resolution, duly seconded, stated by the chair and remarks called for. (Some motions are undebatable and must be voted on without discussion). In discussing a motion, no member should be allowed to speak twice if anyone who has not had an opportunity to speak is asking for the privilege of the floor. Common sense, fairness and courtesy should guide the conduct of the presiding officer.

67. BUSINESS, HOW INTRODUCED. An organization may not take action on or even discuss any matter until it has been officially placed before the assembly. There are three steps which must be followed if a matter is to be officially considered.

1. A motion must be made. This is done by a member addressing the chair, being recognized and saying, "I move that . . . ." It is poor form to use the expression, "I make a motion" or "I move you." When the motion has been made, the chair says, "It has been moved that . . . . " (repeating the motion). "Is there a second?"

2. The motion must be seconded. There are a number of motions that do not require a second but all main motions do. Seconding a motion may be more informal. To be formal, a member addresses the chair, is recognized and says, "I second the motion." However, to second a motion, one does not need to be recognized. He may simply

call out, "I second the motion" or even just "Second."

3. The third step is called "Stating the motion." This is done by the chair saying, "It has been moved and seconded that . . . . " (Again stating the motion). "Is there any discussion?" This question . . . . is there any discussion . . . . is the third step and is called stating the motion. The business is now officially on the floor and is ready to be debated and acted upon.

There are other ways of considering a matter in an organization, such as INFORMAL CONSIDERATION and consideration in COMMITTEE OF THE WHOLE but *official* consideration must follow the above procedure.

68. BUSINESS, ORDER OF. Every permanent organization usually adopts a regular chronological order in which it conducts business. This means that all regular meetings follow the same pattern of procedure except in case of special orders or unless the rules have been suspended. The pattern varies with different societies but is usually consistent within the organization. The usual order of business is as follows:

1. *Call to order.* The presiding officer calls the meeting to order. This he does by attracting attention (usually by rapping sharply with a gavel) and saying, "The meeting will please come to order."

2. *Roll call.* The roll is called by the secretary. This is not always necessary and many societies omit it, but if attendance is required, roll call is necessary. Also, it may be used to determine whether a quorum is present.

3. *Reading the minutes.* The chairman asks the secretary to read the minutes of the previous meeting which are corrected if necessary and then approved.

4. *Treasurer's report.* The chairman calls for the treasurer's report. Except in the case of annual reports of the treasurer, no action on the treasurer's report is necessary.

5. *Reports of standing committees.* The chairman calls for reports of standing committees and the assembly acts on these reports. Sometimes there are no standing committees, in which case this item is omitted.

6. *Reports of special committees.* The chairman calls for reports of special committees and the assembly acts on them. If there are none, this item is omitted.

7. *Correspondence.* The chairman calls for the reading of correspondence. This is done by the secretary or by the corresponding

secretary, if there is one. No action is necessary on this report. If action is necessary on a particular piece of correspondence, it is taken up under "unfinished business" or under "new business," whichever is appropriate depending on whether the matter has previously been considered.

8. *Special orders.* The chairman introduces "special orders," that is, business which has been made a "special order of business" for this meeting. If there is none this item is omitted.

9. *Unfinished business.* All business which was left unfinished at the previous meeting is taken up and disposed of. The chairman should simply ask, "Is there any unfinished business?" The minutes should indicate if there is and the secretary should be alert to introduce it. If there is none, the meeting may pass on to new business.

10. *New business.* New business is transacted. New business is any that has not been introduced at a previous meeting. This is the major job of the meeting.

11. *Announcements.* The chairman calls for any announcements. These may be made by the chairman or by any member of the assembly who has one. No action on announcements is necessary.

12. *Adjournment.* After new business has been completed and announcements made, the assembly adjourns. This requires a motion to adjourn which may be made by any member of the assembly. This motion must be seconded and passed but the meeting is not adjourned until the chairman announces, "The meeting stands adjourned."

69. BUSINESS PRIORITY OF. When several matters are on the docket for consideration at a given meeting and none has priority over another, the chairman is not bound to consider them in any particular order unless the motion is passed to take them up in a certain order. It is wise for the presiding officer to make up an agenda prior to the meeting but such an agenda does not bind the society to follow it in the order listed. In situations where the meeting is likely to be long and the matters to be considered are numerous, an agenda is useful, not only as a guide to the chairman, but also to restrain members from attempting to give priority to a favorite item to the detriment of other equally important matters.

70. BUSINESS, TO CHANGE THE ORDER OF. When a society has adopted a regular order of business and has so stated in their "Rules of Order," no change in procedure can be made without suspending the rules. Such a suspension may be made provided it does not violate either the constitution or the by-laws of the organization. A two-thirds vote is required to suspend the rules of order. Sometimes a society places its order of business in its by-laws. Although the by-laws may not be suspended, any rule relating to the order of business should be allowed to be suspended the same as if it were in the rules of order where it belongs.

Sometimes a society will place its order of business in the standing rules. Although standing rules may be suspended by a majority vote, any rule pertaining to the order of business should require a two-thirds vote for suspension because it requires this vote to suspend rules of order.

When a rule is suspended, the reason should be clearly stated and when the particular business is completed, the rules go back into effect.

71. BUSINESS, UNFINISHED, EFFECT OF ADJOURNMENT UPON.

The effect of an adjournment upon unfinished business is as follows, unless the organization has adopted rules of its own to the contrary:

1. If the adjournment does not end the session (see **SESSION AND MEETING, DISTINCTION BETWEEN**) the interrupted business becomes the first in order at the next meeting after the reading of the minutes. It is treated the same as if no adjournment had taken place because an adjourned meeting which does not end a session is legally the continuation of the previous meeting of which it is an adjournment.

2. If an organization has regular sessions as often as quarterly, when the last meeting of a session is adjourned and thus the adjournment closes the session (such as the last meeting of a session of Congress), the same situation as 1 above pertains. That is, the interrupted business is taken up at the first meeting of the next session exactly where it was broken off by the adjournment. The exception to this rule is in elected bodies where either all or part of the membership is elected for a definite term. In this case, the unfinished business which was interrupted by the adjournment, becomes dead with the expiration of the term for which all or part of the organization was elected. For example, if a piece of business is interrupted by adjournment of the last meeting of a session and if there is an election of membership in the interval between that session and the next session, then the interrupted business does not hold over and must be introduced as new business just as though it had not previously been brought up. Thus members of an organization who have been defeated for reelection but who are

continuing to meet while finishing their term cannot force their successors to consider a piece of business, because they cannot postpone it nor make it a special order of business if either an election or change of membership intervenes.

3. If the organization does not meet as often as quarterly and business is interrupted by adjournment which closes a session, the interrupted business is also dead at the end of the session. As in the case of elected bodies, as stated above, the interrupted business may be introduced at the next session just as though it had never been considered previously.

72. BUSINESS, UNFINISHED, ITS PLACE IN THE ORDER OF BUSINESS. Unfinished business is any matter which has been before the assembly previously and was not disposed of or any business which was pending when the previous meeting was adjourned. This includes business "postponed to the next meeting" or "general postponement" which means the same thing. In the order of business, unfinished business follows "special orders" and precedes "new business."

73. BY-LAWS, AMENDMENT OR REVISION OF. The by-laws should contain an article providing for the method by which they may be amended. This article should contain two provisions: (1) the kind of advance notice which must be given prior to the voting on a proposed amendment and (2) the kind of vote required for its passage (majority, two-thirds).

1. The kind of notice required varies widely with different societies. Some specify that no notice is required while others go so far as to require that printed copies of the proposed amendment be sent so each member should know in advance what the proposed amendment is and when it will come up for debate and vote. If advance notice is required and the time for consideration of the amendment arrives, the society must confine itself to a consideration of that amendment contained in the notice. In other words, amendments cannot be proposed which were not contained in the notice.

2. The second provision which should be contained in the by-laws is the vote required for passage of an amendment. This may be a simple majority of those voting or it may go as high as three-fourths of the entire membership. The usual provision is two-thirds of those present and voting provided a quorum is present.

After a set of by-laws has been in effect for a length of time, it is often desirable to make extensive changes in them. The best method to accomplish this is to select a by-laws revision committee. This committee then studies the by-laws and submits a report of suggested changes. These changes may be few in number or they may consist of an entirely new set of by-laws. When the committee reports, this serves as notice and no action can be taken until the time of notice has elapsed as provided for in the old by-laws. When the time arrives for consideration of the proposed changes, each one is taken up and voted on separately.

74. BY-LAWS, CONTENTS OF. The by-laws should contain all the details necessary to insure orderly procedure under the constitution. They serve as a detailed supplement to the constitution. Basically they should provide for the following:

1. detailed requirements for membership.
2. methods of admitting new members.
3. dues.
4. detailed duties of officers.
5. detailed duties of committees.
6. election of officers and committees.
7. provisions for calling and conducting meetings.
8. parliamentary authority.
9. number constituting a quorum
10. method of amending the by-laws.

75. BY-LAWS, NO SUSPENSION OF, UNLESS PROVIDED IN. If the society wishes to make it possible to suspend any by-law, it must be provided for in the by-laws themselves. By-laws relating to the conducting of business such as are usually contained in "rules of order" may be suspended by a two-thirds vote but no other by-law may be suspended unless such suspension is specifically provided for.

76. CALL FOR THE QUESTION. When the members of a society wish to close debate and proceed to a vote on the pending motion, they may do so informally by calling out, "Question, question." This is an informal way of moving (or calling for) the previous question. If no member has or is seeking the floor, the chair, upon hearing the call, "Question," says, "The question has been called for. Are you ready for the question?" If no one claims the floor, the chair proceeds to put the pending motion to a vote. The fact that no member claims the floor indicates that debate has been closed by general consent. If a member does claim the floor, general consent is not given and debate continues.

77. CALL OF THE HOUSE. Call of the house is used to compel members of an organization to attend meetings. Since ordinary societies cannot do this, the motion cannot be used. If the society is of such a nature that it has the right to force members to attend, call of the house is the method by which this is accomplished. Such assemblies usually provide a rule which, when no quorum is present, allows a specified small number to order a call of the house. In Congress, if one-fifth of the members are present, a call of the house may be ordered by a majority vote of those present. If a quorum is present, and it is desired to force absentees to attend, a call of the house can be ordered by a majority vote. In this case the motion has the same rank as a privileged motion but if the call is once rejected, it cannot be renewed at that meeting as long as a quorum remains present.

When no quorum is present, the call of the house takes precedence over everything except the motion to adjourn and once the call has been ordered, the assembly cannot adjourn nor interrupt the proceedings of the call until a quorum is present or it becomes clear that no quorum can be secured for that meeting after which it is possible to adjourn.

When a call of the house has been ordered the procedure is as follows:

1. The secretary or clerk calls the roll of the membership alphabetically and then again calls the names of the absentees.

2. The doors are locked and members are not permitted to leave.

3. The sergeant-at-arms is ordered to take absentee members into custody and bring them before the house.

4. Arrested members are brought before the chairman who gives them an opportunity to make their excuses for being absent without leave.

5. The chairman then orders them to take their seats after a motion is made to discharge them from custody. Sometimes a fee or fine is assessed.

6. If a fee is assessed, it must be paid before the member can vote or be recognized by the chair.

78. CALL SPEAKER TO ORDER. A speaker may be called to order if he violates any rule of the assembly or of parliamentary law or if he is guilty of any indecorum or uses improper language in debate. If it is a simple matter of indecorum or language, the call to order must be made at the time the breach of order occurs, but if it is a matter of an unlawful act, he may be called to order at any time. For example, if a motion is made which violates any of the rules of the assembly, it is never too late to raise a point of order.

The chairman has the right to call a speaker to order or any member may say, "Mr. Chairman, I call the speaker to order." This may interrupt the speaker, does not require a second and is neither debatable nor amendable. It does not require a vote since it is decided by the chair. If the chair is in doubt, he may refer it to the assembly in which case, the matter is decided by a majority vote.

79. CALL TO ORDER. The first order of business in any meeting of any organization is to call the meeting to order. This is done by the presiding officer. He attracts attention (usually by rapping sharply with a gavel) and says, "The meeting will please come to order." This should be done in a very business-like manner. Since there is usually considerable noise and confusion in an assembly prior to the opening of the meeting, a decisive and forceful attitude on the part of the chairman is called for because it will get the meeting under way more quickly and effectively.

80. CHAIRMAN (PRESIDING OFFICER), ADDRESSING THE. In order to speak or make a motion it is necessary for a member to first obtain the floor. This is done by rising and "Addressing the chair." The presiding officer should be addressed by title such as, "Mr. President," "Madam President," "Mr. Moderator." The term chairman is used unless the presiding officer has a specific title. The presiding officer is never addressed by name and the term Madam is always used if the presiding officer is a lady; never Miss or Mrs. The terms "Sister" or "Brother" should not be used because they imply that the person addressing the chair is also a presiding officer. In asking for the floor, the member should address the chair in a firm, dignified voice, loud enough to be easily and distinctly heard.

81. CHAIRMAN CANNOT APPOINT CHAIRMAN PRO TEM FOR A FUTURE MEETING. Even though the president or permanent chairman may know in advance that he is going to be absent from a future meeting, he does not have the right to appoint a chairman pro tem to take his place. The proper procedure is as follows: If the secretary is present, he calls the meeting to order and proceeds to secure the election of a chairman pro tem through the regular method. If the secretary is absent, some other member of the society should call the meeting to order and hold the election. The chairman pro tem then presides for that meeting or until the arrival of the regular chairman or president or until he is replaced, through an election, by another chairman pro tem.

82. CHAIRMAN, DUTIES OF. The presiding officer of an organization may be given any one of a great many titles, the most common being, chairman, president, moderator, chief, director. In addition to these, there are many others, more fantastic and peculiar to the society involved. Regardless of title, however, the duties of the presiding officer in any group remain essentially the same. These duties should be stated in the constitution or by-laws. The more unusual duties, peculiar to the society, are listed and the statement usually ends with a phrase similar to the following: " . . . . and such other duties as are usual to the office of president." These "usual" duties may be listed as follows:

1. to open the meeting at the appointed time.
2. to announce the agenda of business for the meeting.
3. to recognize members who wish the floor.
4. to state all motions which are moved.
5. to put to vote all motions and announce the results of votes.
6. to conduct meetings in accordance with the rules of the society and parliamentary law.
7. to protect the society from annoyance by refusing to recognize persons who are being frivolous or who make dilatory motions.
8. to protect the rights of members.
9. to keep the discussion within the bounds of proper debate.
10. to decide points of order or, if in doubt, to submit the decision to the assembly.

11. to answer points of parliamentary inquiry unless a parliamentarian is used for this purpose.
12. to sign necessary papers and documents.
13. to represent the society in dealing with other individuals or groups.
14. to adjourn the meeting without vote in case of riot, fire, disaster or other serious emergency.

83. CHAIRMAN, ELECTION OF TEMPORARY. When a group of people decide to form a new club, organization or society, they must decide on a time and place for the first meeting, who shall be invited to the meeting, who shall call the meeting to order and who shall explain the purpose of the organization. Sometimes also, they decide who shall be nominated as temporary chairman and who shall do the nominating.

When the persons have gathered at the meeting place (sometimes it is desirable to delay a few minutes to be sure all have arrived who are coming) the person picked to do the job steps to the front and calls the meeting to order. After this, the first business is the election of the temporary chairman. There are two methods which may be used at this point.

1. The presiding officer may call for nominations (sometimes he makes this nomination himself) and then declares the first person whose name was heard by him nominated and calls for a vote on that name. If the name secures a majority vote, he is declared elected and takes the chair as temporary chairman. If he does not receive a majority, the presiding officer calls for another nomination and vote. This is continued until some person is elected and takes the chair.

2. The presiding officer may call for nominations from the floor and when a number of names have been nominated and the nominations closed in the usual manner, the names are voted on and the person receiving the most votes is declared elected as temporary chairman.

84. CHAIRMAN, OF A COMMITTEE, HOW SELECTED. Committees are selected in one of three ways:
1. they are appointed by the presiding officer.
2. they are named by the person who moves that a matter be referred to a committee.
3. they are elected by the assembly.
Whether appointed or elected, one person is usually designated as

chairman. If no one is named as chairman, it is generally assumed that the first named person is to act in this capacity and in his absence, the second named should take over. However, if the assembly does not specifically name a chairman, the committee has the right to elect its own.

One of the duties of the chairman is to call meetings of the committee but if he fails to do so, any two members may call meetings. It is also his duty to turn over to the secretary of the club all papers which were given to the committee by the society, when the committee's work is finished. The committee is not obligated to turn over its own papers, including minutes and books, however.

85. CHAIRMAN OF A COMMITTEE OF THE WHOLE. When an organization decides to consider a matter in committee of the whole, the presiding officer usually appoints another member of the society as chairman rather than act in this capacity himself although it is his right to do so if he wishes. The committee chairman immediately calls the committee to order and it considers the matter referred to it. It may not take up any other matter. A committee of the whole follows the same procedure as any other committee. When it has finished discussing the matter referred to it, the committee votes on the report it will make and then "rises" (adjourns); the presiding officer then reconvenes the assembly and the chairman of the committee makes his report and the assembly votes on it. It would seem unnecessary to take this vote since the same people voted on the same matter in the committee but it is a definite rule that a committee cannot take final action for the organization, therefore the second vote is required.

86. CHAIRMAN, RIGHT OF, TO VOTE WHEN IT AFFECTS RESULT. The chairman has the right to vote if the vote is cast by written ballot, however, his ballot must be cast with the rest of the membership and not after the polls are closed or the tellers have commenced to count the ballots. In all other methods of voting, the presiding officer may vote, if his vote will change the result. There are four conditions under which this is the case.

1. · When the issue requires a majority vote to pass and the actual vote is a tie, the chairman may vote in the affirmative but not in the negative. A tie vote does not give a majority to the issue and therefore the motion is lost. An affirmative vote by the chairman will cause the issue to be passed and thus change the outcome.

2. When the issue requires a majority vote to pass and the affirmative has one more vote than the negative (yes — 16 .... no — 15, for example) the chair may cast a negative vote but not affirmative. An affirmative vote will not change the result because the issue has passed anyway but a negative vote will create a tie and cause the issue to be lost.

3. When the issue requires a two-thirds vote to pass and it lacks one (yes — 15 .... no — 8, for example) the chair may vote yes but may not vote no. A no vote would not change the decision since the issue is lost anyway but a yes vote would give the affirmative two-thirds and thus cause it to pass.

4. When the issue requires a two-thirds vote to pass and has exactly that (yes — 16 .... no — 8, for example) the chair may vote "no" but may not vote "yes" because, since the issue already has two-thirds, it has passed anyway but a no vote would prevent a two-thirds majority and thus change the decision.

87. CHAIRMAN, TEMPORARY OR PRO TEM.

A person who acts temporarily for the chairman is called a temporary chairman or chairman pro tempore (for the time being). This term, however, does not apply to the vice-president nor to any other officer who succeeds to the chairmanship by virtue of his office. The rules of a society usually provide that in the absence or incapacity of the president, the vice-president shall take over his duty. Also, usually if the president wishes to relinquish the chair temporarily, (to make or discuss a motion, for example) he asks the vice-president to take over. The term pro tempore does not apply in this case.

However, if the vice-president or any other officer who would normally succeed the president is not available, then the president may appoint a chairman from among the membership. This is called "chairman pro tem." The office of chairman pro tem may be terminated in any one of three ways.

1. the president may elect to resume the chair.
2. adjournment terminates the office.
3. the assembly may choose to elect another chairman and thus terminate the office.

88. CLERK.

There are several titles by which the recording officer may be called. Some of these are clerk, secretary, recording secretary if there

is also a corresponding secretary, recorder and scribe. (For duties see
SECRETARY, DUTIES OF.)

89. CLOSE AND REOPEN NOMINATIONS. If carried, the motion to close nominations prevents any further nominations from being made. The chair should refuse to entertain this motion as long as there are any who wish to make further nominations.

When nominations have been made by a nominating committee or from the floor or both and when it appears to the chair that there are no further nominations, he should ask if there are any further nominations. If none are forthcoming, he may declare the nominations closed and proceed with the election.

If a motion to close nominations is made from the floor, it requires a second, is undebatable and can have no secondary motions applied to it except that it can be amended as to the time of closing. Because it deprives members of their right to make nominations, it requires a two-thirds vote. It yields to all privileged motions.

If it is desired to reopen nominations after they have been closed, it may be done by a motion to that effect. This motion requires a second, is undebatable and can have no secondary motions applied to it except that it can be amended as to time. It yields to all privileged motions and requires a majority vote to pass.

90. CLOSE AND REOPEN POLLS. When an assembly is voting by secret ballot and the presiding officer observes that all have voted who intend to do so, he may declare the polls closed after inquiring if all have voted. He may then order the tellers to count the ballots.

Sometimes, though not often in the ordinary society, a formal motion to close the polls is made. Obviously, the chair should not recognize such a motion until he is sure all have voted. The motion requires a second, is undebatable and requires a two-thirds vote. It can have no subsidiary motions applied to it except that it may be amended as to the time of closing.

Occasionally it is desired to reopen the polls. For example, if members come into the meeting after the polls are closed and desire to vote, a motion to reopen the polls is in order. This motion has the same status as the motion to close the polls except that it requires only a majority vote to pass.

91. CLOSE DEBATE. The motion to close debate is called the "previous question." If the motion were properly named, it would be called the "motion to close debate." Previous question is not only a misnomer but is confusing because frequently when a vote is called for on the previous question, many people think they are voting on the pending motion. This is not true. They are simply voting to close debate on the pending motion and must then proceed to vote on this motion. This confusion is due to the fact that in England where the previous question originated (as did most of our parliamentary law) the call for the previous question means something entirely different. Originally, in the United States the motion meant the same as it does in England but in this country it has gradually undergone great changes although the original name has been kept. Only its present use in the United States will be considered here.

There are several forms of the previous question. The *informal* form means that when members of the assembly believe the group is ready to vote, they simply call out, "Question." It is unnecessary to rise or be recognized for this, but they may not interrupt a speaker. When someone (or several) calls "Question," the chairman says, "Question has been called. If there is no objection, we will proceed to vote on the motion before the house which is . . . . " (stating the immediately pending motion). This is called "general consent." One objection by a member of the assembly will prevent this action. (See **GENERAL CONSENT**.)

The more *formal* unqualified form means that the previous question is stated in the form of a motion. A member of the assembly rises, addresses the chair, is recognized and then says, "I call for (or move or demand) the previous question." This motion requires a second, may not interrupt a speaker and requires a two-thirds vote to pass. Obviously, it is undebatable because to debate it would defeat its purpose which is to stop debate. The two-thirds vote is required because the previous question is a violation of the basic parliamentary rule of full and free debate. When this motion is made, it applies *only* to the immediately pending question. Suppose, for example, that there is pending a main motion, an amendment to the main motion and an amendment to the amendment. If the unqualified form of the previous question is used, it applies only to the immediately pending question which is the amendment to the amendment. The chairman says, "The previous question has been called for (or moved or demanded) and seconded on the immediately pending question which is . . . . (stating the amendment to the amendment). All those in favor of closing debate on this motion make it known by raising your right hand (or rising)." A show of hands or rising vote is generally used on motions requiring a two-thirds vote because it is easier to determine the count. If the previous question gets the necessary two-thirds vote, the chair immediately proceeds to take a vote on the amendment to the amendment and then opens the floor for debate on the amendment to the main motion which is the next matter to be considered by the assembly.

The *qualified* form of the previous question specifies the motion to which it is to be applied, "the previous question on all pending business," for instance. Suppose again there is a pending main motion, an amendment to the main motion and an amendment to the amendment. Now suppose a member says, "I call for the previous question *on all pending business.*" If this passes, the chair must call for a vote first on the amendment to the amendment, then, without debate, they must vote on the amendment to the main motion and then, again without debate, on the main motion. Or in the example above, a member may say, "I call for the previous question on the amendment to the amendment and the amendment to the main motion." If this passes, the chair would call for a vote on the two amendments and then open the main motion for further debate.

The previous question takes precedence over all other motions except privileged motions, incidental motions and the motion to lay on the table to all of which it yields.

92. CLUB. The words club, assembly, society and organization are used synonymously to mean any organized body of persons banded together for a purpose and using parliamentary rules as a basis for conducting meetings.

Technically the word assembly indicates a meeting of such a group. The words mean any deliberative body. Whenever a group has a name, that name should replace the more general terms when motions are made or other reference is made to the body.

93. COMMIT, FORMS OF MOTION TO. The forms of the motion to refer to a committee vary all the way from the simple, unqualified motion, "I move that this matter be referred to a committee," to the completely qualified motion which specifies all the details such as, "I move that this matter be referred to a committee of three consisting of Mr. A. as chairman, Miss B and Mr. C and that the committee be instructed to make a complete investigation and report all details at our next meeting."

If the unqualified form is made, the chairman must determine the wishes of the organization on such details as follows:

1. the size of the committee.
2. how it shall be secured; appointed by the chair or elected by the society, and if elected, he must conduct the election.
3. what instructions are to be given to the committee.
4. when the committee shall be prepared to report.

The motion to commit may be qualified in another manner also. It is possible to refer only a part of the subject to a committee or to refer different parts of the same subject to different committees. Suppose it is moved that the club hold a picnic and a committee is appointed to investigate possible dates, another committee to investigate possible places and a third committee to investigate places to get food at a discount. This would be three committees assigned to three different parts of the same subject.

94. COMMIT, MOTION TO. The motion to commit or refer is a motion to refer a matter to a committee. If the matter to be committed or referred is pending, that is, if it is on the floor or before the assembly, the motion to commit is a secondary motion. Suppose the society is considering the question of building a clubhouse and it is moved to refer the matter to a committee; then this motion is a secondary motion. On the other hand, if the matter is not before the assembly, and the motion is made to refer it to a committee, then the motion to commit is a main motion. For example, a member moves that a committee be appointed to investigate the possibilities of building a clubhouse.

The motion to refer cannot be applied to secondary motions. It cannot be laid on the table nor postponed but both these motions take precedence over it and if either is applied to the main motion and is passed while the motion to commit is pending, then the motion to refer goes with the main motion. Such motions as the previous question, to limit debate, to extend limits of debate and to amend may be applied to it and not affect the main motion. For example, if a matter is before the assembly and the motion is made to refer it to a committee and then the motion is made to limit debate to ten minutes, this does not limit debate on the main motion but only on the motion to refer. This indicates that the motion to commit is debatable which is true but the debate must be confined to the matter of referring to a committee and cannot include debate on the main motion. In the United States Congress, the motion to refer or commit is not debatable.

When an amendment is pending and the motion is made to refer the main motion to a committee, the amendment goes to the committee with the main motion. If a committee has begun consideration of a matter referred to it, it is too late to reconsider the motion to commit. Prior to that time, however, the motion to reconsider may be applied to it.

The motion to commit or refer is used also when it is desired to go into committee of the whole and when it is desired to consider a matter informally. For committee of the whole the proper form is, "I move that the assembly resolve itself into a committee of the whole to consider . . . . ." (Name the matter.) For informal consideration, the proper motion is, "I move that . . (name the subject) be considered informally." Both these motions have the same status as the motion to refer to a committee.

95. COMMIT, WHEN A MAIN MOTION. Usually the motion to refer to a committee is a secondary motion because it is applied to a matter which is pending but if a matter which is not pending is referred to a committee then the motion to commit is a main motion and has the same status as any other main motion.

96. COMMITTEE, EX-OFFICIO MEMBERS OF. "Ex-officio" is a Latin term meaning "from office" or "by virtue of office." Thus officers of a society, especially the president, are frequently made ex-officio members of committees by virtue of their office. Not infrequently the president is made an ex-officio member of all committees. An ex-officio member has all the rights and privileges of a regular member of a committee including the right to attend meetings, make motions, debate and vote. On the other hand, when the ex-officio member of the committee may, but is not required to attend meetings, he is not included when counting a quorum.

In some instances, an individual is an ex-officio member of a committee of an organization of which he is not a member. For example, the govenor of a state may be made an ex-officio member of the governing board of a college or university. In such a case, the same rules apply. He has all the rights and privileges of a regular member of the committee, including the right to vote, but is not counted in determining a quorum unless he is under the authority of the society.

An officer of an organization is never an ex-officio member of any committee or of all committees unless the rules of the society provide for it or unless he is elected to the ex-officio membership by a majority vote of the society. Even though the rules provide that an officer is ex-officio member of all committees, he should never serve as such on a nominating committee if he is a candidate either for re-relection or for any other office.

Occasionally an officer will be made ex-officio chairman of a committee. When this happens, he is entitled to preside over committee meetings but in his absence the committee has the right to choose a chairman pro tem who may preside when the ex-officio chairman is absent.

When an officer is ex-officio member of a committee by virtue of the office he holds, his ex-officio membership automatically expires when his term of office is concluded.

97. COMMITTEE, MANNER OF CONDUCTING BUSINESS IN. One of the purposes of referring a matter to a committee is so it may be considered informally, therefore, the manner of conducting business in a committee should be as informal as possible. The degree of formality necessary will depend to a large extent on the size of the committee. Small committees can operate with less formality. Insofar as practicable, the rules of the parent organization apply to its committees but the rules of parliamentary procedure do not apply any more than is necessary. Members do not need to obtain the floor in order to speak or make motions, nor are they required to stand. Matters may be discussed without the necessity of a formal motion but a motion introducing business is permitted. If a motion is made, it may be seconded but a second is not required. Unlike a regular assembly, the chairman is permitted to make motions and to discuss business without relinquishing the chair. Give and take conversation is permitted as long as it is germane to the matter under consideration.

Two formal motions are required in committees. They are the motion which adopts the report to be made to the society and the motion to adjourn. The committee may adopt the report it intends to make by a majority of those present provided all members have been notified of the meeting and a quorum is present. If a meeting cannot be held to adopt a report, it may be adopted by a majority vote of the committee membership.

When a committee has held its last meeting and is ready to report, the motion "to rise" is substituted for the motion to adjourn.

Although it is not required by parliamentary law, it is generally wise for a committee to keep minutes. This may be done by any member appointed by the chairman. These minutes are the property of the committee which cannot be required to submit them to the parent organization although the committee may do so if it wishes. The minutes and other papers belonging to the committee may be filed or destroyed or disposed of in any way the committee desires when its work is finished.

A committee may create sub-committees of its own members. These sub-committees are responsible to and report to the committee and not to the parent organization. Also, if a committee is charged with the responsibility of carrying out a course of action, it may appoint sub-committees from the general membership of the society. For example, if a committee is created for the purpose of making all arrangements for a picnic, the committee might appoint an entertainment committee, a refreshment committee and a transportation committee. All of these would be responsible to the arrangements committee which, in turn, would be responsible to the parent organization.

98. COMMITTEE, OBJECT OF MOTION TO REFER TO. Matters are referred to committees for one of three purposes.

1. Investigative purposes: It may be necessary for an organization to have more information on a subject before it can intelligently consider what action should be taken. In this case, it may assign to a committee the job of gathering and reporting the simple facts. For example, suppose a club was considering the possibilities of holding a picnic but lacked information on where such an event could be held. It would be logical to assign to a committee the job of investigating the various parks and picnic grounds available and reporting to the club the facts so the club could consider them and make a decision on where to hold the event. Such a committee would be an investigative or fact finding committee. Its job would be merely to report the facts and let the club make the decision.

2. Action recommending purposes: The club may wish to place upon the committee the responsibility of making a decision, after investigation, and offering that decision to the society for its adoption. In the case above, the committee might be charged with the job of

studying the facts concerning the various possible places for holding the picnic and deciding which spot it thinks would be most suitable to the needs of the club. Under these circumstances, the club might instruct the committee concerning the facilities it desired such as soft ball diamond, picnic tables, swimming beach, cooking facilities, etc. and asking that the committee recommend the place it feels that would best suit the desires of the club. Such a committee might be called an action recommending committee. In this case, the club would move to adopt the report of the committee and, if passed, the decision of the committee would be carried out by the club.

3. Action purposes: Sometimes a matter is referred to a committee with full power to act. In this case, the society is bound by and responsible for whatever action is taken by the committee. Again to use the example above, the club wishing to hold the picnic might assign to the committee the responsibility of deciding on a place for the picnic and giving it the responsibility of making the necessary contacts, reservations or contracts for securing the place. Another type of action committee would be one in which the club has decided where it wishes to hold the picnic and then assigning to a committee the job of making the contact, reservation or contract and any other negotiations necessary for securing the desired place. In all such cases, the society must assume responsibility for any action taken by the committee.

99. COMMITTEE OF THE WHOLE. Sometimes a society wishes to consider a matter with more freedom and with less formality than is allowed in a regular parliamentary assembly. When this is the case or when the society does not wish to refer a matter to a committee and yet needs to work the matter over before it is ready for formal consideration and needs the freedom of an ordinary committee to do it, it may go into a committee of the whole. Someone then moves that the matter be considered in committee of the whole. If this motion is passed, the presiding officer appoints a chairman of the committee of the whole who takes over the meeting while the presiding officer takes his place as a regular member of the society.

The only motions that may be made in a committee of the whole are the motions to adopt a report, to amend and to rise and report. The committee cannot close or limit debate nor change the limits of debate if any have been set by the society before going into committee. The committee of the whole has no right to refer any matter to a committee or sub-committee. The committee cannot change a motion or resolution referred to it but if the committee itself formulates a resolution it has the right to amend or alter it. The committee cannot consider any matter except the one referred to it.

When the committee has completed its deliberations, the motion is made to "rise and report." If this motion is passed, the presiding officer again takes over and reconvenes the regular session and the chairman of the committee of the whole reports. This report is then acted upon in the same manner as any other committee report.

100. COMMITTEE OF THE WHOLE, QUASI. The word quasi means "as if in" so the term quasi committee of the whole means "as if in committee of the whole." When it is desired to use this informal method of considering a matter, someone moves as follows: "I move that this matter be considered as if in committee of the whole." When this motion is passed, the society automatically goes into quasi committee of the whole. The presiding officer of the society becomes the chairman of the committee and the secretary of the society becomes the secretary of the committee. A quasi committee of the whole operates in much the same manner as a regular committee of the whole operates except that it cannot make any motions except the motion to amend. It may debate and amend the motion referred to it but may make no other motions. The secretary should keep minutes but they are temporary and should not be made a part of the regular minutes of the society. When the committee has finished debating and amending the matter referred to it, the chairman announces that the assembly has had the matter under consideration as if in committee of the whole and reports what has been done. The assembly then acts on this report in the same manner as if it were a report from a committee of the whole. The motion to rise is not necessary to discontinue a quasi committee of the whole.

101. COMMITTEE ON RESOLUTIONS. Resolutions may be offered for the consideration of an assembly in either one of two ways.

1. Any member may offer a resolution in the same manner as he would offer any main motion.

2. Or a resolutions committee may be charged with the responsibility of drawing up resolutions for the society. A resolutions committee is more frequently used in mass meetings and conventions. It is less common in a society which meets regularly and frequently. A resolutions committee may be provided for in the rules of a society, in

which case it is usually appointed well in advance of the meeting and prepares resolutions at its convenience. If no provision for such a committee exists in the rules, a committee on resolutions may be created in the same manner as any other committee.

When the resolutions committee has been appointed (or elected), it should retire from the meeting and draft whatever resolutions are desired. When the committee returns, it should be prepared to report as soon as the pending business on the floor at the time is disposed of. The chairman of the committee (or the reporting member if other than the chairman) obtains the floor, reads the resolutions, moves their adoption and hands them to the presiding officer or the secretary. They are then acted upon by the assembly. Resolutions may be amended, debated and in general, dealt with in the same manner as any other committee report.

102. COMMITTEE, PROGRAM. In the ordinary club or society, the program committee is usually a standing committee whose function is to arrange the programs or entertainment during the term of its office. Many organizations, such as luncheon clubs, church groups, service clubs and women's clubs, devote a part of their meeting time to a business meeting and a part to entertainment. Frequently the program committee adopts a general theme for a year and centers the program for each meeting around this theme.

In conventions, the program committee has a different function. It is its function to prepare a program for the business of the convention which may last over several days. Usually the committee, which should be appointed well in advance of the convention, has the program printed and distributed to the members. When the presiding officer calls for it, the chairman of the program committee makes his report or submits the printed program and moves that it be adopted. This motion is debatable and may be amended. It requires a majority vote for adoption but once adopted, the program cannot be changed or deviated from except by a two-thirds vote of those voting or a majority vote of the entire membership. The report of the program committee is usually called for immediately following the report of the credentials committee.

103. COMMITTEE, QUORUM IN. A committee is the creation of the parent organization, therefore, it has no powers except those delegated to it by its creator. This includes determining the number constituting a quorum. The society may state the number necessary for a quorum or it may specifically delegate this right to the committee. If there is no statement to the contrary, a majority of the committee constitutes a quorum and is the number which must be present to conduct business. For example, in a committee of seven, a quorum of four could officially conduct business.

104. COMMITTEE, REPORTING MEMBER OF. The usual reporting member of a committee is the chairman, however, there are situations where the chairman does not make the report. Of course, in the absence of the chairman, another member must report. Also, if there is disagreement on the committee and both a majority and minority report are to be made and the chairman is with the minority, it becomes necessary for the majority report to be made by someone else although, in this case, the chairman may make the minority report. Also, if the committee is large or its work is complicated and it has a secretary, it is sometimes better to have him make the report because the records are more available to him and he may be more familiar with them. Under any circumstances, it is necessary that the committee agree on who is to make the report before it is due.

When the time comes and the report is called for, the reporting member secures the floor and reads the report or states the gist of it without reading it. If desired or if the report is at all complicated, a written copy should be handed to the presiding officer or secretary of the assembly. Usually the reporting member moves the adoption or acceptance of the report but if he does not, any member of the society may do so.

It requires a two-thirds vote to receive a report out of the regular order of business because this is the same as a suspension of the rules. If there is no provision in the regular order of business for receiving a given report, when the report is ready, the reporting member may obtain the floor and state that the report is ready. The chair may state that if there is no objection the report will be received or he may put it to a vote by asking the assembly, "Shall the report be received now?" A majority vote is required and the question is undebatable. Usually it is not necessary to vote on receiving a report since the matter is ordinarily settled by general consent.

105. COMMITTEE REPORTS, ADOPTION OR ACCEPTANCE OF. When a committee report has been presented to the organization, it is said to have been "received" and must be disposed of in one of several ways depending upon its content. In some instances, the motion for the disposal of the report is made by the reporting member of the committee and in other cases the motion should come from some other member of the assembly.

1. When the report contains only information or facts for the assembly, it is only proper for another member to move to "accept" the report. Actually such a motion is not necessary but it is usually used to indicate approval of the report or the work of the committee and has the effect of endorsing its contents. If the assembly does not approve the report, the motion to "accept" should be defeated since its passage makes the organization responsible for it.

2. If the committee has made a recommendation but has not placed it in the form of a motion, the proper form is to move to "adopt" the recommendation. This motion may be made by the reporting member of the committee or by any other member of the assembly.

3. If the recommendation is in the form of a motion or resolution or resolutions, the proper form is to move to "adopt" and again may be made by anyone but is usually made by the reporting member. A word of warning is important here. If the motion to "adopt" is passed in this instance or in the case of 2 above, it means that the assembly agrees to carry out the recommendation contained in the motion. Therefore, if the assembly does not wish to take the action recommended in the motion or resolution presented by the committee, the motion to "adopt" must be defeated. The parent body need not adopt an entire committee report. It may eliminate parts or adopt with reservations but it may not add to a committee report since then it is not the report of the committee.

The motion to "adopt" is the same as "to agree to." Thus the motion to "accept" a report applies if no action is involved but the assembly accepts responsibility; whereas, the motion to "adopt" means to agree to the report and to carry out its recommendations. Frequently these two motions . . . . to "accept" and to "adopt" are used interchangeably, however the above distinction is preferable.

106. COMMITTEE REPORTS, AMENDMENT OF. When the report of a committee includes a recommendation for action, it should be accompanied by a motion to adopt the report. When this is done, the motion to adopt becomes an ordinary main motion and may be treated as such. This being the case, the recommendation may be amended in the same manner as any other regular main motion. It should be pointed out, however, that if the matter was referred to the committee in the first place, objection to consideration of the motion to adopt may not be made since the matter was previously considered at the time it was referred. Also, it should be made clear that any amendments which are applied or attached to the recommendation are acts of the assembly and are not a part of the committee's report. The assembly has no right to change the report of the committee in any way although it does have the right to alter what it adopts. Thus if the picnic committee recommends that the society hold a picnic on July fourth at three-thirty in the afternoon and this recommendation is amended to change the time to one o'clock in the afternoon, the minutes should clearly indicate that the recommendation of the committee was three-thirty because the recommendation of the committee cannot be altered by the society. Since the time was changed to one o'clock by the society, this should be indicated as an act of the society not as the recommendation of the committee. The committee's report should be recorded exactly as it was made and any alterations in it made by the assembly should be indicated as such.

107. COMMITTEE REPORTS, FORMS OF. The forms used by committees in making their reports are almost as varied as the number of committees but there are certain rules which should be followed if a written report is submitted. In most clubs the usual report is made verbally and no written report is necessary but if the report contains recommendations, resolutions or any other material which should be in the records of the society, a written report should be submitted. When a written report is submitted, it should begin by stating the name of the committee, its purpose and the date it was appointed. At the end of the report, the expression "respectfully submitted" is no longer used although there is some disagreement among parliamentarians on this point. The report should end with the word "signed" which should be followed by the signatures of the members of the committee. The name of the chairman should be the first but should not be followed by the word "chairman." The committee may authorize the chairman to sign the report. In this case, his is the only signature that appears and is followed by the word "Chairman." There are several kinds of committee reports depending upon the nature of the committee.

1. *Report of fact.* When a committee is charged with the responsibility of investigating a matter for the purpose of getting information only, it makes a report of fact without recommendation for action as follows:

Podunk, Michigan
May 13, 19——

To the Podunk Civic Society:

The committee appointed May 6, 19 . . . . to investigate possible sites for holding the annual picnic begs leave to submit the following report:

1. Clark Park has boating, fishing and swimming facilities. Adequate picnic tables and camp stoves with a supply of fuel are available. There are two soft-ball diamonds and facilities for horse-shoes and volley-ball. It is located twenty-five miles from town and is usually crowded on week-ends.

2. Jones Park has no water sports . . . . swimming, boating, etc. The picnic facilities are considerably better than Clark Park and it is located in a wooded area with opportunity for hiking. It has three soft-ball diamonds, two volley-ball courts and ample opportunity for horse-shoe pitching. It is located ten miles from town.

Signed,
George Smith
Helen Brown
Harry Boyd

2. *Report recommending action.* When a committee is charged with the responsibility of investigating a matter for the purpose of recommending a course of action, it reports as follows:

Podunk, Michigan
May 13, 19——

To the Podunk Civic Society:

The committee appointed May 6, 19—— to investigate and recommend a site for holding the annual picnic begs leave to submit the following report:

1. Clark Park has boating, fishing and swimming facilities. Adequate picnic tables and camp stoves with a supply of fuel are available. There are two soft-ball diamonds and facilities for horseshoes and volley-ball. It is located twenty-five miles from town and is usually crowded on week-ends.

2. Jones Park has no water sports – swimming, boating, etc. The picnic facilities are considerably better than Clark Park and it is

located in a wooded area with opportunity for hiking. It has three soft-ball diamonds, two volley-ball courts and ample opportunity for horseshoe pitching. It is ten miles from town.

Signed,
George Smith
Helen Brown
Harry Boyd

Recommendation

The committee recommends the adoption of the following resolution:

Whereas, a poll of the membership shows that a large percentage wish to participate in boating and swimming activities; and

Whereas, Clark Park has such facilities; and

Whereas, this is the only park with such facilities within a reasonable distance of Podunk; therefore be it

Resolved, that the Podunk Civic Society hold its annual picnic at Clark Park.

Signed,
George Smith
Helen Brown
Harry Boyd

3. *Action report.* Frequently a committee is given the responsibility of exercising its judgment in arriving at a decision and carrying out whatever action results from that decision. For example, the Podunk Civic Society, in the illustration above, might give its committee full power to decide on a place for the picnic and to make whatever arrangements are necessary. In this case, the committee would report as follows:

Podunk, Michigan
May 13, 19——

To the Podunk Civic Society:

The committee appointed May 6, 19—— to secure a suitable site for the annual picnic begs leave to submit the following report:

The committee polled the members to determine the kind of facilities desired. This poll indicated that the members were interested in boating, swimming and soft-ball; that the members want suitable cooking facilities and adequate picnic tables.

After investigation of the various park and recreation areas, the committee unanimously agreed that Clark Park was the most suitable to the desires of the society.

The committee then contacted the Department of Parks and Recreation and reserved sufficient space and equipment, including boats and soft-ball equipment as well as tables and stoves. The committee took the responsibility of signing the necessary forms required by the Department of Parks and Recreation.

Signed,

George Smith

Helen Brown

Harry Boyd

4. *Minority report.* Sometimes the members of a committee disagree among themselves. This is especially true when the committee is recommending action. One of the reasons for appointing an odd number of persons on a committee is so that if there is disagreement, there can be both a majority and a minority report. They cannot split evenly. When a committee disagrees, the minority may also submit a report as follows:

Podunk, Michigan

May 13, 19——

To the Podunk Civic Society:

A minority of the committee appointed on May 6, 19—— to investigate possible sites for holding the annual picnic begs leave to submit the following report:

1. Clark Park has boating, fishing and swimming facilities. Adequate picnic tables and camp stoves with a supply of fuel are available. There are two soft-ball diamonds and facilities for horseshoes and volley-ball. It is located twenty-five miles from town and is usually crowded on week-ends.

2. Jones Park has no water sports — swimming, boating, etc. The picnic facilities are considerably better than Clark Park and it is located in a wooded area with opportunity for hiking. It has three soft-ball diamonds, two volley-ball courts and ample opportunity for horseshoe pitching. It is ten miles from town.

Signed,

Walter Black

Mary McAndrews

Recommendation

Whereas, it is true that Jones Park does not have water facilities, and

Whereas, Jones Park does have much better picnic facilities, and

Whereas, Jones Park offers facilities not available at Clark Park such

97

as hiking, bird watching and nature study, and

Whereas, Jones Park is located only ten miles from town and with excellent bus service; Therefore be it

Resolved, that the Podunk Civic Society hold its annual picnic at Jones Park.

Signed,
Walter Black
Mary McAndrews

5. *Executive committee report.* A small organization which has an executive committee frequently does not require a written report but, just like any other committee, if the report contains any material which should be preserved in the records of the society, a written report should be submitted. Usually such a report is made annually or periodically, covering a certain stated period of time. Following is an example of such a report:

Podunk, Michigan
April 1, 19——

To the members of the Podunk Civic Society:

The Executive Committee begs leave to submit the following report for the first quarter of 19—— beginning January 1, 19—— and ending March 31, 19——.

Since it was decided by the Society that its activities during the year 19—— would be confined to a study of highway accidents, the Executive Committee has likewise confined its efforts to this area. The Committee has attempted to accomplish the following general objectives:

1. to study major accidents in our city in order to determine major causes.

2. to promote highway safety in an effort to reduce accidents.

3. to publicize causes of highway accidents in order to make the public aware of these causes.

The Committee has recommended action upon the following activities:

1. the appointment of a committee to study the causes of accidents.

2. the appointment of a publicity committee.

3. the election of a Safety Director to work with the City Commission and Police Department.

The Executive Committee is pleased to report that favorable action was taken by the Society and that progress is being made in the entire area of highway safety.

Signed,
Joseph Sears
William Conrad
Louise Collins
Gerald Yates

108. COMMITTEE REPORTS, MINORITY. Frequently committee members disagree and sometimes this disagreement is strong enough so that the minority may wish to make a separate report. When the majority report has been received by the society and a motion made for its adoption or acceptance, a member of the minority (usually the leader) asks leave to make a minority report. (see **COMMITTEE REPORTS, FORM OF**.) Usually societies allow minority reports without any objection but if there is an objection by any member, the motion to receive the report requires a majority vote to pass and the motion is undebatable. When the minority report has been made and handed to the chairman or secretary, two possibilities are open to the assembly. A motion may be made to substitute the minority for the majority report. Such a motion is really in the nature of an amendment to the motion to adopt or accept the majority report. As such, it may be debated and requires a majority vote.

If no motion to substitute is made, the minority report is simply considered as debate on the main motion and the society acts on the majority report. Even if the minority report is not read, any member of the society, including a minority member of the committee, may move to substitute the resolutions favored by the minority for the resolutions in the majority report.

Sometimes even the members of the minority cannot agree among themselves and several minority reports are submitted. Also, sometimes a committee member will agree with all but one part of the committee report. In this case, after the other members have signed, the dissenting member writes at the end of the report that he agrees with all but the part which he specifies, then he signs the report.

109. COMMITTEE REPORTS, PLACE OF, IN THE ORDER OF BUSINESS. If the society has not adopted a different order of business, committee reports should follow the treasurer's report and should precede correspondence, as follows:

1. call to order.
2. roll call.
3. reading of the minutes of the last meeting.
4. treasurer's report.
5. reports of standing committees.
6. reports of special committees.
7. correspondence.
8. special orders.
9. old business.
10. new business.
11. announcements.
12. adjournment.

110. COMMITTEE REPORTS, RECEPTION OF. Many organizations adopt a standard agenda or order of business which they follow in all regular meetings. When this is done, there is usually a place provided for reports of committees. When the time for reports arrives, the chair calls for reports of standing committees in the order provided for in the rules. Then he calls for reports of special committees in the order in which they were appointed. When a report is called for, the reporting member (usually but not necessarily the chairman of the committee) obtains the floor in the usual manner, reads the report and hands it to the chairman or secretary. If the report requires action by the society, the reporting member (or some other member of the society) moves that the report be accepted or adopted, whichever is appropriate.

If there is no provision in the order of business for committee reports, the report may be made at any time the committee is ready, provided no business is pending and the society is willing to receive the report. The reporting member obtains the floor and states that the committee has agreed upon a report and is ready to present it. The chair may then direct him to make the report if he believes the assembly is ready to receive it. The report is read, handed to the chair or secretary and the appropriate motion is made for its adoption or acceptance; if the chair is not sure whether the society is ready to receive the report, he should put it to a vote. If a majority are in favor, the report is received. The motion to receive a report is undebatable. If a majority are opposed to receiving the report, a time should be set for its reception.

111. COMMITTEE, TO DISCHARGE A. There are several reasons for discharging a committee.

1. The committee may be failing to fulfill its responsibilities.

2. The society may change its mind and decide not to refer the matter. This cannot be done if the committee has started work.

3. The committee may have completed its work, made its report and therefore have no further need for existing.

If the reason for discharging the committee is either because it has been remiss in doing its work or because the society has changed its mind about referring the matter, the motion may be made "to discharge the committee from further consideration of the question." Such a motion should be stated like this: "I move that the special committee appointed to (state the matter referred) be discharged from further consideration of the matter." This motion requires a second and is debatable and amendable. If the motion to discharge is made at the same meeting that the matter was referred, it requires either a two-thirds vote of those voting or a majority vote of the entire membership to pass. If the motion is made at a later meeting, it requires the same vote if previous notice was given or a two-thirds vote if no previous notice was given.

Passage of the motion to discharge takes the matter out of the hands of the committee and if there is no further reason for its continued existence, it is automatically dissolved.

When a committee is discharged and it is desired to consider the matter referred to it, this must either be included in the motion to discharge or stated in a separate motion.

When a committee has completed its work and made its report, it is automatically discharged and no motion to discharge is necessary.

112. COMMITTEES, APPOINTMENT OF. The following methods may be used for choosing the membership of a committee:

1. The person making the motion to refer may use the qualified form and name the members of the committee, thus: "I move that this matter be referred to a committee of three consisting of Mr. A as chairman, Miss B and Mr. C." If this motion is passed, the three named persons constitute the committee.

2. The unqualified motion to refer may be amended by another member who qualifies it by adding the names, thus: "I move that the motion to refer the matter to a committee be amended by adding 'and that they consist of Mr. A. as chairman, Miss B and Mr. C.' " If both the

amendment and main motion are passed, the committee is named.

3. After the unqualified motion to refer has been passed, a member may move that the committee consist of certain persons, thus; "I move that the committee be made up Mr. C as chairman, Miss B, and Mr. A." This is a main motion and is subject to debate and amendment. If the motion passes, the committee is selected.

4. The committee may be entirely appointed by the chair. This is one of the most usual methods.

5. The committee may be nominated by the chair and elected by the assembly. In this case, if the names nominated by the chair or any of them are not elected, the chair must continue to make nominations until a full committee has been elected.

6. The committee may be both nominated and elected by the assembly. If only the exact number of names are nominated as are needed to fill the committee, no vote is necessary and the chair may declare the names elected but if more names are nominated than are needed, the names are voted on in the order nominated until enough are elected. Both an affirmative and negative vote must be taken on each name in order to determine which names receive a majority.

Great care should be taken in selecting a committee. If possible, persons should be selected who are interested in the matter referred, who have some knowledge of the matter and who will be willing to do the work.

113. COMMITTEES CLASSIFIED. Much of the work of many organizations is done in committees. In the United States Congress and in the State Legislatures no bill may be debated on the floor until it has first been considered in committee. Also, large national societies depend upon committees, especially the executive committee, to carry out the major work of the society. And even the ordinary small club must depend upon committees to do some of the work. A committee is a relatively small group of persons appointed or elected by the parent organization to carry out tasks, make studies and investigations or do whatever work may be assigned to it. There are four classifications of committees.

1. Executive committees which go under various titles such as board of directors, board of managers, board of trustees, and others. (see **COMMITTEE, EXECUTIVE AND BOARDS**)

2. Standing committees which are usually elected, serve for a definite term and are assigned a given area of the society's work such as

program committee, finance committee and membership committee. (see **COMMITTEES, SPECIAL AND STANDING**)

3. Special committees which are usually temporary in nature and are assigned a specific job and which are dismissed when the job is finished.

4. Committee of the whole which consists of the entire society which resolves itself into a committee in order to consider a matter in a more informal manner. (see **COMMITTEE OF THE WHOLE**)

114. COMMITTEES, COMPOSITION OF. In many ways a committee is a miniature assembly although it is not bound by all the same rules of parliamentary law and usually has more freedom and less formality in its meetings. On the other hand, a committee is restricted by its ties to the parent organization since it must follow instructions and concern itself only with those matters referred to it. The officers of most committees consist of only a chairman, although, if the work is complicated a secretary may be needed also. Even more rarely a vice chairman and treasurer may be necessary officers of a committee. In most cases these officers, with the exception of the chairman, are elected by the committee itself and in some instances the chairman is selected in this way. The duties of the committee officers are essentially the same as similar or equivalent officers in a society.

115. COMMITTEES, EXECUTIVE AND BOARDS. There are several names by which an executive board may be designated. Among them are the following:

1. board of managers.
2. board of directors.
3. board of trustees.
4. governing board.
5. executive committee.
6. executive board.
7. administrative committee.

All such boards are small deliberative groups which represent a larger parent organization and they derive all their power and authority from the parent society. They do not have any inherent power of their own. The authority of the board may be stated in the constitution or in the by-laws or be given to it by a vote of the society. Such things as duties, quorum, time of meeting, officers and procedures are determined by the parent organization. The by-laws and other rules governing the board are adopted by the parent society unless the board is authorized to adopt its own.

The purpose of such a board is to represent the parent body, to conduct the business of the society between meetings and to carry on such other business as is assigned to it. In societies which meet infrequently, such as quarterly or annually, a board is vitally important.

116. COMMITTEES, INSTRUCTIONS TO. Since a committee is the creation of the parent society, it is the right of the parent to direct or instruct the committee in any way it may wish. These instructions may be included as a part of the motion to commit or as an amendment to this motion. Also, a separate motion to instruct a committee in a certain way may be passed by a majority vote. Suppose a motion has been passed that a committee be appointed to investigate a certain matter. A motion could be made to direct the committee to interview Mr. X in regard to the matter. This would be in the nature of instructions. A committee may be given instructions at any time up to the submission of its final report.

117. COMMITTEES, PROPER SIZE OF. A committee may consist of any number of persons. Usually they range in size anywhere from one to twenty with three, five or seven being the most frequently used number. The number on a committee is generally uneven in order to avoid a deadlock. If the society has agreed on a certain action and is selecting a committee to carry it out, the committee should be small and should be in favor of the action. Any person suggested for such a committee who is opposed to the action should ask to be excused because it is necessary for such a committee to work harmoniously. On the other hand, a deliberative or investigative committee should be fairly large and should be composed of persons representing all of the conflicting points of view of the members of the assembly. The value of such a committee will be greatly reduced if an important point of view is not represented. It should be remembered that the larger the committee, the harder it is to hold meetings and the more unwieldy the meetings become. Therefore, committees should be kept as small as possible, consistent with the above.

118. COMMITTEES, SPECIAL AND STANDING. In many societies it is common practice to have much of the work done by committees.

Such committees are either special or standing depending on the nature of the work assigned to them.

Special committees (sometimes called "Ad hoc" committees, though this is to be deplored) are chosen to do a particular job and are dismissed when the job is completed and a report made. Special committees are usually appointed by the presiding officer but may be elected or may be named by the maker in a qualified motion to refer or commit. In small committees, the chairman generally acts as secretary and keeps notes of the proceedings and actions taken. If the work is complicated or the committee large, a secretary is frequently elected. A special committee may hold several meetings in which case it adjourns at the end of each meeting except the last when the motion is made to "rise" or to "rise and report." To adjourn assumes that the committee will meet again at the call of the chairman; therefore, to adjourn without fixing a time for the next meeting does not disband the committee and all of the meetings are considered as one session. When the motion is made to "rise" or to "rise and report," it is assumed that the committee has completed its work and this will be the last meeting. Meetings may be called by the chairman at any time but if he fails to call meetings, they may be called by any two members if they notify all the other members. A special committee may be discharged by a two-thirds vote of the society but unless this happens, it continues to exist until the work assigned to it is completed.

When a special committee has completed its work, it prepares a report and passes the motion to rise or to rise and report. The report is usually made by the chairman but not necessarily. A committee may disagree on the report, in which case two reports are made—a majority report and a minority report—the chairman making the report with which he agrees. A special committee may not consider any business of the society except that assigned to it. All papers and documents given to it and belonging to the society must be returned to the society but papers belonging to the committee, including minutes of its proceedings, may be retained or destroyed by the committee.

Standing committees are permanent in nature, may be either elected or appointed, are provided for in the rules of the society and their duties and power generally specified. Even though the rules do not provide for them, a standing committee may be established by custom or common practice. Usually the term of office of members of standing committees coincide with the term of office of the officers of the society but frequently the term is longer and staggered so that only a part of the committee goes out of office at a time. This is especially true when it is considered wise to have a nucleus of experienced persons on the committee. Standing committees are often called permanent committees. They do all the work of a particular kind assigned to them and, unlike special committees, often work independently of the parent organization. They may make reports from time to time as called for by the society and usually prepare an annual report which is adopted or accepted by a vote of the society. Acceptance of a report by the society does not disband a standing committee as it does in the case of a special committee. Examples of standing committees are: Finance Committee, Membership Committee, Program Committee, Flowers Committee, Entertainment Committee, Social Committee and Publicity Committee.

119. CONSENT CAN BE GIVEN ONLY WHEN QUORUM IS PRESENT. Only four motions may be made in a meeting when a quorum is not present; they are:
1. motions dealing with an attempt to secure a quorum.
2. the motion to fix the time of the next meeting.
3. the motion to take a recess.
4. the motion to adjourn.

General or unanimous consent cannot be used in the absence of a quorum and any notice given or announcement made is neither valid nor official.

120. CONSENT, GENERAL OR UNANIMOUS. General consent (sometimes called "unanimous consent" or "silent consent") is a device by which the chairman can expedite the conducting of business by avoiding the formality of making motions and/or voting, by assuming that everyone agrees. Much of the business handled in meetings is routine or of little importance and may be handled in this way unless there is an objection. Perhaps the best example of the use of general consent is the approval of the minutes of the last meeting. They are read and the chair says, "Are there any corrections?" He pauses and then says, "Hearing none, the minutes stand approved as read." This assumes two things. First, it assumes that since no one spoke up, there were no corrections to be made. Secondly, it assumes that since there were no corrections, the assembly will approve the minutes as read and, therefore, there is no need to waste time by putting the matter to vote.

The device may be used by the chairman at any time when he

believes that there will be no objection. For example, when a committee announces that it is ready to report, the chair may say, "If there is no objection, we will receive the report of the committee on (naming the subject)."

Objection on the part of any member of the society will prevent the use of this device. If there is objection, the chair simply reverts to the usual method of deciding the matter by putting it to a vote. Even though no objection is made, it does not necessarily mean that every member is in favor of the motion. The opposed member may simply realize that it is useless to object since the matter would be passed anyway and so in the interest of facilitating business, he does not object.

121. CONSIDERATION BY PARAGRAPH OR SERIATIM. When a number of closely related items are submitted under one motion to adopt, such as a set of rules, a set of by-laws or a series of resolutions, it is not desirable to adopt each one separately because as soon as one is adopted it goes into effect immediately and may affect a later one. Also, it may be necessary, as the result of a later item, to change an earlier one that has already been considered and if the earlier one has been adopted, it can only be changed by a motion to reconsider. A much better method is to consider each one separately but not to vote on it until all have been considered and then to vote on all of them at once. This procedure is called "consideration by paragraph" or "consideration seriatim."

The proper form of this motion, "I move that this matter be considered by paragraph (or seriatim)." The word article, resolution or section may be substituted for the word paragraph if it is more appropriate. While considering each separate paragraph, amendments may be offered and these amendments may be adopted. Also, it is possible to return to a previously considered paragraph and make other changes if it is desired. This cannot be done if each paragraph is voted on separately at the time it is considered.

122. CONSIDERATION OF QUESTION, INFORMAL. Informal consideration of a question works better in groups where the meetings are not large. In such groups, informal consideration is better and easier than going into committee of the whole or quasi committee of the whole. The motion "I move that the question be considered informally," if passed, opens the main question and any amendments that may be attached to it to free debate in the same manner as if the society was in committee of the whole. The number and length of speeches may be limited by a two-thirds vote and the previous question may be passed in the same manner but unless this is done, the debate is completely open although this freedom of debate is limited to the one question and its amendments. Any other matter that is brought before the assembly is subject to the same limitations of debate as in a regular meeting of the society. In granting the floor to members who wish to speak, the chairman should give the preference to members who have not previously spoken. In other words, a member who has already spoken should not speak a second time, if there are others who wish to speak. Although the consideration of the question is informal, all votes are formal the same as in a regular session. As soon as the question which is being considered informally is disposed of, the informal consideration stops. No motion is necessary to revert back to the formal meeting.

123. CONSIDERATION OF QUESTION, OBJECTION TO. Any member of a society may object to the consideration of any original main motion provided the objection is made before there has been any debate on the question and provided no secondary motions have been applied to it. The proper form for making this motion is, "Mr. Chairman, I object to the consideration of this question." This motion may interrupt a speaker and the maker does not need to secure the floor before making it. It does not require a second and is undebatable. It may not be amended, reconsidered or renewed. When objection to consideration is made, the chair should say, "Objection to consideration of this question has been made. Shall we consider the question? All those in favor of considering the question make it known by (name the method of voting)." A two-thirds vote in the negative is necessary to prevent consideration. If the objection to consideration is upheld, the question to which it is applied is dropped and may not be considered again at that meeting. It may be introduced again at a succeeding meeting. If the objection is not upheld by a two-thirds vote, the consideration of the question is continued exactly as if no objection had been made.

124. CONSTITUTION, ADOPTION OF. When the constitution committee is ready to report, it makes this fact known to the presiding officer of the assembly who then calls for the report of the committee.

The constitution is adopted in the following manner which should be followed rigidly:

1. The chairman (or reporting member) of the constitution committee reads the proposed constitution *as a whole* and presents it to the secretary with the motion that it be adopted.

2. The secretary reads the constitution *article by article and section by section.* The presiding officer asks after each whether there are any amendments to be proposed. Proposed amendments are either incorporated by permission of the committee or are voted on as they are offered. The article or section is not voted on at this time. The preamble is always considered last.

3. When the final article (or preamble) has been read, the secretary again reads the constitution *as a whole* as it then stands including any amendments which may have been made.

4. The presiding officer then asks if there are any further amendments to be made to any part of the constitution. If there are, they are incorporated at this time.

5. The presiding officer then calls for a vote on the original motion made at the beginning by the chairman of the constitution committee that the constitution be adopted. If the majority vote favorably, the constitution is adopted.

125. CONSTITUTION, AMENDMENT OR REVISION OF. Every constitution, set of by-laws and set of standing rules should contain an article providing a method by which they may be amended. If they do not contain such an article, they may be amended at any regular (but not special) meeting of the society by a majority vote of the *entire* membership. If a copy of the proposed amendment was submitted in writing at the immediately preceeding regular meeting, then they may be amended by a two-thirds vote *of those voting* if a quorum is present. The above is the basic parliamentary rule for amending these documents. Beyond this rule, each organization may and should set up its own rules. (For more specific details see **AMENDMENT OF CONSTITUTION, BY-LAWS AND RULES OF ORDER.**)

126. CONSTITUTION, CONTENTS OF. The constitution of a society is its basic law and, therefore, should contain nothing which the society may wish to suspend although, if the article dealing with the election of officers provides that the election is to be by ballot, the article should also provide that by unanimous agreement officers may be elected other than by ballot if there is only one candidate. The following items are the basic content of a constitution:

1. Preamble. The preamble consists of a brief statement of the aims and purposes of the organization.

2. Article I states the name of the organization and, if the preamble is omitted, contains a brief statement of the purposes of the organization.

3. Article II states the requirements for membership.

4. Article III contains a list of the officers, defines their term of office, and method of election, and determines their duties.

5. Article IV provides for a board of directors or an executive committee and for the method of selecting. This article may also provide for other committees.

6. Article V states the time and place for regular meetings and provides a method by which special meetings may be called.

7. Article VI contains a statement of the method of amending the constitution and the vote required for such amendment.

The articles of a constitution may be sub-divided into sections if desired.

127. CONVENTION, MINUTES OF. When a society holds frequent regular meetings and also an annual convention, the minutes of the last regular meeting should be read and approved at the convention and conversely, the minutes of the convention should be read and approved at the next regular meeting following the convention. When a society meets only once a year in an annual convention which lasts several days, the minutes should not be held over from one annual meeting to the next. Rather, the minutes of the preceding day should be read each day at the beginning of the meeting. On the last day of the convention, the minutes should be read at the end of the meeting. However, frequently there is neither time nor interest enough at the end of the convention. In this case, the executive committee may be authorized to approve the minutes or a special committee may be appointed for this purpose.

128. CONVENTION, ORGANIZING AND CONDUCTING. Conventions may be of two kinds, namely:

1. An *organized convention* which is a convention of a society already organized such as the convention of the American Medical Association, the American Management Association, the Speech

110

Association of America, Unions, etc.

2. A *convention not yet organized* is a convention of delegates called for the purpose of organizing a permanent or semi-permanent society and holding its first convention. The procedure in the two is considerably different.

An organized convention should have already adopted a constitution and/or by-laws and previously elected officers. A well planned convention is much more likely to be a successful one and the job of planning and carrying out a convention is placed in the hands of a number of committees appointed at the previous convention or shortly thereafter by the executive committee or the president of the society or by whatever method is prescribed in the rules. The following committees are the ones that bear the brunt of the work of the convention:

1. Credentials and/or registration.
2. Program.
3. Resolutions.
4. Transportation.
5. Rules.
6. Public Relations.
7. Housing.
8. Arrangements.
9. Courtesy.
10. Decorations.
11. Entertainment.

The work of these committees must be planned before the convention and the work of some of them must be completed by then. The last five committees named above are usually assisted by local committees in the convention city.

The Credentials or Registration committee should prepare facilities for the registration of members or delegates, for checking credentials, if necessary, and should supervise the registration. This is a big job and in a large convention, will involve considerable clerical assistance. In a small convention, the work may be handled entirely by the committee. When he registers, it is usual for the credentials committee to furnish each delegate or member with an identification card or badge which admits him to the meetings. Also this committee keeps a record of those registered for its report later. All this work will require that the committee be on hand early or, in large conventions lasting several days, even a day or two before the opening meeting. The report of the credentials committee is usually made immediately following the opening exercises and consists of a list of the delegates and their alternates. The list should not contain any names of delegates who have not yet registered. The list does contain the names of registered ex-officio members. The report of the committee is read either by the chairman of the committee or the secretary of the society or an official reader, if there is one. If there is a contest between two delegates or sets of delegates, the Credentials Committee may decide the contest and place on the list the names of the delegates that should be seated. If the committee is in doubt, the names of both sets of delegates is omitted from the list and the fact of the contest reported to the convention and the issue settled on the floor with neither set of contesting delegates being allowed to vote. When the credentials or registration committee has reported, it is not dismissed as in the case of ordinary committees because it may be needed to handle late registrations and make supplementary reports.

The function of the program committee in conventions is to prepare a program for the business of the convention which may last over several days. Usually the committee has the program printed and distributed to the members. When the presiding officer calls for it, the chairman of the program committee makes his report or submits the printed program and moves that it be adopted. This motion is debatable and may be amended. It requires a majority vote for adoption but once adopted, the program cannot be changed or deviated from except by a two-thirds vote of those voting or by a majority vote of the entire membership. The report of the program committee is usually called for immediately following the report of the credentials committee. Like the credentials committee, the program committee is not dismissed when its report is made because speakers may fail to appear and it may be necessary to get substitutes.

When the time arrives for the opening meeting of the convention to convene, the presiding officer (usually the President) calls the meeting to order. There is usually considerable confusion, especially in large conventions, therefore, the President must use tact and firmness to get the meeting under way. After the meeting has come to order, there are usually some opening exercises which generally consist of a prayer or invocation, a welcoming speech and a response. Following the opening exercises, the report of the credentials committee is received and acted upon. No delegate is allowed to vote either at this time or later until he has registered and his name is on the list of official delegates. Following the report of the credentials committee, the program committee reports and its report is adopted. From this point on the convention follows the adopted program and at the end it adjourns sine die.

A convention not yet organized is like a mass meeting because it has no constitution, by-laws or other rules and no officers, but in a mass meeting everyone may vote while in a convention only official delegates may do so. It may be difficult to determine who the official delegates are. In a convention of this type, much preliminary work must be done, such as setting a time and place for the meeting, notifying delegates, securing a hall and all the other details necessary for the preparation. Since there are no previously appointed committees this work is usually done by the group of persons interested in promoting the convention. In addition to this, the group should decide who is to call the meeting to order, who will explain the purpose of the convention, who is to be nominated as temporary chairman and who will make the nomination. It is not a good idea to leave the temporary chairmanship to chance because, if a weak one is elected, it can jeopardize the entire convention.

When it is time to convene, the person chosen to do the job calls the meeting to order and a temporary chairman and secretary are chosen in the same manner as in any temporary organization. The first business is to appoint a credentials committee which must go to work immediately checking credentials since official business cannot be conducted until it is determined who may vote. The committee must examine all credentials and report to the convention the names of the eligible delegates. While this is being done, the temporary chairman should appoint three committees; (1) a nominating committee to nominate a slate of officers for the convention, (2) a committee on rules; and (3) a program committee. These committees should be appointed by the chair and no one should be placed on a committee if there is any doubt about his right to a seat in the convention. The rest of the time, while waiting for the credentials committee to report, is spent in listening to speeches. Meanwhile, the other three committees have been active and following the report of the credentials committee, their reports are received and acted upon. The convention is now organized and ready to conduct business since it has officers, rules and a program. If it is not intended to form a permanent organization, this is all that is needed.

If it is intended to form a permanent organization, a constitution committee is appointed instead of a rules committee and is appointed far enough in advance of the convention to prepare a proposed constitution which is adopted before the report of the nominating committee. If the constitution committee is not appointed until the convention opens, those who have prepared a proposed constitution in advance are placed on it.

129. CONVENTIONS, ORDER OF BUSINESS IN. The setting up of a program for a convention is usually entrusted to a program committee which is appointed well ahead of the convention time and which prepares a program. Generally, this program is printed and mailed to the members along with the notice of the convention. The program is not official, however, until it has been adopted by the convention. After the credentials committee has reported, the report of the program committee is received and adopted, with or without amendment. Once the program has been adopted, it becomes the order of business of the convention and may not be changed or deviated from except by a two-thirds vote of the convention.

130. CORRESPONDING SECRETARY. Small organizations usually have only one secretary whose title is "Secretary" and whose duty, among other things, is to carry on any correspondence of the organization including sending out notices of meetings. When an organization is large or has a large amount of correspondence due to its nature, it is desirable to have a corresponding secretary. It is his duty to send out notices of meetings, write and receive all correspondence and report any correspondence which may require action by the society. He may be assigned other duties but if so, they should be specified in the rules of the society. The word "corresponding" should always be used when referring to this officer because the word "secretary" when used alone always refers to the recording secretary.

131. CREDENTIALS COMMITTEE. The credentials or registration committee of a convention should prepare facilities for the registration of members or delegates, for checking credentials, if necessary, and should supervise the registration. This is a big job and, in large conventions, will involve considerable clerical assistance. In a small convention, the work may be handled entirely by the committee. When he registers, it is usual for the credentials committee to furnish each delegate or member with an identification card or badge which admits him to the meetings. Also, the credentials committee keeps a record of those registered for its report later. All this work will require that the committee be on hand early or, in large conventions lasting several days. even a day or two before the opening meeting. The report of the credentials committee is usually made following the opening exercises and consists of a list of delegates and their alternates. The list should not contain any names of delegates who have not yet registered. The list does contain the names of the registered ex-officio members. The report of the committee is read either by the chairman of the committee or the secretary of the convention or by an official reader, if there is one. If there is a contest between two delegates or sets of delegates, the credentials committee may decide the contest and place on the list the names of the delegates who should be seated. If the committee is in doubt, the names of both sets of delegates is omitted from the list and the fact of the contest reported to the convention. When the credentials or registration committee has reported, it is not dismissed as in the case of ordinary special committees because it may be needed to handle late registrations and make supplementary reports.

132. DAY, ORDERS OF THE. Orders of the day may be established in any one of several ways. If a matter is postponed to a certain time, it becomes the order of the day, for that time. The same is true if a matter is made a special order of business for a certain day and hour. Also, if an agenda of items to be considered at a meeting has been adopted, those items become the orders of the day. When an agenda has been adopted, it cannot be changed except by a two-thirds vote. Matters that are postponed to a certain time or are made a special order of business for a certain time, cannot be considered before that time except by a two-thirds vote.

133. DEBATE. In parliamentary language, the word "debate" is used to designate any discussion on a motion. While frequently discussion is argumentative, often it is not. It may be and frequently is explanatory. Therefore, the term debate should be recognized as meaning any discussion of the pending question, whether argumentative or not. Unless it is being considered informally or in committee, no ordinary matter is open to debate until three steps have been taken. First a motion must be made; second, the motion must be seconded; third, discussion must be called for by the chairman. When these three steps have been taken, the matter is open for debate.

Debate must be germane to the immediately pending question. For example, if a main motion is pending and an amendment has been properly placed on the floor, the immediately pending question is the amendment and debate must be limited to that until it is disposed of or until a motion which takes precedence over it is placed on the floor. Debate on the main motion is not germane.

Speakers should always address their remarks to the chairman, not to another member of the assembly. Profane language and discourteous remarks are unparliamentary. A speaker should always speak of another member in the third person. Courtesy, fair play and good ethics are important in debate.

134. DEBATE, CLOSING AND PREVENTING BY CHAIR. The presiding officer of an assembly should be constantly alert to the temper of the assembly over which he is presiding. When he believes the debate on a motion is finished, he should ask; "Is there any further discussion? Are you ready for the question?" If no one claims the floor, the chair, after a brief pause, should put the question (call for a vote). This does not actually close debate because any time before the negative vote is taken, a member may claim the floor and continue the debate even if the affirmative vote has been taken. If this happens, it is necessary to take the entire vote over. When it appears to the chairman that this is being done merely to delay the vote, the chair must protect the assembly by declaring the member out of order in the same manner he would handle any other dilatory act. If both the affirmative and negative votes have been taken, but it is necessary to vote over because the chair is in doubt or because a division of the house has been called for, debate is closed and may not be reopened except by general consent.

135. DEBATE CONFINED TO IMMEDIATELY PENDING QUESTION. When there is more than one motion before the assembly, debate must be confined to the immediately pending question. This is the motion last stated by the chair; when both a motion and an amendment are on the floor, the immediately pending question is the amendment. When there are two motions on the floor and one takes precedence over the other, the one taking precedence is the immediately pending question and must be debated first. Since there can never be two motions of equal rank on the floor at the same time, the question of precedence is no problem.

136. DEBATE, DECORUM IN. Proper decorum in debate applies not only to the speaker who has the floor, but to the other members of the assembly as well. The following rules are standard parliamentary law:

1. Debate must be germane to the immediately pending question. The speaker must confine his remarks to the matter before the assembly.

2. The speaker must avoid personalities. Any remark which is derogatory or which reflects upon the character of another member or the assembly is not permitted unless that is the subject of the debate.

3. A member should avoid using the name of another member. He should be referred to by title or by some other designation. For example; "The gentleman from Indiana," "The Senator from Texas," "The speaker who just left the floor."

4. Remarks or questions should never be directed to another member, but always to the presiding officer; for example; "Mr. Chairman, will the speaker yield to a question?" Not; "Mr. Jones, will you yield to a question?"

5. The speaker is entitled to courteous attention. While a member

is speaking, unnecessary noise, talking, whispering, moving and walking about are unparliamentary.

6. Profane language and language unbecoming to the dignity of the assembly is out of order.

7. If a speaker is called to order either by the chair or another member, he should take his seat until the point is settled. If the speaker's remarks are decided to be improper, he may not continue to speak without permission of the assembly.

8. If a speaker's words are disorderly and he cannot justify them and will not apologize for them, the assembly must act. The offender must leave the room while the case is discussed.

9. If the disorderly words concern another member, both must leave the room except if disorderly words concern an officer, he need not leave.

10. If any business has been conducted following an unparliamentary act and before the act is objected to, it is too late to object unless the act is of such a nature that it will cause the assembly to continue to be unparliamentary.

11. Disturbance is not permitted during debate, while a motion is being made, while the chairman is speaking nor while a vote is being taken.

12. Dilatory remarks are out of order. Speaking for purpose of delaying progress is unparliamentary.

137. DEBATE, MEMBER INTRODUCING SUBJECT MAY CLOSE. If he wishes, the member introducing a matter or making a motion has the right to be the last speaker on that subject before a vote is taken. This gives him the chance to conclude the argument and answer the opponents of the measure. However, if there is a limit on debate and he has exhausted his allotted time or if he has already spoken twice and for a total of twenty minutes, the assembly has the right to deprive him of this privilege.

138. DEBATE, NUMBER AND LENGTH OF SPEECHES ALLOWED IN. Originally in parliamentary law, a member was entitled to speak as long and as many times as he could obtain the floor. The only restriction was that his remarks must be germane and he could not read, repeat nor speak with undue slowness.

In modern parliamentary procedure, it has been found desirable to place some restrictions on the number and length of speeches that may be made by any one member on a given question. Any society may make its own rules concerning debate and these rules may be changed by a two-thirds vote of those voting. If the society has no rules concerning debate and if no restrictions have been placed on a given motion by the assembly, parliamentary practice dictates that no member shall speak more than ten minutes at a time nor more than twice on a given matter. Also a member should not be allowed to speak a second time as long as a member who has not spoken wishes to do so. The maker of a motion should be allowed to speak first if he wishes and also to close the debate if he has not exhausted his twenty minutes.

If a member, while speaking, yields the floor to another, the time is charged against the speaker just as though he had continued speaking. On the other hand, if the speaker is interrupted by a point of order or other matter that may interrupt a speaker, the time taken by the interruption is not charged against him.

139. DEBATE, PRINCIPLES REGULATING THE EXTENT OF.
Debate is allowed, prohibited or limited according to certain basic rules.

1. All regular main motions are debatable. Since main motions introduce business on the floor of the assembly, it is deemed wise to allow unlimited debate. By unlimited debate is meant limited only by the rules of the society and parliamentary law.

2. Motions of high privilege are undebatable because their high privilege indicates that they are urgent and should be settled without delay. This includes all incidental motions such as appeal, point of order, parliamentary inquiry, withdraw a motion, suspend the rules, objection to consideration, division of the question and division of the assembly. Also the privileged motions to adjourn (when unqualified), to recess (when privileged) and orders of the day. To rise to a question of privilege is undebatable, but when the request is stated as a motion, it is debatable.

3. Motions that suspend the rules or have the same effect are undebatable. Therefore, all motions dealing with limiting debate, extending debate, and closing debate are not debatable.

4. The motion to close debate requires a two-thirds vote, therefore, an appeal made while the previous question is in effect, is undebatable.

5. The motions to amend and to reconsider are debatable if the motion to which they apply is debatable, otherwise they are not.

6. Secondary motions are debatable or not depending upon the

119

extent to which they prevent the assembly from considering the motion to which they are applied. For example, to postpone indefinitely prevents the assembly from considering a question, therefore, it is subject to free debate. To refer to a committee allows the assembly to again consider the question when the committee reports, therefore, to refer is debatable only as to the desirability of referring and instructing the committee. To postpone to a certain time has the same status. When a motion is laid on the table, the assembly may take it up at any time, so this motion is not debatable.

140. DEBATE, TO CLOSE NOW. The motion to close debate is called the "previous question." If the motion were properly named, it would be called "the motion to close debate." Previous question is not only a misnomer, but is confusing because frequently when a vote is called for on a previous question, many people think they are voting on the pending motion. This is not true. They are simply voting to close debate on the pending motion and must then proceed to vote on this motion. This confusion is due to the fact that in England where the previous question originated (as did most of our parliamentary law) the call for the previous question means something entirely different. Originally, in the United States the motion meant the same as it does in England, but in this country it has gradually undergone great changes although the original name has been kept. Only its present use in the United States will be considered here.

There are several forms of the previous question. The *informal* form means that when members of the assembly believe the group is ready to vote, they simply call out, "question." It is unnecessary to rise or be recognized for this, but they may not interrupt a speaker. When someone (or several) call "question," the chairman says; "Question has been called. If there is no objection, we will proceed to vote on the motion before the house which is . . . .," (stating the immediately pending motion). This is called "General Consent." An objection by a member of the assembly will prevent this action. (see **GENERAL CONSENT.**)

The more *formal* unqualified form means that the previous question is stated in the form of a formal motion. A member of the assembly rises, addresses the chair, is recognized and then says; "I call for (or move or demand) the previous question." This motion requires a second, may not interrupt a speaker and requires a two-thirds vote to pass. Obviously it is undebatable because to debate it would defeat its

120

purpose, which is to stop debate. The two-thirds vote is required because it is a violation of the basic parliamentary rule of free and full debate. When this motion is made it applies *only* to the immediately pending motion. Suppose for example, that there is pending a main motion, an amendment to the main motion and an amendment to the amendment. If the unqualified form of the previous question is used, it applies only to the immediately pending motion which is the amendment to the amendment. The chairman says; "The previous question has been called for (or moved or demanded) and seconded on the immediately pending question which is .... (stating the amendment to the amendment). All those in favor of closing debate on this motion make it known by raising your right hand (or rising)." A show of hands or rising vote is generally used on motions requiring a two-thirds vote because it is easier to determine the count. If the previous question gets the necessary two-thirds vote, the chair immediately proceeds to take a vote on the amendment to the amendment and then opens the floor for debate on the amendment to the main motion which is the next motion to be considered by the assembly.

The *qualified* form of the previous question states the motion to which it is to be applied: "The previous question on all pending business," for instance. Suppose again there is pending a main motion, an amendment to the main motion and an amendment to the amendment. Now suppose a member says; "I call for the previous question *on all pending business.*" If this passes, the chair must call for a vote first on the amendment to the amendment then, without debate, they must vote on the amendment to the main motion and then, again without debate, on the main motion. Or a member, in the example above, may say: "I call for the previous question on the amendment to the amendment and the amendment to the main motion." If this passes, the chair would call for a vote on the two amendments stated and then open the main motion for further debate.

The previous question takes precedence over all other motions except privileged motions, incidental motions and the motion to lay on the table, to all of which it yields.

141. DEBATE, TO LIMIT OR EXTEND LIMITS OF. To limit debate and to extend the limits of debate are actually two sets of motions which have exactly the opposite effect. Therefore, although the rules concerning them are identical, they must be considered separately.

1. The motions to limit debate. In parliamentary law there is a basic rule limiting debate to two ten-minute speeches for each member. (see **DEBATE, NUMBER AND LENGTH OF SPEECHES ALLOWED IN)** Also every society has the right to incorporate in its rules a rule limiting debate. Therefore, consideration of the question of limiting debate must be taken to mean further limitations than existing rules allow. Further, it should be recognized that the motion to limit debate is not a motion to close debate. It is not a call for the previous question.

A motion to limit debate is usually made in the interests of saving time or preventing filibustering. Debate may be limited as to the number of speeches allowed. For example, a motion may be made to limit debate to two speeches for each side. Also a limit may be set on the length of speeches thus: "I move that speeches on this motion be limited to three minutes each." Or there may be a combination of these as: "I move that debate on this motion be limited to two speeches of three minutes each for each side." Also the total time may be limited thus: "I move that debate on this question be limited to thirty minutes." Finally, a closing time may be set as a limitation of debate like this: "I move that debate on this question be closed at four o'clock."

Motions to limit debate are themselves undebatable and require a two-thirds vote to pass. They may be applied to any debatable motion or series of motions. If not specified otherwise, they apply only to the immediately pending motion and to any secondary motions that may be applied to it after the motion to limit has been passed. They yield to the motion to lay on the table and the previous question as well as to all incidental and privileged motions. One motion to limit debate may be applied to another as an amendment. For example, suppose it was moved to limit debate to two speeches for each side. This motion could be amended by inserting the words "of three minutes each" after the word "speeches" thus limiting both the number and length of speeches. Since these motions require a two-thirds vote and are really a form of suspension of the rules, a second motion to limit debate may be made even after one is adopted and even if the second conflicts with the first. For instance, suppose the motion has been passed to limit the debate to three speeches for each side. It is not out of order to move to limit debate to two speeches for each side. The motion to reconsider may be applied to these motions at any time. If the motion to reconsider is lost, it may be renewed after reasonable progress in debate. The motion to limit debate lasts only for the duration of the session. That is, if debate has been limited and is still in progress when the meeting is adjourned, the motion to limit debate does not apply when debate is resumed at the next meeting.

2. The motions to extend limits of debate have the opposite effect from limiting debate. The limits of debate may be extended by increasing the length of speeches, by increasing the number of speeches allowed, by increasing the time allowed for debate and by extending the time of closing debate. To illustrate each of these: "I move that the length of speeches be increased from three to five minutes," "I move that the number of speeches be increased from two to three for each side," "I move that the time allowed for debate on this question be increased from thirty minutes to one hour," "I move that the time for closing debate on this question be extended from four o'clock to five o'clock".

All the rules that apply to motions to limit debate also apply to motions to extend limits of debate.

142. DEBATE, TWO-THIRDS VOTE REQUIRED TO LIMIT OR EXTEND. Any motion to limit or extend the limits of debate is actually in the nature of a suspension of the rules. Also limiting debate violates the general rule of full and free debate. For these reasons, a motion to limit debate, close debate or extend the limits of debate require a two-thirds vote of those voting to pass.

143. DEBATE, WHAT PRECEDES. Before any matter may be debated, three steps must be taken.

1. A motion must be made. The only exception to this is in committees where a subject may be discussed without the formality of a motion.

2. The motion must be seconded. Some motions do not require a second, but if the motion does require a second, it must be done before debate is allowed.

3. The motion must be stated by the chair. Until this is done, the motion is the property of the maker who may modify it or withdraw it without permission from anyone. Once it has been stated by the chair, however, the motion becomes the property of the assembly and may be debated.

When a motion has been made and seconded, the chair must either rule it out of order or state it and call for discussion. This is done in the following manner: "It has been moved and seconded that . . . . Is there any discussion?" There are two reasons for stating a motion; (1) to prevent the maker from withdrawing it without permission after debate has started, and (2) to make clear to the assembly what is the immediately pending question. This is important because confusion can result both in debate and in voting, if the assembly does not clearly understand what is immediately before them.

It is permissible and frequently saves time to allow a little informal consultation before the motion is stated, but the chair should be careful to prevent such consultation from becoming discussion or debate.

144. DECISION OF THE CHAIR, APPEAL FROM. It is the responsibility of the presiding officer to make rulings on all matters of decorum, parliamentary procedure, germaneness of motions and debate, violations of the constitution, by-laws, standing rules and rules of order. In all such cases, when a member violates any of these rules, he is declared "out of order." If a member who has been declared out of order by the chair, does not agree with the decision, he may appeal "from the decision of the chair" unless there is already another appeal pending at the time, in which case, the second appeal must wait until the first appeal has been decided. Appeal must be made at the time the chair made the decision or ruling. If a member does not appeal immediately, that is if any business or debate takes place before the appeal is made, it is too late to appeal.

Any appeal from the decision of the chair may interrupt a speaker, requires a second and may not be amended. However, an appeal yields to orders of the day, lay on the table, question of privilege and adjourn. Appeals may be made without the maker being recognized by the chair. If the appeal is on a matter of indecorum, it is not debatable. In all other cases it is debatable. Whether debatable or not, the chairman may state his reasons for the decision without leaving the chair. The procedure in appeal is as follows:

1. The chair makes a decision.
2. The member, without waiting to be recognized, says; "Mr. Chairman, I appeal from the decision of the chair."
3. The appeal is seconded.
4. The chair says, "Appeal from the decision of the chair on (states the matter) has been made and seconded. All those in favor of the decision of the chair make it known by (state the method of voting such as raising the right hand). Those opposed. The ayes have it

and the decision of the chair is sustained." (or the "nos have it and the decision of the chair is overruled.")

A majority vote in the negative supports the appeal and overrides the chair. A tie vote or a majority vote in the affirmative will support the chair and override the appeal. The vote on any appeal may be reconsidered, but an appeal may not be renewed.

If a motion is on the floor at the time an appeal is made, the motion may or may not adhere to the appeal depending on whether or not the decision of the chair affects the status of the main motion. For example, if a matter is on the floor and a member is declared out of order because his remarks are not germane, the status of the main motion is not at stake and it does not adhere to the appeal. On the other hand, if a member makes a motion and he is declared out of order because his motion is in violation of the constitution, then the fate of the motion is affected by the decision and will adhere to the appeal. If the main motion does not adhere to the appeal, the consideration of the main motion is continued as soon as the appeal is decided.

145. DECORUM IN DEBATE. Proper decorum in debate applies not only to the speaker who has the floor, but to the other members of the assembly as well. The following rules are standard parliamentary law:

1. Debate must be germane to the immediately pending question. The speaker must confine his remarks to the matter before the assembly.

2. The speaker must avoid personalities. Any remark which is derogatory or which reflects upon the character of another member or the assembly is not permitted unless that is the subject of the debate.

3. A member should avoid using the name of another member. He should be referred to by title or by some other designation. For example; "The gentleman from Indiana," "The Senator from Texas," "The speaker who just left the floor."

4. Remarks or questions should never be directed to another member, but always to the presiding officer. For example, "Mr. Chairman, will the speaker yield to a question?"

5. The speaker is entitled to courteous attention. While a member is speaking, unnecessary noise, talking, whispering, moving and walking about are unparliamentary.

6. Profane language and language unbecoming to the dignity of the assembly is out of order.

7. If a speaker is called to order either by the chair or another

member, he should take his seat until the point is settled. If the speaker's remarks are decided to be improper, he may not continue to speak without permission of the assembly.

8. If a speaker's words are disorderly and he cannot justify them and will not apologize for them, the assembly must act. The offender must leave the room while the case is discussed.

9. If the disorderly words concern another member, both must leave the room except that if disorderly words concern an officer, he need not leave.

10. If any business has been conducted following an unparliamentary act and before the act is objected to, it is too late to object unless the act is of such a nature that it will cause the assembly to continue to be unparliamentary.

11. Disturbance is not permitted during debate, while a motion is being made, while the chairman is speaking nor while a vote is being taken.

12. Dilatory remarks are out of order. Speaking for the purpose of delaying progress is unparliamentary.

146. DEFER ACTION. There are several motions which will defer the consideration of a question. Which one to use must be determined by the effect which the maker wishes to accomplish.

1. To postpone indefinitely delays action permanently. To pass this motion means that the matter to which it is applied is killed and cannot be considered again unless it is introduced by a new motion. This cannot be done at the same session.

2. To lay on the table lays a question aside, but reserves the right to take it up again at any time the assembly wishes as long as no business is pending and motions of its class or unfinished business or new business is in order. A motion laid on the table must be taken up either at the same session or at the next session if the society meets as often as quarterly.

3. If it is desired to set a matter aside, but to fix a time for it to be taken up again, the proper motion is to postpone to a certain time. When the time to which it was postponed arrives, if there is no business pending, a member calls for the orders of the day and the postponed matter must be taken up. However, if there is business on the floor, the postponed matter must wait until the pending business is finished.

4. The motion to make a special order of business for a certain time has exactly the same effect as the motion to postpone to a certain

time except that when the time arrives, the special order may interrupt pending business. A matter that is either postponed to a certain time or made a special order for a certain time cannot be taken up before that time except by suspending the rules which requires a two-thirds vote.

147. DELEGATE, CREDENTIALS OF. When a delegate attends a convention which requires credentials, these credentials are furnished by the society or group of constituents which he represents. At the beginning of the convention or when he registers, the credentials are checked by a credentials committee and if in order, he is allowed a seat in the convention and his name is placed on the official list of delegates.

148. DELEGATE, DEFINITION OF. A delegate is an individual who has been appointed or elected to represent a society or group of constituents at a convention. In certain types of conventions (political conventions, for example) a delegate must have credentials affirming his right to represent his constituents.

149. DELEGATES, REGISTRATION OF. The registration of delegates or members of a convention is an important and often complicated procedure. The job is usually handled by a registration committee and in large conventions requires the assistance of considerable clerical help. The machinery for registration should be set up well in advance and should be in full operation a day or two before the opening of the convention. The work not only involves getting the names and addresses of the delegates, but may include issuing badges, getting addresses or hotel room numbers of out of town delegates, collecting dues or registration fees, distributing programs, giving out information and serving as a general clearing house for the members of the convention.

150. DILATORY, ABSURD OR FRIVOLOUS MOTIONS NOT PERMITTED. One of the basic purposes of parliamentary law is to facilitate the orderly conducting of business. Whenever a member uses it for the purpose of obstructing progress, he is out of order. It is the responsibility of the chairman to protect the society from such acts. When the chair feels that a member is making motions or using any other parliamentary form for the purpose of obstructing progress he should declare the member out of order. If the member appeals the decision and the chair is upheld, the chair has the right to refuse to

127

recognize the member and to refuse to entertain another appeal as long as he is satisfied that the member is using this means to obstruct progress since the member is violating the rule that no dilatory, absurd or frivolous motions may be made.

151. DIRECTORS, BOARD OF. There are several names by which a board of directors may be designated. Among them are the following:

1. Board of Managers.
2. Board of Directors.
3. Board of Trustees.
4. Governing Board.
5. Executive Committee.
6. Executive Board.
7. Administrative Committee.

All such boards are small deliberative groups which represent a larger parent organization and they derive all their power from the parent society. They do not have any inherent power of their own. The authority of the board may be stated in the constitution or in the by-laws or be given to it by vote of the society. Such things as duties, time of meeting, officers and procedure are determined by the parent organization. The by-laws and other rules governing the board are adopted by the parent society unless the board is authorized to adopt its own.

The purpose of such a board is to represent the parent body, to conduct the business of the society between meetings and to carry out such other business as may be assigned to it. In societies which meet infrequently, such as quarterly or annually, a board is vitally important.

152. DISCHARGE COMMITTEES. There are several reasons for discharging a committee.

1. The committee may be failing to fulfill its responsibilities.
2. The society may change its mind and decide not to refer the matter.
3. The committee may have completed its work, made its report and therefore, have no further need for existing.

If the reason for discharging the committee is either because it has been remiss in doing its work or because the society has changed its mind about referring the matter, the motion may be made "To discharge the committee from further consideration of the question." Such a motion should be stated like this; "I move that the special

128

committee appointed to (state the matter referred) be discharged from further consideration of the matter." This motion requires a second and is debatable and amendable. If the motion to discharge is made at the same meeting that the matter was referred, it requires either a two-thirds vote of those voting or a majority vote of the entire membership to pass. If the motion is made at a later meeting, it requires the same vote if previous notice was given or a two-thirds vote if no previous notice was given.

Passage of the motion to discharge takes the matter out of the hands of the committee and if there is no further reason for its continued existence, it is automatically dissolved.

When a committee is discharged and it is desired to consider the matter referred to it, this must be either included in the motion to discharge or stated in a separate motion.

When a committee has completed its work and made its report, it is automatically discharged and no motion to discharge is necessary.

153. DISPENSE WITH THE READING OF THE MINUTES. When the chair calls for the reading of the minutes of the last meeting, a member may move to dispense with the reading of the minutes. This is a fairly common practice in small organizations which meet frequently, but should be used sparingly. The minutes are a record of the actions of the society and it is responsible for them. Therefore, the minutes should not be passed over lightly. On the other hand, if there is good reason why they need not be read, it may be dispensed with. The motion to dispense is an ordinary main motion, but actually has the effect of laying on the table because later a motion may be made to read them. The motion to dispense is debatable, requires a second and majority vote.

154. DIVISION OF THE ASSEMBLY. When a vote has been taken and the result announced, if a member questions the announced result, he may call for a division of the assembly or house. This means that the vote must be taken over. The person calling for a division does not need to be recognized by the chair. He merely says, "I call for a division of the house," or he may say, "I doubt the vote," or merely call out, "Division." This call must be made, however, before any other business has been announced. It does not require a second, is not debatable or amendable and may not be reconsidered. It is not voted on, but is decided by the chair who must proceed immediately to take a re-vote.

If the original vote was by voice or a show of hands, another method such as rising must be used for the second vote. Where there is any doubt about the outcome of a vote, any member has the right to insist on a division. However, the chair should not allow this privilege to be misused. If the decision of the first vote was perfectly clear, the chair should refuse to entertain a call for a division. He may do this by stating that a division is unnecessary. If the member still insists, he must do so by appealing from the decision of the chair which will probably die for want of a second or if it does get a second, will certainly lose when the appeal is voted on. If a member wishes for a roll call vote or a vote by ballot, he may move to that effect. This requires a second and a majority vote.

Originally a division of the house meant exactly that. All those in favor of the proposition moved to the right side of the hall and those opposed to the left and each side was counted. This practice is still followed in Canada.

155. DIVISION OF THE QUESTION. When a motion or resolution consists of two or more independent or semi-independent parts, it may be wise to divide the question in order to allow the assembly to consider each part separately. This can be done only if the parts are independent enough so each can stand as a separate motion; for example, a motion, "that this club hold a picnic and that hot dogs be served as refreshment," could not be divided because the second part is entirely dependent on the first. Thus, if the part "to hold a picnic," fails, the second part "to serve hot dogs," becomes foolish. On the other hand, a motion, "that this club hold a picnic on Saturday afternoon and a dance on Saturday night," could be divided because either part of the motion could be carried out without the other.

The proper form of this motion is: "I move that this question be divided into two parts, the first part that . . . , and the second part that . . . ." Or it may be state: "I move that the pending question be divided as follows . . . ." The motion to divide takes precedence over the pending question, the motion to amend and to postpone indefinitely. It yields to all other secondary motions and to all privileged and incidental motions. It requires a second, is not debatable, may interrupt a speaker and may not be reconsidered. It may be amended only with respect to the method of division and requires a majority vote if necessary, but is usually adopted by general consent.

Each part of the divided question is debated and voted on

130

separately, but it is not necessary to move the adoption of each since the original main motion to adopt covers all the parts.

156. DUTIES OF OFFICERS. The duties of the various officers of a society are covered under the heading of each officer separately.

157. EJECT PERSONS, RIGHT OF ASSEMBLY TO. Every organization, society or assembly has the right to determine who may or who may not attend its meetings. This determination may be made in the constitution, by-laws or standing rules of the society. It may be made by a vote of the assembly. Thus, either by a rule or a vote, the society may decide to eject a person or persons. When this decision is made it is the responsibility of the presiding officer to carry out the decision and he may use whatever force necessary to see that it is done.

If the society has a sergeant-at-arms, he may be called on by the presiding officer to eject the unwelcome person and he may request whatever assistance necessary to carry out the order. If there is no sergeant-at-arms, the chairman may appoint members to do the evicting.

Force may be used to eject a party, but care should be exercised because if the members should be unnecessarily forceful, they may be liable for damages. This liability applies only to the ejecting persons and does not apply to the presiding officer or to the society because they did not exceed their legal rights in ordering the ejection.

158. ELECTION OF OFFICERS. In any permanent organization, the method of electing officers should be prescribed in the constitution or by-laws. These methods may be very simple or extremely complicated. The most common ones are suggested here:

1. Nominations are made from the floor. Nominations are closed and a vote taken.

2. A nominating ballot is cast. Those receiving the most votes are nominated. Another vote is cast on those thus nominated. The winner on this vote is elected.

3. A nominating committee picks a slate and it is presented. The floor is opened for further nominations. Nominations are closed and the vote cast.

4. A nominating convention is held, candidates are picked, a campaign is carried out and a final election is held.

5. A public primary election is held and the candidates nominated in the primary conduct a campaign and are voted on in the final election.

The first three of these methods are used in ordinary societies. The fourth and fifth are the methods used in political elections. When an election is held by ballot, the ballots should be kept a "reasonable" length of time before being destroyed. The specific time should be stated in the by-laws of the society. A defeated candidate has the right to challenge (which is really a demand for a recount) and must be given time to do so if he wishes. Some organizations hold election ballots for a year but others designate a much shorter period.

159. ERRORS IN ACTING UPON REPORTS. After a committee report has been presented, it is common to move that it be received. This is an error. Receiving a report means allowing it to be presented. Therefore, the motion to receive should be made (if at all, since it is usually done by general consent) only to determine whether the assembly wishes the report to be presented. To move to "receive" is the same as moving to "hear" the report or the motion that the report be presented.

Another common error is to move to "adopt" when the report contains only facts and there is no recommendation for action. The motion in this case, should be to "accept" although no motion is actually necessary. Also, the motion to "accept" should not be applied to a motion recommending action. The motion in this case should be to "adopt."

160. EXCUSED FROM DUTY, TO BE. When an individual joins an organization or society, he usually assumes certain obligations and responsibilities. These should be clearly stated in the rules and must be made clear to the member. Beyond these responsibilities, however, a member cannot be required to perform tasks which he is unable or unwilling to perform.

If a member is nominated for an office or appointed on a committee and is unable or unwilling to serve, he should make this fact known before the election or before the appointment goes into effect. This assumes that he is present at the time. If he fails to decline immediately, he has, by his silence, accepted the duty and is obligated to perform until there has been reasonable time for the society to accept his resignation. If the member was not present at the time of election or appointment, he should resign as soon as he learns of the matter. A society has no right to force an office on an unwilling member; therefore, it is not good policy to refuse to accept a resignation. Usually resignations are presented to and accepted by the presiding officer, but if a motion is made, it is an ordinary main motion. It yields to incidental and privileged motions, is debatable,

133

requires a second and a majority vote and may have secondary motions applied to it.

A good method in common practice to avoid misunderstanding is to approach the member in advance and secure his acceptance to serve before his name is proposed for duty or office. This is almost always done when a nominating committee is used.

161. EXECUTIVE COMMITTEE. There are several names by which an executive board may be designated. Among them are the following:
1. Board of Managers.
2. Board of Directors.
3. Board of Trustees.
4. Governing Board.
5. Executive Committee.
6. Executive Board.
7. Administrative Committee.

All such boards are small deliberative groups which represent a larger parent organization and they derive all their power and authority from the parent society. They do not have any inherent power of their own. The authority of the board may be stated in the constitution or in the by-laws or be given to it by vote of the society. Such things as duties, quorum, time of meeting, officers and procedures are determined by the parent organization. The by-laws and other rules governing the board are adopted by the parent society unless the board is authorized to adopt its own.

The purpose of such a board is to represent the parent body, to conduct the business of the society between meetings and to carry on such other business as is assigned to it. In societies which meet infrequently, such as quarterly or annually, a board is vitally important.

162. EXECUTIVE SECRETARY. An executive secretary is not ordinarily necessary in a small club or organization. On the other hand, large local societies as well as state and national organizations usually make use of one. He is usually a paid official who devotes much or all of his time to the job. He may be a member of the organization, but often is not. He must be a good organizer and administrator. He serves under the direction of the executive committee and is usually hired by them. The executive secretary serves as assistant to the officers and executive committee, carries on the business of the society, tends the business office and maintains continuity of policy.

134

163. EX-OFFICIO MEMBERS OF BOARDS AND COMMITTEES.

"Ex-officio" is a Latin term meaning "from office" or "by virtue of office." Thus officers of a society, especially the president, are frequently made ex-officio members of committees by virtue of their office. Not infrequently the president is made ex-officio a member of all committees. An ex-officio member has all the rights and privileges of a regular member of a committee including the right to attend meetings, make motions, debate and vote. On the other hand, if the president is made a member ex-officio of all committees he may, but is not required to attend meetings. He is not included when counting a quorum.

In some instances an individual is an ex-officio member of a committee of an organization of which he is not a member. For example, the Governor of the state may be made an ex-officio member of the governing board of a college or university. In such a case, the same rules apply. He has all the rights and privileges of a regular member of the committee, including the right to vote, but is not counted in determining a quorum unless he is under the authority of the society.

An officer of an organization is never an ex-officio member of any committee or of all committees unless the rules of the society provide for it or unless he is elected to the ex-officio membership by a majority vote of the society. Even though the rules may provide that an officer is ex-officio member of all committees, he should never serve as such on a nominating committee if he is a candidate either for re-election or for any other office.

Occasionally an officer will be made ex-officio chairman of a committee. When this happens, he is entitled to preside over committee meetings, but in his absence the committee has the right to choose a chairman pro tem who may preside when the ex-officio member of a committee is absent.

When an officer is ex-officio member of a committee by virtue of the office he holds, his ex-officio membership automatically terminates when his term of office is concluded.

164. EXPULSION OF MEMBERS REQUIRE TWO-THIRDS VOTE.

Listed among the punishments which a society may impose on a member is expulsion. This is done by a vote of the members. It should require a two-thirds vote with at least a quorum voting. This means that even though a quorum is present, a member should not be expelled if enough members refrain from voting so that the total votes cast is less than a quorum. The vote should be by either general consent or secret ballot.

165. EXPUNGE, MOTION TO. The motion to expunge is very rarely used. Only once in the entire history of the United States Congress, for example, has it been used. The effect of this motion is to express very strong disapproval of a motion or portion of a motion that has been previously passed. It is usually used in conjunction with the motion to rescind, thus: "I move to rescind and expunge from the minutes . . . ." It is debatable and may be amended. It can be reconsidered only if it has failed to pass. It always requires a two-thirds vote. A matter is expunged by drawing a line around the part to be expunged and writing across it the words: "Expunged by order of the assembly." This should be dated and signed by the secretary. To expunge does not mean to erase or eliminate the matter from the minutes, but only to express disapproval by indicating that it has been rescinded and expunged. The matter should not be so blotted that it cannot be read.

166. EXTEND LIMITS OF DEBATE, MOTION TO. The motion to extend limits of debate have the opposite effect from limiting debate. The limits of debate may be extended by increasing the length of speeches, by increasing the number of speeches allowed, by increasing the time allowed for debate and by extending the time of closing debate. To illustrate each of these: "I move that the length of speeches be increased from three to five minutes," "I move that the number of speeches allowed be increased from two to three for each side," "I move that the time allowed for debate on this question be increased from thirty minutes to one hour," "I move that the time for closing debate on this question be extended from four o'clock to five o'clock."

Motions to extend debate are themselves undebatable and require a two-thirds vote to pass. They may be applied to any debatable motion or series of motions. If not specified otherwise, they apply only to the immediately pending motion and to any secondary motions that may be applied to it after the motion to extend has been passed. The motion to extend debate may be amended, but can have no other secondary motions applied to it. It yields to the motion to lay on the table and the previous question as well as to all incidental and privileged motions. One motion to extend debate may be applied to another as an amendment. Since these motions require a two-thirds vote, and are really a form of suspension of the rules, a second motion to extend debate may be made even after one is adopted and even if the second conflicts with the first. The motion to reconsider may be applied to these motions at any time. If the motion to reconsider is lost, it may be renewed after reasonable progress in debate. The motion to extend debate lasts only for the duration of the session. That is, if debate has been extended and is still in progress when the meeting is adjourned, the motion to extend debate does not apply when debate is resumed at the next meeting.

167. FILLING BLANKS, AMENDMENT BY. Amendments proposed for the purpose of filling blanks are not treated in exactly the same manner as ordinary amendments since different members of the assembly may propose several names or number to fill the blank. Of course, no one member may propose more than one name or number unless by general consent. Any number of names or numbers may be proposed without a second.

For example, suppose the motion is before the assembly to authorize the refreshment committee to spend "blank" amount of money. Several members propose varying amounts of money—ten dollars, fifteen dollars, twenty dollars, twenty-five dollars. All these amounts are proposed as suggestions not as amendments. In this case, the presiding officer would start the vote with the highest amount (twenty-five dollars). If this amount did not receive a majority vote, he would then proceed to twenty dollars and so on down until he reached an amount that was approved by the majority. Thus, he would arrive at the highest amount that would be approved by the majority of the assembly. On the other hand, suppose the club decided to sell the clubhouse and the "blank" to be filled was to determine the asking price. Several amounts are suggested. The chair would start the vote on the lowest amount to determine how many would be willing to sell for that price and would continue to vote on each successively higher amount until he reached the amount where the majority would be willing to sell. Thus in the case of filling the blank with numbers, the vote is started at one end of the scale (either the lowest or highest, depending on which is least likely to receive a majority) and proceeds on up or down until a majority is reached. It is a good general rule to start with the largest sum and proceed downward.

In the case of filling the blank with a date, it is wise to start with the most distant and proceed toward the present.

When the blank is to be filled with a time, the chair usually starts with the longest. For example, suppose a contractor is to be allowed a "blank" amount of time to do a job. The question is, what is the maximum time to be allowed. Suggestions are made—two years, one year, six months. The chair starts with two years. If a majority is not willing to allow that much time, the chair proceeds to the next suggested time until he gets a majority vote.

If the blank is to be filled with a name, the chair calls for a vote on each name in the order suggested until one name receives a majority

138

vote. If the blank is to be filled with several names, say three, and only three names are proposed, it does not require a vote. The three proposed names are automatically inserted. But if the blank is to be filled with three names and five are suggested, the chair calls for a vote on each successively in the order suggested until three have received a majority. If the number of names to be inserted is not specifically stated, all names that receive a majority are inserted in the blank.

The purpose of making a motion which includes blanks is to make it possible to offer several suggestions for filling the blanks without the formality of offering separate amendments. Also, if the amendment process is used, only two (an amendment and an amendment to the amendment) are possible; whereas, in filling blanks, any number of suggestions may be offered and each considered in turn until one receives majority support. For example, suppose the motion is made to sell the clubhouse. In debate the question arises, "What shall be the asking price?" Someone moves to amend the motion by adding the words, "for $5,000." Then someone else moves to amend the amendment by substituting "$7,500" for "$5,000." In this case no further suggestions can be added and the club must consider only two amounts. On the other hand, if a blank is created and the original motion is made, "to sell the clubhouse for 'blank' amount," then any number of suggestions may be made as to the amount to be filled in the blank; $5,000, $7,500, $10,000, $12,000. Since the least likely asking price is $5,000, the chairman would start with this amount. If it received a majority vote, that would be the amount inserted to fill the blank. But if it did not receive a majority, the chairman would then proceed to the next higher amount until he arrived at an amount that did get a majority vote and that amount would fill the blank.

A good basic rule for the chairman to follow is always to begin with the item least likely to be adopted and to proceed until one item receives a majority vote. That item is then used to fill the blank.

Ordinarily, blanks should be filled before the main motion or resolution is voted upon, but if it is obvious that the main motion is opposed by a large majority, the previous question may be called for before the blank is filled. This would force a vote on the main motion before its blank had been filled. Thus, if the motion is made to sell the clubhouse for "blank" amount and the motion is obviously unpopular and the previous question is passed, a vote is immediately taken on selling the clubhouse. Usually this would be defeated and that would end the matter. But if the motion *should* be passed to "sell the clubhouse for 'blank' amount," then it would be necessary to fill the blank in the manner described above.

168. FLOOR, APPEAL FROM DECISION IN ASSIGNING. If there is dissatisfaction or objection to the way the chairman is assigning the floor to members for motions or debate, any two members may appeal. One makes the appeal and the other seconds it. Such an appeal is handled in the same way as any appeal from the decision of the chair. If the chair himself is in doubt as to who should be given the floor, he may put it up to a vote of the assembly. The member receiving the most votes is given the floor.

169. FLOOR, OBTAINING. With certain exceptions, a member is not entitled to speak or present a matter to the assembly until he has obtained the floor, that is, until he has been recognized by the presiding officer. This is done in the following manner; the member rises and says; "Mr. Chairman" or "Mr. President" or whatever the title of the presiding officer may be. In very large assemblies, he also states his name. He then waits to be recognized. The chair recognizes him by calling him by name or by title or by indicating in some other manner that the member has the floor. Sometimes the chair recognizes the member by some such statement as: "The member from Alabama has the floor." When more than one member seeks the floor at the same time, the chair exercises his discretion in giving the floor to one of them.

170. FLOOR, YIELDING. When a member addresses the chair and is recognized by him, he is said to have the floor and is entitled to it for the purpose of debate or to make a motion or for any other legal reason or purpose. If another member wishes to interrupt the one who has the floor, he asks him to yield the floor. He addresses the chair and says; "Will the member yield the floor?" The chair relays the request and if the member yields the floor, it is turned over to the one requesting it. If a member wishes to ask a question of the speaker, he says, "Mr. Chairman, will the speaker yield to a question?" If the request is granted, the question is asked, answered and the speaker continues as if no interruption had taken place. The time consumed in asking and answering the question is deducted from the speaking time of the speaker.

140

171. FORM OF AUDITOR'S REPORT. Financial reports are for the information of the members of a society. Too much detail in the way of specific receipts and disbursements only serve to confuse and do not enlighten. It is the duty of the auditing committee to go into these details, but the report to the membership need not contain them. The amount of such detail must be determined by the society itself.

At the end of the regular financial report of the treasurer, the auditing committee merely makes the following statement:

Examined and found correct

George Smith
Helen Brown
Auditing Committee

172. GAVEL, USE OF. The gavel is the symbol of authority of the presiding officer and should be used by him in asserting that authority, but it should be used sparingly and with dignity. Excessive use of the gavel is not in keeping with the dignity of the officer and furthermore, like a constantly scolding parent, the overuse of the gavel will soon result in its use being ignored entirely and, therefore, will lose its effectiveness. In opening the meeting, the presiding officer should strike sharply three times and say: "The meeting will please come to order." If the meeting becomes disorderly, the gavel should be used by striking once, sharply but not too hard. The chairman usually strikes once when he declares the meeting adjourned or when he declares a recess. In very large assemblies, the chair often uses the gavel, by striking once with it, to indicate the ending of the consideration of a piece of business or in declaring the result of a vote. For example, "The ayes have it and the motion is carried." (One rap with the gavel.)

173. GENERAL CONSENT. General consent (sometimes called "unanimous consent" or "silent consent") is a device by which the chairman can expedite the conducting of business by avoiding the formality of making motions and/or voting by assuming that everyone agrees. Much of the business handled in meetings is routine or of little importance and may be handled in this way unless there is an objection. Perhaps the best example of the use of general consent is the approval of the minutes of the last meeting. They are read and the chair says, "Are there any corrections?" He pauses and then says, "Hearing none, the minutes stand approved as read." This assumes two things. First, it assumes that since no one spoke up, there were no corrections to be made. Secondly, it assumes that since there were no corrections, the assembly will approve the minutes as read and therefore there is no need to waste time by putting the matter to vote.

This device may be used by the chairman at any time when he believes that there will be no objection. For example, when a committee announces that it is ready to report, the chair may say, "If there is no objection, we will receive the report of the committee on (naming the subject)."

Objection on the part of any member of the society will prevent the use of this device. If there is an objection, the chair simply reverts to the usual method of deciding the matter by putting it to a vote. Even though no objection is made, it does not necessarily mean that every member is in favor of the motion. The opposed member may simply realize that it is useless to object since the matter would be passed anyway and so in the interest of facilitating business he does not object.

174. GENERAL ORDERS. When a matter is postponed to a certain meeting, day or hour, it becomes a general order for that meeting, day or hour. There are several ways of making this motion:

1 "I move this matter be postponed to the next meeting."

2. "I move this matter be made a general order for the next meeting."

3. "I move this matter be postponed to January fifth."

4. "I move this matter be made a general order for January fifth."

5. "I move this matter be postponed to four o'clock this afternoon."

6. "I move this matter be made a general order for four o'clock this afternoon."

It will be noticed that the first two are simply different ways of saying the same thing. They postpone to a certain meeting. The next two say the same thing, but postpone to a certain day and the last two postpone to a certain hour. All these are merely different ways of creating a general order. The motion to create a general order requires a second, may be amended, is debatable, may be reconsidered and may be renewed after progress. It requires a majority vote.

When a matter is postponed to a certain meeting or day and the day arrives, the matter is taken up as the last step under unfinished or old business unless the order of business of the society provides for "orders of the day" in which case, it is taken up then. If the matter is postponed to a certain hour, it is taken up when that hour arrives. In no case, however, can it interrupt business that is on the floor at the time it is due. For example, suppose a matter is postponed or made a general order for four o'clock on January fifth. If there is other business on the floor at four o'clock, the postponed matter must wait until the business on the floor is finished, then it is considered. If a meeting adjourns and a general order is not disposed of, it then becomes the first matter to be considered under unfinished business at the following meeting. A general order cannot be taken up before its appointed time except by a two-thirds vote because to do so would be the same as suspending the rules.

If several general orders are made for the same time, they are taken up in the order in which they were created. If several general orders are created *at* the same time and *for* the same time, they are taken up in the order in which they were listed when created. For example, suppose the following motion is made; "I move that matters A, B, and C be made a general order for four o'clock." At four o'clock matter A would be considered, then B and finally C.

175. GERMANE, AMENDMENTS MUST BE, TO SUBJECT TO BE AMENDED.

The word germane is defined as "related to, akin to, or relevant to." An amendment must be germane to the motion which it is intended to amend. That is, it must be "related to, akin to, relevant to," the subject to which it is applied. This is true also of an amendment of the second degree, that is an amendment to an amendment must be germane not only to the amendment to which it is applied, but also, through it, to the main motion. An amendment which changes the main motion in such a way that it becomes a new motion is not germane nor can a new motion be introduced under the guise of an amendment. On the other hand, an amendment may conflict completely with the spirit of the main motion to which it is applied and still be germane. For example, a motion "to thank" an individual may be amended by substituting the word "condemn" for the word "thank" because it is relevant to the main motion and therefore is germane.

Following are examples of amendments that are germane and are not germane:

1. An amendment adding the words "and ping pong paddles" to the motion "to purchase a ping pong table" is germane, but it would not be germane to add the amendment "to hire a ping pong coach."

2. If the motion "to pay the expenses of the president to the national convention" were pending, it would be germane to amend by inserting the words "and vice-president" after the word "president." It would not be germane to move an amendment "to thank the national committee for the invitation to attend."

3. A motion "to purchase a typewriter for the secretary" could be amended by adding "a typewriter table" and this in turn could be amended by an amendment of the second degree "to include a chair for the table." But the main motion could not be amended by adding a motion "to increase his salary."

4. A motion to thank two members for their work on a certain project could be amended by adding the name of a third member provided it was for the same project but the third name could not be added if he were to be thanked for a different project.

144

176. HANDS, VOTE BY SHOW OF. Of the several methods of voting, the "show of hands" is one of the most common. When an issue is put by the chairman, he says, "All those in favor make it known by raising your right hand." The hands are raised and counted by the chairman or secretary or both if it is desired to double check. The chairman then says; "Down hands. All those opposed raise your right hand." The negative vote is counted and the vote announced. This method of voting is more accurate than a voice vote, but less accurate, especially in large assemblies, than a standing vote or a vote by ballot. One difficulty is that people do not raise their hands high enough to be certain that they are voting. Also hands are frequently lowered before they are counted.

177. HISTORIAN, DUTIES OF. The office of historian is frequently created for the purpose of collecting publicity and compiling an over-all summary of the activities of the society. Sometimes the historian is charged with the responsibility of bringing up-to-date and compiling a history of the origin, antecedents and development of a society and of keeping this history currently up-to-date. Frequently the job consists of compiling scrapbooks and collecting programs and other material and organizing this material into a chronological history of the society.

178. HONORARY MEMBERS AND OFFICERS. If a society wishes to show its appreciation to an individual or to honor him for his fine character or for some service he has performed, it may do so by making him an honorary member or officer of the society. Colleges and universities, for example, often confer honorary degrees. If the person is not a member of the society, the usual thing is to make him an honorary member of the society. Frequently an officer who has served long as an officer of a society and is retiring, will be made an honorary officer. An honorary officer or member has no responsibility or obligation to fulfill. Although he may attend meetings and speak, he does not have the right to vote nor to make motions by virtue of his honorary position.

179. HONORARY OFFICERS, DUTIES OF. A member of a society who is given an honorary office is not obligated in any way by the honor. He has no duties imposed on him by virtue of the office. The fact that he holds the honorary office does not prevent him from holding another regular office.

180. HOUSE, DIVISION OF THE. When a vote has been taken and the result announced, if a member questions the announced result, he may call for a division of the assembly or house. This means that the vote must be taken over. The person calling for a division does not need to be recognized by the chair. He merely says: "I call for a division of the house" or he may say: "I doubt the vote" or merely call out: "Division." This call must be made, however, before any other business has been announced; it does not require a second, is not debatable or amendable and may not be reconsidered. It is not voted on, but is decided by the chair who must proceed immediately to take a re-vote.

If the original vote was by voice or a show of hands, another method such as rising must be used for the second vote. Where there is any doubt about the outcome of a vote, any member has the right to insist on a division. However, the chair should not allow this privilege to be misused. If the decision of the first vote was perfectly clear, the chair should refuse to entertain a call for a division. He may do this by stating that a division is unnecessary. If the member still insists, he must do so by appealing from the decision of the chair which will probably die for want of a second or if it does get a second, will certainly lose when the appeal is voted on. If a member wishes for a roll call vote or a vote by ballot, he may move to that effect. This requires a second and a majority vote.

Originally a division of the house meant exactly that. All those in favor of the proposition moved to the right side of the hall and those opposed to the left and each side was counted. This practice is still followed in Canada.

181. IMMEDIATELY PENDING QUESTION, MEANING OF. A piece of business is before an assembly only after a motion concerning it has been made and seconded and the chairman has stated it to the society. It is then said to be pending, that is, ready to be considered. When several matters are pending, the last one stated by the chairman must be the first one acted on by the society. It is the immediately pending question. For example, if a main motion is on the floor and an amendment is made to it, the amendment is the immediately pending question. If an amendment to the amendment is made, then the amendment to the amendment becomes the immediately pending question.

182. IMPROPER AMENDMENT. An amendment is improper and out of order and may not be made when:

1. It is not germane to the subject to be amended.

2. It changes the affirmative to the negative or the reverse. For example, if the motion is made "that we sell our clubhouse," the amendment to insert the words "do not" before the word "sell" would be out of order because it reverses the motion and changes the affirmative to the negative. Likewise if the motion was that "we do not sell our clubhouse," the amendment to strike out the words "do not" would not be in order because it changes the motion from the negative to the affirmative.

3. It is the same as another motion already decided at the same session. Suppose the motion has been passed "that we sell the property adjacent to the clubhouse." Then later in the same session, it is moved "that we sell our clubhouse." An amendment to add the words "and the property adjacent to" would be out of order. This would be just as true if the motion to sell the adjacent property had failed earlier because it had been considered at the same session.

4. It changes one form of an amendment for another form. If an amendment is made to "strike out" an amendment to the amendment cannot be made "to strike out and insert" since this is a different form of amendment.

5. It substitutes one form of amendment for another form.

6. It strikes out the word "resolved" in a resolution.

7. It changes the meaning of the main motion in such a way as to leave no reasonable motion before the group.

8. It is frivolous or absurd.

147

183. INCIDENTAL MAIN MOTIONS. Main motions that are incidental or related to the business of the assembly or that deal with past action of the assembly are called "incidental main motions." These are not to be confused with "incidental motions" which are entirely different. When a standing committee reports and the motion to adopt or to accept is made, it is an original main motion, but when a committee reports on a matter previously referred to it and the motion to adopt or accept is made, it is called an incidental main motion. Outside of the fact that objection to consideration cannot be applied to it, there is no difference in procedure between incidental main motions and original main motions. The following are incidental main motions:

1. accept a committee report on a matter referred to it.
2. adopt a committee report on a matter referred to it.
3. the motion to fix the time at which to adjourn.
4. the motion to fix the time to which to adjourn.
5. the motion to adjourn if qualified in any way.
6. the unqualified motion to adjourn if the assembly has no provision for a future meeting.
7. the motion to fix the time and/or place of the next meeting.
8. any motion to amend a rule or set of rules already adopted such as, the constitution, by-laws, rules of order, standing rules and resolutions.
9. any motion to ratify or confirm action already taken.
10. the motion to rescind action already passed.
11. the motion to rescind and expunge action already passed.
12. the motion to reconsider.
13. the motion to take from the table.

184. INCIDENTAL MOTIONS. Incidental motions are motions that arise incidentally in the conducting of business. They are incidental to pending business and although they have no precedence over each other, they do take precedence over the motion out of which they arise. Incidental motions are generally not debatable because they are in order only when a situation occurs that requires one of them and should be settled as quickly as possible in order to make way for the real business at hand. They yield to privileged motions. The following are incidental motions:

1. point of order.
2. objection to consideration.
3. suspension of the rules.

148

4. appeal from the decision of the chair.
5. consider by paragraph.
6. division of the house.
7. division of the question.
8. parliamentary inquiry.
9. leave to withdraw a motion.
10. to be excused from duty.

185. INCORPORATE, HOW TO. Any organization may incorporate by adopting rules or articles of incorporation which comply with the state law that provides for incorporation of that kind of society. The Secretary of State of the state in which the corporation is to be formed will give information concerning the conditions under which the society may become incorporated and will furnish the necessary forms. Incorporation is a simple procedure, but the articles of incorporation must be correctly drawn, therefore, a lawyer should be obtained.

The articles of incorporation of an incorporated society correspond to the constitution of an unincorporated organization. These articles and the by-laws of an incorporated society may be amended only as provided by the law of the state in which the corporation is located.

There are certain advantages to incorporation. The organization has exclusive right to the use of its name within the state. It may buy, own and sell real property and may bring legal action. Individual members of an incorporated society are protected against liability or responsibility for the debts of the society.

186. INDECORUM, LEAVE TO CONTINUE SPEAKING AFTER. When a speaker has been found guilty of indecorum, the member is allowed to continue speaking only under certain conditions. If the member did not realize he was committing a breach of decorum or if the breach was a minor one and the member apologizes, he is generally allowed to continue. If it was a serious breach such as deliberate abuse of another member or the use of improper language, the speaker may be punished as well as being deprived of his right to continue speaking. In any case of indecorum, either major or minor, a member cannot continue speaking if any member objects, except by a majority vote of the assembly.

187. INDEFINITE POSTPONEMENT. The term "postpone indefinitely" is actually a misnomer because the purpose of this motion is not to postpone, but to kill the main question. It is used by the enemies of the main question primarily as a test of strength without risking a vote. If the enemies of the main question can muster enough voting strength to pass the motion to postpone indefinitely, they have succeeded in killing the main motion. On the other hand, if they do not have strength enough to pass the motion to postpone indefinitely, they have not hurt their position and they now know they do not have strength enough to defeat the main question if it comes to a vote. Also they learn who is in favor and who is opposed to the main motion and whether it is worthwhile to continue the fight against it.

The motion to postpone indefinitely is debatable and since, if passed, it kills the main motion, it actually opens debate on the main question. Therefore, a member who has exhausted his speaking time on the main question can actually speak again under the guise of debating the motion to postpone indefinitely.

The motion to postpone indefinitely takes precedence over the main motion and nothing else. It yields to all other secondary motions and to all privileged and incidental motions. It cannot be amended and the only motions that may be applied to it are the previous question and motions limiting or extending limits of debate. It can be applied only to main motions. It may be reconsidered if passed, but not if lost and if lost, it may not be renewed. It requires a majority vote to pass. If the main question is referred to a committee while the motion to postpone indefinitely is pending, the postponing motion does not go to the committee, but is simply ignored.

188. INFORMAL CONSIDERATION OF QUESTION. Informal consideration of a question works better in groups where the meetings are not large. In such groups, informal consideration is better and easier than going into committee of the whole or quasi committee of the whole. The motion: "I move that the question be considered informally" if passed, opens the main question and any amendments that may be attached to it to free debate in the same manner as if the society were in a committee of the whole. The number and length of speeches may be limited by a two-thirds vote and the previous question may be passed in the same manner, but unless this is done, the debate is completely open although this freedom of debate is limited to the one question and its amendments. Any other matter that is brought before the assembly is subject to the same limitations of debate as in a regular meeting of the society. In granting the floor to members who wish to speak, the chairman should give the preference to members who have not previously spoken. In other words, a member who has already previously spoken should not speak a second time if there are others who wish to speak. Although the consideration of the question is informal, all votes are formal the same as in a regular session. As soon as the question which is being considered informally is disposed of, the informal consideration stops. No motion is necessary to revert back to the formal meeting.

189. INFORMAL OR NOMINATING BALLOT. In electing officers many organizations, especially small ones, do not go thru the formality of nominating candidates. Instead ballots are passed out and the members write the name of one person for each office to be filled. If the same name receives a majority of votes for the same office, he is declared elected. On the other hand, if several names receive votes for the same office and no one name receives a majority, all names are considered nominated and a second vote is taken on these names. If on this second ballot a name receives a majority, he is declared elected. If not, a motion is passed to eliminate all but the two names receiving the most votes and a third vote is taken. Obviously one of these two will receive a majority and thus will be elected. On rare occasions a tie will occur in which case the decision is made by lot unless the society decides to solve the problem in some other manner.

190. INFORMATION, REQUEST FOR. During debate on a question, it often occurs that a member may wish to get information or clarification of a point by asking a question. He may seek this information from the chairman or from the speaker if another member has the floor or from another member if no one has the floor. The inquirer rises and says, "Mr. Chairman, I rise for information," or "I rise to a point of information." The chair then directs him to state his point which he does. If the question is directed to the chair, it is answered by him. If the question is directed to another member, the chair requests that person to answer. If the question is directed to the speaker, the chair asks if he will yield to a question and if he consents, the inquirer addresses his question to the chair and the speaker by saying, "Mr. Chairman, I should like to ask the gentleman . . . ." The reply of the speaker is made the same way, that is, through the chair who, however, remains silent during the conversation. The time consumed by the inquiry and answer is charged against the time of the speaker.

191. INQUIRY, PARLIAMENTARY. A member who seeks information concerning parliamentary law may make a parliamentary inquiry as follows, "Mr. Chairman, I rise to a point of parliamentary inquiry." He does not wait to be recognized after he says, "Mr. Chairman." The chair then directs him to state his point and the chair answers the inquiry. If the point is one that requires immediate attention, it may interrupt a speaker. If the inquiry is made when another has the floor, but the chair believes it is not pertinent enough to require immediate attention, he may defer his answer until the speaker has finished. If the society has a parliamentarian, the chair may refer the point to him for answer.

192. INSERTING OR ADDING OR STRIKING OUT AN ENTIRE PARAGRAPH, AMENDMENT BY. When it is desired to amend a motion or a resolution by inserting or striking out an entire paragraph or by substituting one paragraph for another, it is important to prepare the new paragraph in its best possible form before proposing it so that it will appear at its best and will require as few changes as possible. Once a paragraph has been inserted into a motion or resolution, it cannot be changed except by adding to it. Furthermore, once it has been inserted by amendment, a paragraph cannot be struck out later except in conjunction with other paragraphs so it is essentially a new amendment. This is to prevent an opposed minority from immediately moving to strike out as soon as a paragraph has been inserted and thus delay action on the main motion or quibbling over an already settled issue.

Likewise, once an amendment to strike out a paragraph has been passed, the paragraph cannot be reinstated and an amendment to do so is out of order unless it has been changed to such an extent that it has virtually become a new question.

If the motion to insert a paragraph is lost, it does not prevent another amendment to insert a part of the paragraph or the same paragraph provided it is reworded so it is essentially different or the objectionable parts are corrected.

Also if the motion to strike out a paragraph is lost, it is still in order to amend by striking out parts of the paragraph. Thus even

152

though an assembly may refuse to strike out an entire paragraph, it still may strike out parts of it by means of another amendment.

193. INSERTING OR ADDING WORDS, AMENDMENT BY. It is possible to amend a motion or a resolution by inserting words or by adding words. If the words come within a sentence or paragraph, the expression "to insert" is used. When the proposed words are to be placed the end of a sentence, paragraph or motion, the term "to add" is used.

When such an amendment is made and seconded in the proper manner, those who favor it should make certain that the proposed words say exactly what is wanted. This should be done by an amendment to the amendment and before the amendment has been voted on because once a vote is taken, it is much more difficult to make further alterations. For example, if the amendment is passed, it becomes impossible to eliminate the same words except by eliminating only a part of them or by eliminating all of them along with either words from the original motion. In the same way, if the amendment is rejected, it becomes impossible to propose the same words again unless they are included with other words or are substituted for words in the original motion and then only if this presents an essentially new motion to the assembly.

The proper form of this amendment is; "I move to amend the motion by inserting the words 'X Y Z' after the word 'C' so the motion will read 'A B C X Y Z D E'."

194. INSTRUCTIONS TO COMMITTEES. Since a committee is the creation of the parent society, it is the right of the parent to direct or instruct the committee in any way it may wish. These instruction may be included as a part of the motion to commit or as an amendment to this motion. Also a separate motion to instruct a committee in a certain way may be passed by a majority vote. Suppose a motion has been passed that a committee be appointed to investigate a certain matter. A motion could be made to direct the committee to interview "Mr. X" in regard to this matter. This would be in the nature of instructions. A committee may be given instructions at any time up to the submission of its final report.

195. INTRODUCTION OF BUSINESS. An organization may not take action or even discuss any matter until it has been officially placed before the assembly. There are three steps which must be followed, if a matter is to be officially considered.

1. A motion must be made. This is done by a member addressing the chair, being recognized and saying, "I move that . . . ." It is poor form to use either the expression, "I make a motion" or "I move you." When the motion has been made, the chair says, "It has been moved that . . . . (repeating the motion). Is there a second?"

2. The motion must be seconded. There are a number of motions that do not require a second, but all main motions do. Seconding a motion may be more informal. To be formal, a member addresses the chair, is recognized and says, "I second the motion." However, to second a motion, one does not need to be recognized. He may simply call out, "I second the motion" or even just, "Second."

3. The third step is called, "stating the motion." This is done by the chair saying, "It has been moved and seconded that . . . . (again stating the motion). Is there any discussion?" This is the third step and is called stating the motion. The business is now debated and acted upon.

There are other ways of considering a matter such as informal consideration and consideration in committee of the whole, but *official* consideration must follow the above procedure.

196. IRREGULAR BALLOT. Irregularities on ballots such as misspellings, errors in grammar or punctuation, or putting a check mark in place of an X should be ignored as long as the meaning is clear. In the case of elections, the candidate for whom it was intended should be credited with the vote even though his name is misspelled or the directions on the ballot are not followed exactly.

If there is real doubt concerning the intent of the ballot, the tellers may invalidate it or they may submit it to the assembly for instructions. In any case, the tellers should report all irregularities.

197. JOURNAL. Although the record of the proceedings of a society is usually called the minutes, the term journal is sometimes used. Minutes and journal are identical in parliamentary usage.

198. LAY ON THE TABLE, EFFECT OF. When the motion to lay a matter on the table is passed, it has the effect of stopping all consideration of the matter until it is taken from the table. Also it has the effect of killing the motion to which it is applied if it is not taken from the table at the same or the next session. Naturally, if the motion to lay on the table is not carried, the main motion is not set aside and is still open for further discussion and disposition.

199. LAY ON THE TABLE, IMPROPER USE OF. The motion to lay on the table is sometimes used for the purpose of setting aside a matter with no intention of taking it up again. This has the same effect as postponing indefinitely and is an improper use of the motion to lay on the table because it is a violation of a basic parliamentary principle. This principle is that any motion which has the effect of killing a matter on the floor must be debatable and require a two-thirds vote. Since the motion to lay on the table is undebatable and needs only a majority vote, it should never be used to postpone a matter when there is no intent to take it from the table either at the same session or the next. If a matter is left on the table beyond the session following the one when it was placed there, it is killed.

200. LAY ON THE TABLE, MOTION TO. The motion to lay on the table is the highest ranking of all the secondary motions. It is a method of postponing business. The proper form is, "I move to lay the motion on the table". A tabled motion cannot be considered again until a motion is passed "to take from the table." A motion laid on the table may be taken up again either during the same session or the next session in a society meeting as frequently as quarterly. The motion to lay on the table cannot be amended and is undebatable. It may not be reconsidered but may be renewed after progress. It requires a majority vote.

201. LAY ON THE TABLE, OBJECT OF. It is frequently desired to lay aside a piece of business temporarily in order to consider some more pressing matter and yet to retain the right to resume its consideration at the same session or the next, at the convenience of the society. The motion to lay on the table accomplishes this.

202. LEAVE TO CONTINUE SPEAKING AFTER INDECORUM. When a speaker has been found guilty of indecorum, the member is allowed to continue speaking only under certain conditions. If the member did not realize he was committing a breach of decorum or if the breach was a minor one and the member apologizes, he is generally allowed to continue. If it was a serious breach such as deliberate abuse of another member or the use of improper language, the speaker may be punished as well as being deprived of his right to continue speaking. In any case of indecorum, either major or minor, a member cannot continue speaking, if any member objects, except by a majority vote of the assembly.

203. LEAVE TO WITHDRAW OR MODIFY A MOTION. Before a motion has been stated by the chair, the maker of the motion may withdraw or modify it without permission. After it has been stated, it is the property of the assembly and the maker must be granted leave or permission to withdraw or modify it. If a motion has been made and seconded and the maker modifies it before it has been stated by the chair, the seconder may withdraw his second, if he does not favor the motion as modified. After the motion has been stated, if permission is granted the maker to modify his motion, the second may be withdrawn.

If the maker wishes to withdraw his motion after it has been stated by the chair, he says, "Mr. Chairman, I ask leave to withdraw the motion." The chair asks whether there is any objection and if there is none, the permission is granted. If there is objection, the request is put to a vote and can be granted by a majority vote. Also, another member can move to grant leave to withdraw a motion. This motion does not require a second because it is presumed that the maker favors the withdrawal and this constitutes a second. Leave to withdraw a motion can be granted any time up to the taking of a vote and may be made even while incidental and secondary motions are pending. If the main motion is withdrawn, all secondary and incidental motions connected with it are also withdrawn. The motion to withdraw cannot be amended or have any secondary motions applied to it. It is undebatable. If a motion has been divided, one part may be withdrawn without affecting the rest of the motion.

204. LIMIT DEBATE, MOTION TO. In parliamentary law there is a basic rule limiting debate to two ten-minute speeches for each member. (see **DEBATE, NUMBER AND LENGTH OF SPEECHES ALLOWED IN**) Also every society has the right to incorporate in its rules a rule limiting debate. Therefore, consideration of the question of limiting debate must be taken to mean further limitations than existing rules allow. Further, it should be recognized that the motion to limit debate is not a motion to close debate. It is not a call for the previous question.

A motion to limit debate is usually made in the interests of saving time or preventing filibustering. Debate may be limited as to the number of speeches allowed. For example, a motion may be made to limit debate to two speeches for each side. Also, a limit may be set on the length of speeches, thus, "I move that speeches on this motion be limited to three minutes each." Or there may be a combination of these, as "I move that debate on this motion be limited to two speeches of three minutes each for each side." Also, the total time may be limited, thus, "I move that debate on this question be limited to thirty minutes." Finally, a closing time may be set as a limitation on debate like this, "I move that debate on this question be closed at four o'clock."

Motions to limit debate are themselves undebatable and require a two-thirds vote to pass. They may be applied to any debatable motion or series of motions. If not specified otherwise, they apply only to the immediately pending motion and to any secondary motions that may be applied to it after the motion to limit has been passed. Motions to limit debate may be amended but can have no other secondary motions applied to them. They yield to the motion to lay on the table and the previous question as well as to all incidental and privileged motions. One motion to limit debate may be applied to another as an amendment. For example, suppose it was moved to limit debate to two speeches for each side. This motion could be amended by inserting the words "of three minutes each" after the word "speeches" thus limiting both the number and length of speeches. Since motions to limit debate require a two-thirds vote and are really a form of suspension of the rules, a second motion to limit debate may be made even after one is adopted and even if the second conflicts with the first. For instance, suppose the motion has been passed to limit the debate to three speeches for each side. It is not out of order to move to limit debate to two speeches for each side. The motion to reconsider may be applied to these motions at any time. If the motion to reconsider is lost, it may be renewed after reasonable progress in debate. The motion to limit debate lasts only for the duration of the session. That is, if debate has been limited and is still in progress **when the meeting is** adjourned, the motion to limit debate does not **apply when debate is** resumed at the next meeting.

205. MAIL, VOTE BY. When the membership of an organization is so scattered that it is virtually impossible to get them to a meeting or when it is desired to get as nearly a unanimous vote as possible, vote by mail is the only solution. Also, this method is used even when the membership is not scattered but when it would be a waste of valuable time to call a meeting merely for the purpose of voting on a single issue. Some organizations such as the faculty of a large university, use this method almost exclusively. It has the advantage of being convenient but there is the disadvantage of not being able to hold open debate on the issue before the vote is cast.

When an amendment to the constitution or by-laws or a proposal is to be voted on, the proposed amendment or proposal should be printed on the ballot or on a separate sheet enclosed with the ballot. Also, it is sometimes permitted to include the arguments for and against the proposal. A return, self-addressed envelope should be enclosed. In fact, usually two return envelopes are enclosed, one marked, "Ballot for . . . " (state the issue) to be placed inside the self-addressed one. The voter should place his signature on the inner envelope. In order for the tellers to prevent fraudulent voting, it is necessary for them to check the envelopes against a list of the names of the membership. For this reason, vote by mail cannot be a strictly secret ballot.

206. MAIN MOTIONS. A main motion is one that brings a piece of business before the assembly. They are subdivided into original main motions and incidental main motions.

An original main motion brings a subject before the assembly for the first time. It may be a simple motion or in the form of a more complicated resolution. If it is the latter, it should be submitted in writing.

An incidental main motion is one that is incidental to the business of the assembly or brings before the assembly a matter that has been acted upon previously or has been before the assembly and postponed or referred. Examples are a motion to amend an already adopted rule such as a by-law, a motion to take from the table, a motion to reconsider. (see **INCIDENTAL MAIN MOTIONS.**)

A main motion cannot be made when any other business is pending. It takes precedence over nothing and yields to all incidental, privileged and secondary motions. A main motion cannot be made that violates the rules of the society nor can it be made if it is the same as or conflicts with any other motion either passed or rejected at the same meeting. Main motions are debatable and amendable and can have secondary motions applied to them. They usually require a majority vote to pass although those that deal with the amendment of existing rules, require whatever vote the rules dictate.

207. MAIN MOTIONS, INCIDENTAL. Main motions that are incidental or related to the business of the assembly or that deal with past action of the assembly are called "incidental main motions." These are not to be confused with "incidental motions" which are entirely different. When a standing committee reports and the motion to adopt or accept is made, it is an original main motion, but when a committee reports on a matter referred to it and the motion to adopt or accept is made, it is called an incidental main motion. Outside of the fact that objection to consideration cannot be applied to it, there is no difference in procedure between incidental main motions and original main motions. The following are incidental main motions:

1. accept a committee report on a matter referred to it.
2. adopt a committee report on a matter referred to it.
3. the motion to fix the time at which to adjourn.
4. the motion to fix the time to which to adjourn.
5. the motion to adjourn if qualified in any way.
6. the unqualified motion to adjourn if the assembly has no provision for a future meeting.
7. the motion to fix the time and/or place of the next meeting.
8. any motion to amend a rule or set of rules already adopted such as the constitution, by-laws, rules of order, standing rules and resolutions.
9. any motion to ratify or confirm action already taken.
10. the motion to rescind action already passed.
11. the motion to rescind and expunge action already passed.
12. the motion to reconsider.
13. the motion to take from the table.

208. MAJORITY DEFINED. In voting, a majority is defined as one vote more than fifty percent of the votes cast. Blank ballots are not counted as a vote cast but illegally marked ballots are counted.

209. MAJORITY VOTE, MOTIONS REQUIRING ONLY. When it is not indicated otherwise, motions require only a majority vote. All motions not listed as requiring a two-thirds vote may be passed by a majority vote. (see **TWO-THIRDS VOTE, MOTIONS REQUIRING.**)

210. MASS MEETING DEFINED. A mass or occasional meeting includes any meeting of persons other than an organized society. The term mass meeting is used regardless of the size of the group because the size does not affect the organizational procedure nor the method of conducting the meeting. The term does not include a mob because the latter has no order and follows no rules and, therefore, cannot be called a meeting. The organizational procedure in a mass meeting is the same as that used in forming a temporary organization. (see **TEMPORARY ORGANIZATION.**)

211. MASS MEETING, HOW TO CONDUCT. The major difference between a mass meeting and a convention not yet organized is that in the latter only official delegates or members may vote while in a mass meeting all who attend may do so. The meeting is called to order by a person previously agreed upon by the ones calling the meeting. When he has called the meeting to order, he then explains the purpose of the meeting and proceeds to the election of officers in the same manner as is done in the formation of a temporary organization. The officers take over and the meeting is ready to conduct whatever business they were called together to consider. Since the mass meeting has no rules of its own, it operates under the rules of common parliamentary law. When the business is completed, the meeting is adjourned. Since such a group does not intend to meet again, it does not set a time for another meeting and so adjourns sine die.

212. MEETING, DISTINCTION BETWEEN SESSION AND. The term meeting is used to mean the coming together of the members of a society in a single assembly during which they do not separate except to recess and which is terminated by adjournment. Thus, if an organization starts a meeting in morning, takes a recess for lunch and reconvenes again in the afternoon, it is the same meeting and they take up after lunch exactly where they left off in the morning. On the other hand, if they meet in the morning, adjourn at twelve o'clock, eat lunch and meet again at one o'clock, it constitutes two separate meetings but only one session.

The term session may apply to a single meeting as in the case of a society that meets regularly once a week or once a month or some other stated interval. Each meeting constitutes a session. On the other hand, a session may constitute a whole series of meetings as a session of Congress. A series of meetings held over a period of several days in a convention would make up one session. A session is terminated by the adjournment of a meeting without providing for another meeting. Also, in a society holding regular meetings, a session is terminated by the adjournment of a meeting until the next regular meeting.

213. MEETING, HOW TO CONDUCT A REGULAR. The success of any business meeting rests largely in the hands of the presiding officer. If he is efficient, business-like, knows the order of business to be followed, has an agenda and moves briskly from one item to another, the meetings will run smoothly and much will be accomplished.

The procedure in different organizations varies greatly but most societies follow a fairly standard order of business. It is as follows:

1. call to order
2. roll call.
3. reading of the minutes.
4. treasurer's report.
5. reports of standing committees.
6. reports of special committees.
7. reading of correspondence.
8. special orders.
9. unfinished business.
10. new business.
11. announcements.
12. adjournment.

Obviously, all societies do not use all of these. Many societies do not call roll, for example. Any society is free to adopt any order of business it desires but the above order is standard practice.

The proper procedure in carrying out each of the above steps will be found under that heading.

214. MEETINGS, REGULAR. Practically all permanently organized societies provide for regular meetings in the constitution and/or by-laws. Regular meetings are meetings that are so provided for and that occur at regularly stated intervals ... "Each Friday at seven-thirty p.m.," "On the first Saturday of each month, September through June," for example. Regular meetings follow an adopted order of business which should be provided for in the rules of the society.

163

Usually one regular meeting is designated as the "annual" meeting and is generally the last meeting of the fiscal year. Annual reports of officers and standing committees are received. Elections are sometimes held and/or officers installed if previously elected.

215. MEETINGS, SPECIAL. Most permanent organizations provide in their rules for the calling of special meetings. A special meeting is one that is called in addition to and at a different time from regular meetings. They do not follow the regular order of business because they are usually called for the purpose of handling an emergency problem or some matter that cannot wait for a regular meeting. Only definitely specified business is transacted at special meetings. Provision for the calling of special meetings must appear in the rules (usually the by-laws) of the society. If no such provision is made, special meetings cannot be called. The usual provision is that special meetings may be called by the president on his own initiative or by the executive committee or by the president, if requested by a certain percent of the members. When a special meeting is called, all members must be notified, and the notice must state the specific business to be considered. A copy of the call should appear in the minutes of the special meeting. If a member is intentionally not notified of a special meeting, the business transacted at that meeting is illegal. No business may be transacted except that which was stated in the call.

216. MEMBERS NOT PRESENT DURING DEBATE CONCERNING THEMSELVES. It is a general rule of parliamentary law that a member should not be present when any matter pertaining to himself is under consideration. For this reason, a member should withdraw voluntarily whenever such a matter comes up. If he refuses to do so, he may be ejected by the society.

217. MEMBERS, PERSONAL INTEREST OF, DEBAR FROM VOTING. It is a generally accepted rule that a member should refrain from voting on matters which concern him directly, either personally or financially. If a member is on trial, he is theoretically under arrest and so is deprived of his rights of membership. Even if he is not under arrest, a sense of propriety prevents him from voting on matters concerning himself. There are so many exceptions, however, that the right to vote on such matters is not prohibited but merely established by the delicacy of the situation. For example, a member has the right to vote for himself when he is a candidate for office or membership on a committee. Also, he has the right to vote when his vote will affect the decision. Furthermore members have the right to vote when others are involved with them. If this were not the case, a small minority could bring charges against the rest of the membership and, since the majority could not vote, they could even be deprived of membership. If members could never vote on any matter involving themselves, the society could never vote on any matter involving itself, which would benefit its members. The members could not vote to decrease the dues, for example, because each member would benefit financially from such a decrease.

218. MINORITY REPORTS OF COMMITTEES. Frequently committee members disagree and sometimes this disagreement is strong enough so that the minority may wish to make a separate report. When the majority report has been received by the society and a motion made for its adoption or acceptance, a member of the minority (usually the leader) asks leave to make a minority report. (see **COMMITTEE REPORTS, FORMS OF**) Usually societies allow minority reports without any objection but if there is an objection by any member, the motion to receive the report requires a majority vote to pass and the motion is undebatable. When the minority report has been read and handed to the chairman or secretary, two possibilities are open to the assembly. A motion may be made to substitute the minority for the majority report. Such a motion is really in the nature of an amendment to the motion to adopt or accept the majority report. As such, it may be debated.

If no motion to substitute is made, the minority report is simply considered as debate on the main motion and the society acts on the majority report. Even if the minority report is not read, any member of the society, including a minority member of the committee, may move to substitute the resolutions favored by the minority for the majority report.

Sometimes even the members of the minority cannot agree and several minority reports are submitted. Also, sometimes a committee member will agree with all but one part of the committee report. In this case, after the other members have signed, the dissenting member writes at the end of the report that he agrees with all but the part which he specifies, then he signs the report.

165

219. MINUTES, ACCESS TO. All records and papers, including the minutes of meetings, belonging to a society are in the custody of the secretary unless otherwise assigned. Some exceptions are the treasurer's books which are the responsibility of the treasurer and papers placed in the charge of an archivist or librarian. All records must be available to all members at all reasonable times. If records are needed by a committee they are turned over to its chairman but must be returned when no longer needed. The records of a committee are the property of that committee and must be available to any member of it but need not be made available to any other member of the society.

220. MINUTES, CORRECTION OF, AFTER APPROVAL. Since it is vitally important that the minutes of a society be correct in every possible respect, it is permitted to correct them even after they have been approved and regardless of how much time has elapsed. In this case, however, the correction is not made as a correction or addition and merely inserted in the minutes as would be the case if the correction was made before approval. It is made in the form of a main motion and as such, it has no privilege and takes precedence over nothing. It is debatable and amendable, yields to all privileged and incidental motions and can have all secondary motions applied to it. It takes a majority vote.

221. MINUTES, CORRECTION OF, BEFORE APPROVAL. Opportunity should always be given to correct the minutes of a meeting before they are approved. The minutes are a record of the business conducted by the society and should be accurate. After they have been read, the chairman says, "Are there any corrections to the minutes?" If none are forthcoming, the chair says, "There being none, the minutes stand approved as read."

If there are corrections, they are incorporated into the minutes by the secretary, unless there is opposition to them. When a correction has been made, the chairman says, "Are there any further corrections?" This continues until all corrections have been made, then the minutes are declared approved. If there is opposition to or difference of opinion on a correction, it is voted on by the assembly.

222. MINUTES, DISPENSE WITH READING OF. When the chair calls for the reading of the minutes of the last meeting, a member may move to dispense with the reading of the minutes. This is a fairly common practice in small organizations which meet frequently but should be used sparingly. The minutes are a record of the actions of the society and it is responsible for them. Therefore, the minutes should not be passed over lightly. On the other hand, if there is good reason why they need not be read, it may be dispensed with. The motion to dispense is an ordinary main motion but actually has the effect of laying on the table because later a motion may be made to read them. The motion to dispense is debatable, requires a second and majority vote.

223. MINUTES, FORM AND CONTENT OF. The amount of detail which the secretary should put in the minutes of a meeting is determined to a large extent, by the nature and desires of the society. In some societies and under certain circumstances, it is necessary to have a complete transcript of everything that is done and said and by whom. In most organizations, however, complete details are unnecessary and only serve to confuse and clutter up the record. Generally the following basic items are all that is necessary:

1. the kind of meeting, regular or special.
2. the name of the organization.
3. the time and place of meeting.
4. the fact that the regular chairman and secretary were present or if not, the names of the substitutes.
5. number present or names of those absent.
6. whether the minutes of the last meeting were approved or their reading dispensed with.
7. all motions and disposition made of them.
8. the time of convening and adjournment and manner of adjournment.
9. secretary's signature.

Much of this can be condensed to the point where it is easy to understand and not too bulky to keep. A sample follows:

June 15, 19––

The regular meeting of the Podunk Self Improvement Club was called to order by the president at 7:30 p.m. at the clubhouse.

In the absence of the secretary, the minutes were read by Mary Smith. The minutes were approved as read.

It was moved and seconded to hold a picnic on July 4th. Motion carried.

Moved and seconded to secure an outside speaker for the July meeting. Referred to the Program Committee.

Moved and seconded that the club go on record as opposed to the new zoning law proposed by the City Commission. Motion lost.

Meeting adjourned at 9:45 p.m.

Signed,
Mary Smith
Secretary-Pro Tem

224. MINUTES IN CONVENTION. When a society holds frequent regular meetings and also an annual convention, the minutes of the last regular meeting should be read and approved at the convention and conversely, the minutes of the convention should be read and approved at the next regular meeting following the convention. When a society meets only once a year at an annual convention which lasts several days, the minutes should not be held over from one annual meeting to the next. Rather, the minutes of the preceding day should be read each day at the beginning of the meeting. On the last day of the convention, the minutes should be read at the end of the meeting. However, frequently there is neither time nor interest enough at the end of the convention. In this case, the executive committee may be authorized to approve the minutes or a special committee may be appointed for this purpose.

225. MINUTES, WHEN PUBLISHED. It is not often that ordinary clubs or organizations have occasion to publish their proceedings or minutes of their meetings. Large organizations and learned societies, however, frequently publish the proceedings of their conventions. When this is done, the publication not only should contain a strict record of what was done but also the names of speakers with either an abstract of the speeches or the speeches in full. Other material also should be complete and exact. Committee reports should be printed in full. If additions or deletions are made, the additions should be in italics and the deletions in brackets with an explanation of this fact at the beginning. Usually when the proceedings of a society are published, the job is placed in the hands of a publishing committee with the power to edit.

226. MODERATOR. The term moderator is a title sometimes given to the presiding officer. In addressing the chair, a member should use the title of the presiding officer. On the other hand, the presiding officer speaks always of himself, not by title, but by using the term "the Chair."

227. MODIFICATION OF MOTION BY MOVER. Before a motion has been stated by the chair, the maker of the motion may modify it without permission. After it has been stated, it is the property of the assembly and the maker must be granted leave or permission to modify it. If a motion has been made and seconded and the maker modifies it before it has been stated by the chair, the seconder may withdraw his second if he does not favor the motion as modified. After the motion has been stated, if permission is granted the maker to modify it, the second may be withdrawn.

If the maker wishes to modify his motion after it has been stated by the chair, he says, "Mr. Chairman, I ask leave to modify the motion." The chair asks whether there is any objection and if there is none, the permission is granted. If there is objection, the request is put to a vote and can be granted by a majority vote. Also, another member can move to grant leave to modify a motion. This motion does not require a second because it is presumed that the maker favors the modification and this constitutes a second. Leave to modify a motion can be granted at any time up to the taking of a vote and may even be made while incidental and secondary motions are pending.

228. MOTION, DEFINITION OF A. A motion may be defined as a proposal made to a deliberative assembly. It may be a proposal that the organization take a certain action or assume or express a certain point of view. Motions are divided into four major groups.
1. Main or principal motions.
2. Secondary or subsidiary motions.
3. Incidental motions.
4. Privileged motions.

229. MOTION TO ACCEPT A REPORT. This is actually an unnecessary motion but is usually offered in courtesy to the committee which has reported. It is usually made by someone other than a member of the committee and indicates approval of the report or of the work done. If either the work or the report is not acceptable, the motion to accept should be defeated since its passage makes the organization responsible for it.

169

230. MOTION TO ADOPT A REPORT. Adoption of a committee report by the organization indicates that the assembly not only accepts as its own and assumes responsibility for the report but also agrees to carry out the action recommended in the report. Thus, if the committee recommends that the organization sell its clubhouse and the report is adopted, it means that the assembly has agreed to sell. The adoption of a recommendation of action by a committee is the same as the passage of a main motion to do the same act.

231. MOTION TO BE STATED BY CHAIR BEFORE DISCUSSION. A motion may not be debated until it has been made, seconded and stated by the chairman. When a motion has been properly made and seconded, the chair repeats the motion and calls for discussion in the following manner: "It has been moved and seconded that we do thus and so. Is there any discussion?" This is called "stating the question" and has the effect of bringing it before the assembly for debate.

232. MOTION TO TAKE UP A MOTION OUT OF ITS PROPER ORDER. Because the adopted order of business has the same status as a rule of the society, the motion to take up a matter out of its proper order is the same as a motion to suspend the rules and is treated as such. The form properly is: "I move to suspend the rules that interfere with consideration of . . . . ." (State the matter for which the rule is to be suspended.) Or it may be stated, "I move to suspend the rules and take up . . . ." This motion takes precedence over main motions and all secondary motions and yields to all privileged motions. It is an incidental motion, requires a second and a two-thirds vote. It is not debatable and may not be renewed except by general consent.

233. MOTIONS CLASSIFIED ACCORDING TO OBJECT.
To suppress action on a motion.
1. call for the orders of the day (if in order).
2. object to consideration (if in order).
3. move to lay on the table.
4. move to postpone indefinitely.
5. move to adjourn.
To delay action.
1. move to postpone to a certain time.
2. move to lay on the table.
3. move to amend.

4. move to refer to a committee.
5. move to adjourn.

To stop discussion.
1. call for the previous question.
2. move to limit debate.

To modify or alter a motion.
1. move to commit, refer or recommit.
2. move to amend.

To consider a matter a second time.
1. move to reconsider.
2. move to reconsider and have entered on the minutes.
3. move to rescind or repeal.
4. move to rescind and expunge from the minutes.
5. move to take from the table (if in order).

To secure rights and comforts of members or prevent breaking rules.
1. rise to a question of privilege.
2. rise to a point of order.

To reverse rulings of the chair.
1. appeal from the decision of the chair.

To substantiate a vote.
1. call for a division of the house.

To extend limits of debate.
1. move to extend limits of debate.
2. move to suspend the rules (if in order).

To question a speaker or secure information.
1. rise to a request for information.
2. ask the chair if the speaker will yield to a question.

To prevent action from being carried out.
1. move to reconsider and have entered on the minutes.

234. MOTIONS, DILATORY, ABSURD AND FRIVOLOUS. One of the basic purposes of parliamentary law is to facilitate the orderly conducting of business. Whenever a member uses it for the purpose of obstructing progress, he is out of order. It is the responsibility of the chairman to protect the society from such acts. When the chair feels that a member is making motions or using any other parliamentary form for the purpose of obstructing progress, he should declare the member out of order. If the member appeals the decision and the chair is upheld, the chair has the right to refuse to recognize the member and to refuse to entertain another appeal as long as he is satisfied that the member is using this means to obstruct progress since the member is violating the rule that no dilatory, absurd or frivolous motions may be made.

235. MOTIONS, HOW TO MAKE. Some motions do not require that the maker secure the floor before they are made. The member who wishes to propose such a motion, rises and says, "Mr. Chairman, (then without waiting to be recognized, he continues) I move that . . . ." Most motions cannot be made until the maker has secured the floor. With such motions, the member rises and says, "Mr. Chairman." The chairman recognizes him by calling him by name or otherwise indicating that he has the floor. The member then continues, "I move that . . . ." Or "I move (or propose) the adoption of the following resolution . . . ."

236. MOTIONS, HOW TO PUT. The process of putting the question or motion to a vote involves several steps.
    1. The chair asks, "Are you ready for the question? or "Is there any further discussion?"
    2. The chair restates the motion.
    3. The chair takes the affirmative vote.
    4. The chair takes the negative vote.
    5. The chair announces the result of the vote.
    When it appears to the chair that the discussion on a motion is over, he asks, "Are you ready for the question? or "Is there any further discussion?" If no one claims the floor to speak, he restates the motion and puts it to a vote by saying, "The motion is that we should do thus and so. All those in favor of the motion make it known by saying 'aye' (or whatever method of voting is to be used). Those opposed 'no'." He then announces the result by saying, "The motion is carried" or "The motion is lost." This whole process is called putting the question because it puts the motion to a vote.

237. MOTIONS, INCIDENTAL. Incidental motions are motions that arise incidentally in the conducting of business. They are incidental to pending business and although they have no precedence over each other, they do take precedence over the motion out of which they arise. Incidental motions are generally not debatable because they are in order only when a situation occurs that requires one of them and

172

should be settled as quickly as possible in order to make way for the real business. They yield to privileged motions. The following are incidental motions:

1. point of order.
2. objection to consideration.
3. suspension of the rules.
4. appeal from the decision of the chair.
5. consider by paragraph.
6. division of the house.
7. division of the question.
8. parliamentary inquiry.
9. leave to withdraw a motion.
10. leave to be excused from duty.

238. MOTIONS, ORDER OF PRECEDENCE OF. The following motions are listed in the order of precedence. Each motion takes precedence over all of the motions below it.

Privileged motions.

1. to fix time to which to adjourn.
2. to adjourn (unqualified).
3. to take a recess.
4. to rise to a question of privilege.
5. to call for the orders of the day.

Incidental motions. (These motions have no particular precedence over each other.)

6. to suspend the rules.
7. to withdraw a motion.
8. to read papers.
9. to object to consideration.
10. to rise to a point of order.
11. to rise to a point of parliamentary inquiry.
12. to appeal from the decision of the chair.
13. to call for a division of the house.
14. to call for a division of the question.

Subsidiary or secondary motions.

15. to lay on the table.
16. to call for the previous question.
17. to limit or extend limits of debate.
18. to postpone to a certain time or definitely.
19. to refer to a committee.

20. to amend.
21. to postpone indefinitely.
22. to make a special order of business. (sometimes this is a main motion)

Main motions.

23. original main motions or resolutions.
24. incidental main motions (These motions have no particular precedence over each other.)
25. reconsider.
26. reconsider and have entered on the minutes.
27. rescind.
28. rescind and expunge.
29. to take from the table.
30. to adjourn (when qualified).
31. to fix time at which to adjourn.

239. MOTIONS THAT ARE IN ORDER WHEN ANOTHER HAS THE FLOOR. There are two reasons for allowing a motion to interrupt a speaker.

1. The motion may be subject to a time limit and therefore be urgent.

2. The motion may be of such immediate importance that it cannot be put off.

The following motions may interrupt a speaker or one who has the floor:

1. appeal from the decision of the chair.
2. division of the assembly.
3. division of the question.
4. objection to consideration of the question.
5. point of order.
6. orders of the day.
7. parliamentary inquiry.
8. question of privilege.
9. reconsider.

240. MOTIONS THAT ARE NOT SUBJECT TO AMENDMENT. All original main motions are subject to amendment. All other motions may be amended except the following:

1. to adjourn (except when qualified or when no provision has been made for a future meeting).

2. call for the orders of the day.
3. questions of order and appeal.
4. objection to consideration of a question.
5. call for a division of the house.
6. to grant leave to withdraw a motion.
7. to grant leave to speak after indecorum.
8. a request of any kind.
9. to take up a question out of its proper order.
10. to suspend the rules.
11. to lay on the table.
12. to take from the table.
13. to reconsider.
14. the previous question.
15. to postpone indefinitely.
16. to amend an amendment.
17. to fill a blank.
18. a nomination.
19. a point of order.
20. to ask leave to speak out of order.
21. for the reading of papers.
22. question of privileges.
23. to accept a report.
24. to close nominations.
25. to enter into the minutes.
26. to go into executive session.
27. to place on file.
28. to receive a report.

241. MOTIONS THAT ARE NULL AND VOID EVEN IF ADOPTED UNANIMOUSLY.

Any motion that conflicts with any law of governmental authority, such as the nation, or state, or city in which the society is located, is out of order and if passed, it is null and void. So, also, is any motion that conflicts with the rules of a higher order of the society, such as a motion passed by a local chapter of a national fraternity. Any motion which conflicts with the constitution or by-laws of the society itself is null and void even if passed unanimously. Any motion which is in conflict with any other rule of the society is null and void unless the rule has been legally suspended for the express purpose of adopting the motion. Any rule which affects absentee members cannot be suspended by general or unanimous consent and if it is done, it is null and void because the absentees have not given their consent and, therefore, the vote is not unanimous. The purpose of voting by secret ballot is to enable members to conceal their vote, therefore, if the rules require a vote to be taken by ballot, any motion which defeats the secrecy of the ballot is null and void, if passed. For example, if a secret ballot is required, a motion to allow one person to cast the ballot for all, such as ordering the secretary to cast an unanimous ballot, is out of order because any member voting against it would reveal his vote. Also if the vote is by ballot and the result is not unanimous, a motion to make it unanimous must be voted on by secret ballot or it is null and void.

242. MOTIONS THAT CANNOT BE AMENDED. The motion to amend cannot be applied to any of the following motions:
1. to adjourn (except when it is qualified or when it is made in an assembly with no provision for a future meeting).
2. call for the orders of the day.
3. questions of order and appeal.
4. to object to consideration of a question.
5. call for a division of the assembly or house.
6. to grant leave to withdraw a motion.
7. to grant leave to speak after indecorum.
8. a request of any kind.
9. to take up a question out of its proper order.
10. to suspend the rules.
11. to lay on the table.
12. to take from the table.
13. to reconsider.
14. the previous question.
15. to postpone indefinitely.
16. to amend an amendment.
17. to fill a blank.
18. a nomination.
19. a point of order.
20. to ask leave to speak out of order.
21. for the reading of papers.
22. raising a question of privilege.
23. to accept a report.
24. to close nominations.
25. to enter in the minutes.

26. to go into executive session.
27. to place on file.
28. to receive a report.

243. MOTIONS THAT CANNOT BE DEBATED. The following motions are not open to debate and are put by the chair as soon as they are seconded if a second is required or as soon as they are made if no second is required:

1. fix the time to which to adjourn (when privileged).
2. to adjourn (when unqualified and made in an assembly that has provided for future meeting).
3. take a recess (when privileged).
4. call for the orders of the day.
5. any motion relating to the priority of business.
6. appeal from the decision of the chair.
7. suspension of the rules.
8. objection to the consideration of the question.
9. point of order
10. parliamentary inquiry.
11. leave to withdraw a motion.
12. division of the question.
13. division of the assembly or house.
14. lay on the table.
15. take from the table.
16. previous question.
17. limit debate.
18. extend limits of debate.
19. amend an undebatable motion.
20. reconsider an undebatable motion.
21. dispense with the reading of the minutes.

244. MOTIONS THAT CANNOT BE RECONSIDERED. No motion that can be renewed within a reasonable time can be reconsidered nor can any motion when the same result can be attained in some other way. Any action that has been partially or completely carried out (except the motion to limit debate) cannot be reconsidered. The following motions cannot be reconsidered:

1. any action which the assembly cannot undo.
2. an affirmative vote on a contract when the other party has been notified.

177

3. reconsider.
4. adjourn.
5. take a recess.
6. lay on the table.
7. take from the table.
8. suspend the rules.
9. suspend the order of business.
10. affirmative vote on the orders of the day.
11. affirmative vote to adopt, amend, repeal, or rescind any rule or set of rules of the society such as the constitution, by-laws and rules of order, if previous notice is required.
12. elect to membership if the person affected has been notified and has not declined.
13. affirmative vote to elect to office if the member has been notified and has not declined.
14. affirmative vote to reopen nominations.
15. negative vote to postpone indefinitely.
16. affirmative vote to commit or refer if the committee has taken up the matter referred.
17. approval of the minutes.

245. MOTIONS THAT CANNOT BE RENEWED. If a motion has been withdrawn by the maker, the matter has the same status as though it had never been made, therefore, any withdrawn motion may be reintroduced and the rules on renewal do not apply. With this exception, the following motions cannot be renewed:
1. to adopt an original main motion.
2. to postpone indefinitely.
3. to reconsider.
4. to object to consideration.
5. to fix time to which to adjourn for the same time.
6. to suspend the rules for the same purpose at the same meeting.
7. to amend.
8. to amend an amendment.
9. appeal from the decision of the chair.
10. division of the house.
11. main motion at the same session.
12. to reopen nominations.
13. to rescind.

14. point of order.
15. parliamentary inquiry.

246. MOTIONS THAT DO NOT REQUIRE A SECOND. The following motions do not require a second:
1. rise to a question of privilege.
2. rise to a point of order.
3. objection to consideration.
4. call for the orders of the day.
5. call for a division of the house.
6. filling blanks.
7. nominations.
8. leave to withdraw a motion.
9. rise to a point of parliamentary inquiry.
10. rise to a point of inquiry (for information).

247. MOTIONS THAT OPEN THE MAIN QUESTION TO DEBATE. Of the four motions listed below, the first is a secondary motion and the other three are incidental main motions. They have in common the fact that they all apply to some other question that is or has been before the assembly. Because of the effect they have on the matter to which they are applied, if they are passed, the result of making one of these motions is to open the question to which they are applied for debate.
1. postpone indefinitely.
2. reconsider a debatable motion.
3. rescind.
4. ratify.

248. MOTIONS THAT SHOULD BE IN WRITING. Most motions are simple enough to be easily understood and remembered. On the other hand, if a motion is at all complicated, it should be put in writing if for no other reason than for the convenience of the secretary. The chairman has the right to demand that a motion be put in writing if he feels that it is necessary. This rule applies to resolutions which should always be in writing but it also includes any motion, amendment and instructions to a committee.

249. MOTIONS, WHEN TWO MAY BE COMBINED. It is a positive rule of parliamentary law that two main motions cannot be pending at the same time. Obviously, it follows that a member cannot make two such motions simultaneously. There are a few situations, however, which permit a member to combine two main motions into one. For example, if a member were to move, "That the rules be suspended and debate be extended for one hour," it is really two motions; (1) to suspend the rules and (2) to extend debate. When two matters are so closely allied that both must be passed in order to make either of value, the two may be combined into one main motion.

N

250. NOMINATING OR INFORMAL BALLOT. In electing officers, many organizations, especially small ones, do not go through the formality of nominating candidates. Instead ballots are passed out and the members write the name of one person for each office to be filled. If the same name receives a majority of votes for a given office, he is declared elected. On the other hand, if several names receives votes for the same office and no one name receives a majority, all names are considered nominated and a second vote is taken on these names. If, on this second ballot, a name receives a majority, he is declared elected. If not, a motion is passed to eliminate all but the two names receiving the most votes and a third vote is taken. Obviously, one of these two will receive a majority and thus will be elected. On rare occasions a tie will occur, in which case, the decision is made by lot unless the society decided to solve the problem in some other manner.

251. NOMINATIONS, SECONDING. It is unnecessary to second nominations from the floor but it is not prohibited. When a nomination is made, it is in order to second it and even to make a seconding speech but it is totally unnecessary. It is usually done in political conventions but is not ordinarily done in the usual society.

252. NOMINATIONS, TO CLOSE AND REOPEN. If carried, the motion to close nominations prevents any further nominations from being made. The chair should refuse to entertain this motion as long as there are any who wish to make further moninations.

When nominations have been made by a nominating committee or from the floor or both and when it appears to the chair that there are no further nominations, he should ask if there are any. If none are forthcoming, he may declare the nominations closed and proceed with the election.

If a motion to close nominations is made from the floor, it requires a second, is undebatable and can have no secondary motions applied to it except that it can be amended as to the time of closing. Because it deprives members of their right to make nominations, it requires a two-thirds vote. It yields to all privileged motions.

If it is desired to reopen nominations after they have been closed, it may be done by a motion to that effect. This motion requires a second, is undebatable and can have no secondary motions applied to it except that it can be amended as to time. It yeilds to all privileged motions and requires a majority vote.

253. NOMINATIONS, TREATMENT OF. There are three methods of nominating candidates for an office. They are; (1) by nominations from the floor, (2) by a nominating committee, and (3) by a nominating ballot.

1. The simplest and most common method of nominating candidates is by nomination from the floor. When this method is used, the chairman opens the nominations by saying, "The chair will entertain nominations for 'blank' office." Any member who wishes to make a nomination, rises and addresses the chair. When he is recognized, he says, "I nominate Mr. X." Nominations do not require a second but they are not prohibited. Other nominations are made until there are no more, then someone moves to close the nominations or the chair says, "Are there any further nominations? If not, the chair will entertain a motion to close nominations." When this motion is passed, the society is ready to vote.

2. If a nominating committee is used, it is appointed far enough in advance of the election date to allow it to prepare a slate of candidates. When the time comes, the chair calls for a report of the committee and the slate of candidates proposed by the committee is read by the reporting member. No motion is made to adopt or accept the report unless there are no other nominations since to adopt it would automatically elect the slate. When the slate has been read, the chair calls for further nominations from the floor for each office in turn and the procedure from this point is the same as above.

3. The nominating ballot is effective in small organizations but not in large ones, if the method is to be used during a meeting. On the other hand, if the nominating is done by mail, it is just as effective in large societies. To use this method, ballots are passed out and the members write the name of one person for each office to be filled. If one name received a majority of votes for the same office, he is declared elected. On the other hand, if several names receive votes for the same office and no one receives a majority, all names are considered nominated and a second vote is taken on these names. If on the second ballot, a name receives a majority, he is declared elected. If not, a motion is passed to eliminate all but the two names receiving the most votes and a third vote is taken. Obviously, one of these two will receive a majority and thus will be elected. On rare occasions a tie will occur, in which case, the decision is made by lot unless the society decides to solve the problem in some other manner.

254. NULL AND VOID, MOTIONS THAT ARE, EVEN AFTER ADOPTION. Any motion that conflicts with any law of a governmental authority such as the nation, state or city in which the society is located, is out of order and if passed, it is null and void. So, also, is any motion that conflicts with the rules of a higher order of the society, such as a motion passed by a local chapter of a national fraternity. Any motion which conflicts with the constitution or by-laws of the society itself is null and void, even if passed unanimously. Any motion which is in conflict with any other rule of the society is null and void unless the rule has been legally suspended for the express purpose of adopting the motion. Any rule which affects absentee members cannot be suspended by general or unanimous consent, and if it is done it is null and void because the absentees have not given their consent and therefore, the vote is not unanimous. The purpose of voting by secret ballot is to enable members to conceal their vote, therefore, if the rules require a vote to be taken by ballot, any motion which defeats the secrecy of the ballot is null and void, even if passed. For example, if a secret ballot is required, a motion to allow one person to cast the ballot for all, such as ordering the secretary to cast an unanimous ballot, is out of order because any member voting against it would reveal his vote. Also, if the vote is by ballot and the result is not unanimous, a motion to make it unanimous must be voted on by secret ballot or it is null and void.

255. NULL AND VOID VOTES. Strictly speaking, from the legal point of view, an illegal vote is one cast by a person who is not eligible to vote. In the ordinary society, any vote by ballot is null and void if it is not intelligible or if it is cast for an ineligible candidate. Misspellings do not invalidate a ballot if the intent is clear. Blank ballots are not null and void, they simply are not counted nor listed in the total votes cast. The only time a blank ballot is counted is in determining a quorum.

256. OBJECTION TO CONSIDERATION OF QUESTION. Any member of a society may object to the consideration of any original main motion provided the objection is made before there has been any debate on the question and provided no secondary motions are or have been applied to it. The proper form for making this motion, "Mr. Chairman, I object to the consideration of this question." This motion may interrupt a speaker and the maker does not need to secure the floor before making it. It does not require a second and is undebatable. It may not be amended, reconsidered or renewed. When objection to consideration is made, the chair should say, "Objection to consideration of this question has been made. Shall we consider the question? All those in favor of considering the question make it known by (name the method of voting)." A two-thirds vote in the negative is necessary to prevent consideration. If the objection to consideration is upheld, the question to which it is applied is dropped and may not be considered again at that meeting. It may be introduced again at a succeeding meeting. If the objection is not upheld by a two-thirds vote, the consideration of the question is continued.

257. OBTAINING THE FLOOR. With certain exceptions, a member is not entitled to speak or present a matter to the assembly until he has obtained the floor, that is, until he has been recognized by the presiding officer. This is done in the following manner; the member rises and says, "Mr. Chairman" or "Mr. President" or whatever the title of the presiding officer may be. In very large assemblies, he also states his name. He then waits to be recognized. The chair recognizes him by calling him by name or by title or by indicating in some other manner that the member has the floor. Sometimes the chair recognizes the member by some such statement as, "The member from Alabama has the floor." When more than one member seeks the floor at the same time, the chair exercises his discretion in giving the the floor to one of them.

258. OBTAINING THE FLOOR, PRECEDENCE IN. The general rule for the guidance of the presiding officer in recognizing the members is that the first member who properly asks for the floor should be given it. However, there are a number of exceptions to this rule which should be followed when it is to the best interests of the society to do so.

1. When a debatable motion is immediately pending, the maker of the motion, if he has not already spoken on the motion, should be

given the floor even though he addresses the chair slightly after another member. This same is true of a committee member who has made a report as well as a member who has moved to take a matter from the table or to reconsider.

2. When two members seek the floor at about the same time and one has already spoken on the pending question, the nod should be given to the other even though he is not the first to address the chair.

3. When two members seek the floor at about the same time and they are of opposing points of view on the pending question, the chair should recognize the one whose views are opposite to the member who spoke immediately before even though he is not the first one up. In other words, the chair should seek to alternate sides in debate as much as possible.

4. When a series of questions are to be considered and one has been disposed of, the chair should give the floor to the member who rises for the purpose of introducing the next question even though another has addressed the chair first. As a matter of fact, when a series of questions are to be considered, no other main motion may be introduced until the series has been completed. Also, if a matter is laid on the table in order to make way for another more urgent question, the member who moved to lay on the table should get the floor in order to introduce the urgent business. The same is true of a member who has moved to suspend the rules to make the consideration of a question possible.

5. When no business is pending and a member rises to move to reconsider or take from the table but is not the first one up, he should be given the floor provided he states his purpose when he asks for the floor.

6. When the motion to refer a matter to a committee has been passed, no new business may be introduced until all matters concerning the referral (such as size of the committee, instructions, etc.) have been settled. Therefore, a member who rises after another and who does so to deal with something concerning the referral, should be given the floor over one who rises to make another motion.

If a member does not agree with the decision of the chair in assigning the floor, he may appeal from the decision. If this appeal is seconded, it is handled in the same manner as any other appeal from the decision of the chair.

185

259. OFFICERS. Not all of the officers on the following list are necessary in all societies. In fact, most clubs and small organizations have a maximum of the first four.

1. President (sometimes called Chairman, Moderator, or other title).
2. Vice-President (sometimes a First, Second, or Third).
3. Secretary (sometimes called Recorder, Clerk, or Scribe).
4. Treasurer.
5. Recording Secretary.
6. Corresponding Secretary.
7. Parliamentarian.
8. Sergeant-at-Arms.
9. Reader.
10. Executive Secretary.
11. Historian.
12. Archivist.

260. OFFICERS, DUTIES OF. The duties of the various officers of a society are covered under the heading of each officer separately.

261. OFFICERS, ELECTION OF. In any permanent organization, the method of electing officers should be prescribed in the constitution or by-laws. These methods may be very simple or extremely complicated. The most common ones are suggested here.

1. Nominations are made from the floor. Nominations are closed and a vote taken.

2. A nominating ballot is cast. Those receiving the most votes are nominated. Another vote is cast on those thus nominated. The winner on this vote is elected.

3. A nominating committee picks a slate and it is presented. The floor is opened for further nominations. Nominations are closed and the vote cast.

4. A nominating convention is held, candidates are picked, a campaign is carried out and a final election is held.

5. A public primary election is held and the candidates nominated in the primary conduct a campaign and are voted on in the final election.

The first three of these methods are used in ordinary societies. The fourth and fifth are the methods used in political elections. When an election is held by ballot, the ballots should be kept a "reasonable" length of time before being destroyed. The specific time should be stated in the by-laws of the society. A defeated candidate has the right to challenge (which is really a demand for a recount) and must be given time to do so if he wishes. Some organizations hold election ballots for a year but others designate a much shorter period.

262. OFFICERS, TEMPORARY OR PRO TEM. The term pro tem or pro tempore means "for the time being" and is used to designate officers who are filling the post temporarily. The term is not applied, however, to an officer who is filling the post of another officer because it is his duty to do so. For example, one of the duties of the vice-president is to take the place of the president. When he fulfills this responsibility, he is not called president pro tem. There are three situations when temporary officers are used.

1. The officers of a temporary organization are officers pro tem.

2. In the formation of a permanent society, temporary officers, usually only a chairman and secretary, conduct the business until a constitution has been adopted and permanent officers elected.

3. When a regular officer is absent or wishes to abandon his office temporarily and there is no official substitute, an officer pro tem is appointed. For example, a secretary pro tem may be appointed in the absence of the regular secretary. Or if the president wishes to speak or make a motion and the vice-president is absent, the president may appoint another member to preside. He is then president pro tem.

If an officer knows in advance that he is going to be absent from a meeting, he does not have the right to appoint a substitute. Such substitute must be elected by the society and his office is terminated by adjournament of the meeting or by the entrance of the regular officer.

263. ORDER, CALL TO. The first order of business in any meeting of any organization is to call the meeting to order. This is done by the presiding officer. He attracts attention, usually by rapping sharply with a gavel, and says, "The meeting will please come to order." This should be done in a very business-like manner. Since there is usually considerable noise and confusion in a assembly prior to the opening of any meeting, a decisive and forceful attitude on the part of the chairman is called for because it will get the meeting under way more quickly and effectively.

264. ORDER OF BUSINESS. Every permanent organization usually adopts a regular chronological order in which it conducts business. This means that all regular meetings follow the same pattern of procedure except in cases of special orders or unless the rules have been suspended. The pattern varies with different societies but is usually consistent within the organization. The usual order of business is as follows:

1. *Call to order.* The presiding officer calls the meeting to order. He does this by attracting attention (usually by rapping sharply with a gravel) and saying, "The meeting will please come to order."

2. *Roll call.* The roll is called by the secretary. This is not always necessary and many societies omit it but if attendance is required, roll call is necessary. Also, it may be used to determine whether a quorum is present.

3. *Reading the minutes.* The chairman asks the secretary to read the minutes of the previous meeting which are corrected if necessary and approved.

4. *Treasurer's report.* The chairman calls for the treasurer's report. Except in the case of annual reports of the treasurer, no action on the treasurer's report is necessary.

5. *Reports of standing committees.* The chairman calls for reports of standing committees and the assembly acts on these reports. Sometimes there are no standing committees, in which case this item is omitted.

6. *Reports of special committees.* The chairman calls for reports of special committees and the assembly acts on them. If there are none, this item is omitted.

7. *Correspondence.* The chairman calls for the reading of correspondence. This is done by the secretary or by the corresponding secretary if there is one. No action is necessary on this report. If action is necessary on a particular piece of correspondence, it is taken up under "unfinished business" or under "new business" whichever is appropriate depending upon whether the matter has been previously considered.

8. *Special orders.* The chairman introduces "special orders," that is, business which has been made a special order of business for that meeting. If there is none, this item is omitted.

9. *Unfinished business.* All business which was left unfinished at the previous meeting is taken up and disposed of. The chairman should simply ask, "Is there any unfinished business?" The minutes should

188

indicate whether there is and the secretary should be alert to introduce it. If there is none, the meeting may pass on to new business.

10 *New business.* New business is transacted. New business is any that has not been introduced at a previous meeting. This is the major job of the meeting.

11. *Announcements.* The chairman calls for any announcements. These may be made by the chairman or by any other member of the assembly who has one. No action on announcements is necessary.

12. *Adjournment.* After new business has been completed and announcements made, the assembly adjourns. This requires a motion to adjourn which may be made by any member of the assembly. This motion must be seconded and passed but the meeting is not adjourned until the chair announces, "The meeting stands adjourned."

265. ORDER OF BUSINESS IN CONVENTIONS. The setting up of a program for a convention is usually intrusted to a program committee which is appointed well ahead of the convention time and which prepares a program. Generally this program is printed and mailed to the members along with the notice of convention. The program is not official, however, until it has been adopted by the convention. After the credentials committee has reported, the report of the program committee is received and adopted, it becomes the order of business of the convention and may not be changed or deviated from except by a two-thirds vote of the convention.

266. ORDER OF BUSINESS, PLACE OF COMMITTEE REPORTS IN. If the society has not adopted a different order of business, committee reports should follow the treasurer's report and should precede correspondence as follows:
1. call to order.
2. roll call.
3. reading of the minutes of the last meeting.
4. treasurer's report.
5. reports of standing committees.
6. reports of special committees.
7. correspondence.
8. special orders.
9. old business.

189

10. new business.
11. announcements.
12. adjournment.

267. ORDER OF PRECEDENCE. When several orders have been set for the same time so that they are in conflict, certain rules of precedence will determine the order in which they should be considered.

    1. A special order always takes precedence over a general order.

    2. Among themselves, general orders take precedence according to the time to which they were assigned but if several were assigned to the same time, they take precedence in the order in which they were created.

    3. Among themselves, special orders take precedence in the order in which they were created.

    4. When a time is set for a recess or adjournment, the recess or adjournment is a special order for that time and takes precedence over all others regardless of the time it was created.

268. ORDER, SPECIAL. A special order is any matter that has been assigned to a certain time for consideration. It should be noted that there is a slight difference between the motion to postpone to a certain time and the motion to make a special order for a certain time. The difference is that when the time arrives, the special order may interrupt any business pending at that time except other special orders made before it, questions of privilege and motions relating to a recess or adjournment. On the other hand, a matter that has been postponed to a certain time may not interrupt pending business but must be considered as soon as the pending business is completed. A special order may not be considered before the time assigned to it except by a two-thirds vote. It requires a two-thirds vote to create a special order and no special order may be made so that it interferes with another special order. If the motion to make a special order is applied to a pending question, it is a secondary motion and is debatable and amendable. If there is no motion pending and the motion to made a special order is applied to a matter introduced at that time, then the motion to create the special order is a main motion. If a matter that was made a special order is not called up at the time specified, it loses its privilege and is taken up as unfinished business.

190

269. ORDER, SPECIAL, FOR A MEETING. Occasionally it is desired to devote an entire meeting or the major part of it to a single matter. In this case, the matter is made *the* special order of business for that meeting. When this is done, the chair announces the matter as the order of the day immediately after the minutes of the last meeting are disposed of. Such a special order takes precedence over all other business including other special orders. The motion creating *the* special order is debatable and amendable and takes a two-thirds vote.

270. ORDER, SPECIAL. TAKES PRECEDENCE OVER GENERAL ORDERS. General orders are created by adopting an agenda, in which case, everything on the agenda is a general order. General orders are also created by postponing a matter to a certain time, at which time it becomes a general order. A special order is created by moving that a question be made a special order of business for a specified time. When a general order and a special order are set for the same time, the special order always takes precedence over the general order and must be considered first.

271. ORDERS, GENERAL. When a matter is postponed to a certain meeting, day or hour, it becomes a general order for that meeting, day or hour. There are several ways of making this motion.

1. "I move that this matter be postponed to the next meeting."
2. "I move that this matter be made a general order for the next meeting."
3. "I move this matter be postponed to January fifth."
4. "I move this matter be made a general order for January fifth."
5. "I move this matter be postponed to four o'clock this afternoon."
6. "I move this matter be made a general order for four o'clock this afternoon."

It will be noticed that the first two are simply different ways of saying the same thing. They postpone to a certain meeting. The next two say the same thing but postpone to a certain day and the last two say the same thing and postpone to a certain hour. All of these are merely different ways of creating a general order. The motion to create a general order requires a second, may be amended, is debatable, may be reconsidered and may be renewed after progress. It requires a majority vote.

191

When a matter is postponed to a certain meeting or day and the day arrives, the matter is taken up as the last step under unfinsihed or old business unless the order of business of the society provides for "orders of the day" in which case, it is taken up then. If the matter is postponed to a certain hour, it is taken up when that hour arrives. In no case, however, can it interrupt business that is on the floor at the time it is made or due. For example, suppose a matter is postponed or made a general order for four o'clock on January fifth. If there is other business on the floor at four o'clock, the postponed matter must wait until the business on the floor is finished, then it is considered. If a meeting adjourns before a general order is disposed of, it then becomes the first matter to be considered under unfinished business at the following meeting. A general order cannot be taken up before its appointed time except by a two-thirds vote because to do so would be the same as suspending the rules.

If several general orders are made for the same time, they are taken up in the order in which they were created. If several general orders are created *at* the same time and *for* the same time, they are taken up in the order in which they were listed when created. For example, suppose the following motion is made; "I move that matters A, B and C be made a general order for four o'clock." At four o'clock matter A would be considered, then B and finally matter C.

272. ORDERS OF THE DAY. Orders of the day may be established in any one of several ways. If a matter is postponed to a certain time, it becomes the order of the day for that time. The same is true if a matter is made a special order of business for a certain day and hour. Also if an agenda of items to be considered at a meeting has been adopted, those items become the orders of the day. When an agenda has been adopted, it cannot be changed except by a two-thirds vote. Matters that are postponed to a certain time or are made a special order of business for a certain time, cannot be considered before that time except by a two-thirds vote.

273. ORDERS OF THE DAY, CALL FOR. Orders of the day may be defined as that business which has previously been ordered to be taken up now. Orders of the day are established in either one of the two ways. *General orders* are prescribed by the rules of order and are the established order in which business is always taken up. For example, roll call follows call to order, reading of the minutes follows roll call, treasurer's report follows reading of the minutes, etc. (see **BUSINESS, ORDER OF**). Any change in the prescribed order of business can and should result in a call for the orders of the day, which is simply a demand that the society follow its regular order of procedure, *Special orders* are established by making a given piece of business a special order of business for a certain date and time. When the time arrives, the orders of the day should be called for.

Call for the orders of the day is a privileged motion, the mover does not need to secure recognition by the chair and it takes precedence over all other motions except the motion to adjourn and questions of privilege. It may interrupt a speaker. General orders may be postponed by a majority vote but it takes a two-thirds to postpone special orders. The proper form is to rise and say, "Mr. Chairman, I call for the orders of the day." This motion does not require a second. General orders may not interrupt business which is on the floor but special orders may. Thus, if old business is being considered, one may not call for orders of the day to consider new business. On the other hand, when the time comes to take up special orders that have been made a special order for that time, a call for the orders of the day may interrupt the business on the floor. In this case, the business is set aside until the special orders have been disposed of and then the interrupted business is resumed exactly where it was broken off. No secondary motions may be applied to the call for the orders of the day and it cannot be debated.

It is the responsibility of the presiding officer to see that business is considered in its proper order and to call special orders to the attention of the assembly when they are due. He should be assisted in this duty by the secretary who has access to the minutes and, therefore, should be aware of special orders. If these two officers always carry out their duty, there will never be any need to call for the orders of the day. However, sometimes the chairman will fail to realize that the time has arrived for special orders or he may feel that the pending business is too important to set aside. Whenever the chairman fails to follow the prescribed order of business of the society or whenever he fails to take up special orders when they are due, then any member has the right to call for the orders of the day. When this is done the chair is required to announce the business that is the order of the day. He may put to a vote the question of whether the orders of the day shall be taken up by asking the question, "Will the assembly proceed to the orders of the day?" If the assembly wishes to delay taking up the orders of the day, it has the same effect as suspending the rules and therefore requires a

193

two-thirds vote. In other words, in a vote on the question, "Will the assembly proceed to the orders of the day?" the vote must be two-thirds in the negative. If the orders of the day are set aside or postponed in this manner, they cannot be called for again until the pending business has been disposed of.

If a piece of business is on the floor and the orders of the day are called for, the assembly may decide, by a two-thirds vote, to continue debate on the pending business for a prescribed length of time. Also, after the business which was the orders of the day has been taken up, it may be debated and have secondary motions applied to it. Thus, by a majority vote it may be set aside, postponed, laid on the table or referred to a committee. When this is done or when it has been disposed of in any other manner, the business which it interrupted must be resumed provided there are no other special orders to interfere.

274. ORDERS, SPECIAL, SERIES OF, MADE BY A SINGLE VOTE.
A series of special orders may be created by a single vote by moving that each item be a special order following the one. before it. The motion is made as follows: "I move that the following questions be made successive special orders of business for two o'clock next Friday." Name the questions in the order that it is desired to take them up. In such a case, the series is treated the same as a program and nothing can interrupt until the entire series has been taken up except by a two-thirds vote.

275. ORGANIZATION OF AN OCCASIONAL OR MASS MEETING.
The organizational procedure in setting up an occasional or mass meeting and in forming a temporary organization is the same. The step are as follows:

1. When a group of persons decide to form a temporary organization or hold a mass meeting, they must decide on a time and place for the meeting, who shall be invited to the meeting, who shall call the meeting to order and who shall explain the purpose of the meeting. Sometimes they also decide who shall be nominated as temporary chairman and who shall do the nominating.

2. When those interested or those who have been invited come together, the person chosen to do so takes the chair and calls the meeting to order.

3. When the meeting has been called to order, the first business is

that of securing a temporary chairman. This may be done in either of two ways:

    a. The presiding officer may call for nominations and then declare the person whose name was first heard by him nominated and call for a vote on that name. If the name secures a majority vote, he is declared elected and he takes the chair as temporary chairman.

    b. Or the presiding officer may call for nominations and when a number of names have been nominated and the nominations closed in the usual manner, the names are voted on and the name receiving the most votes is declared elected.

    4. The temporary chairman, having taken the chair, then proceeds to secure a temporary secretary in the same manner.

    5. The necessary officers now having been elected, the organization is complete and it proceeds to conduct whatever business it may wish.

    6. When the business has been completed, the organization adjourns sine die.

276. ORGANIZATION OF A PERMANENT SOCIETY. A permanent society is one that is organized with the intent of continuing its existence indefinitely and which does not intend to disband after the accomplishment of a single task or series of tasks. When a permanent society is to be organized, the first step is to form a temporary organization, then the following steps are taken:

    1. When the temporary officers are elected, the temporary chairman appoints a constitution committee whose duty it is to prepare a constitution and by-laws for the organization. It is helpful to this committee to have a rather full discussion of the purposes, intentions and desires of those present as to the nature of the organization in order that it may consider these in formulating the constitution. The constitution committee may be elected if it is the will of the organization.

    2. A motion fixing the time, date and place of the next meeting should be passed and the constitution committee instructed to report at that time.

    3. The organization then adjourns until the next meeting.

    4. The second meeting should be given over to the adoption of the constitution and by-laws which have been prepared by the

committee. (see **CONSTITUTION, ADOPTING OF.**) The by-laws are adopted in the same manner as the constitution.

5. The next item of business to come before the meeting is the selection of officers provided for in the constitution by the method stipulated in the by-laws. Those elected take office at once.

6. The final step in getting the organization under way is the appointment of any standing committees which have been provided for in the constitution and by-laws and then the organization is a going concern.

7. Unless there is further business, the second meeting is adjourned.

277. ORGANIZATION OF A SEMI-PERMANENT SOCIETY.
Sometimes a temporary organization cannot complete the work for which it was created in one meeting and therefore may wish to form a semi-permanent organization. The organizational procedure is the same as in the formation of a temporary society except that when the temporary officers (usually a chairman and secretary only) are elected, the term pro tem is added to their titles and the next step is the appointment of a nominating committee to nominate semi-permanent officers and a rules committee to recommend a few simple rules for guidance in conducting business. These rules should provide for a time and place of meeting and for a parliamentary authority as well as any others the society may wish to adopt. At the second meeting rules are adopted in the same manner as adopting a constitution or a set of by-laws and the semi-permanent officers are elected. The organization is then a going concern.

P

278. PAPERS IN CUSTODY OF SECRETARY. In addition to preparing and keeping the minutes of meetings, one of the duties of the secretary is to keep in his custody all papers belonging to the society unless provision is made otherwise by the rules. These papers may include a roll of the members, the constitution, by-laws, rules of order, legal documents and many others. It is his duty to furnish these papers to committees, when authorized to do so by the society.

279. PAPERS, READING OF. A member does not have the right to read nor cause the secretary to read from any book or paper as a part of his speech if any member objects. Permission may be granted, upon request or motion, by either general consent or majority vote. When permission is requested, the chair asks if there is any objection and if there is none, it is granted. If there is objection, the matter is put to a vote. The request or motion to grant leave to read papers yields to all privileged motions, cannot be debated or amended or have any secondary motions applied to it.

When papers are placed before the assembly, any member may demand that they be read once and, if they have been amended or the debate on them has been lengthy, he cannot be compelled to vote on them until they have been read again, if he wishes. If it is obvious that the request is for information and not delay, the chair should direct them to be read. If there is objection, however, permission must be granted by a vote of the assembly. A member who was not present when a paper was read cannot demand that it be reread.

280. PARAGRAPH, CONSIDERATION BY. When a number of closely related items are submitted under one motion to adopt, such as a set of rules or by-laws or a series of resolutions, it is not desirable to adopt each one separately because as soon as one is adopted it goes into effect immediately and may affect a later one. Also it may be necessary, as the result of a later item, to change an earlier one that has already been considered and if the earlier one has been adopted, it can only be changed by a motion to reconsider. A much better method is to consider each one separately but not to vote on any until all have been considered and then to vote on all of them at once. This procedure is called "consideration by paragraph" or "consideration by seriatim."

The proper form of this motion is, "I move that this matter be considered by paragraph (or seriatim)." The word article, resolution or section may be substituted for the word paragraph if it is more

197

appropriate. While considering each separate paragraph, amendments may be offered and these amendments may be adopted. Also, it is possible to return to a previously considered paragraph and make other changes if it is desired. This cannot be done if each paragraph is voted on separately at the time it is considered.

281. PARAGRAPHS, NUMBER OF, CORRECTED BY SECRETARY.
In adopting a constitution or set of by-laws with numbered articles or sections or a resolution or any other matter with numbered paragraphs, it frequently happens that, due to amendments, it becomes numbered inaccurately. It is unnecessary to offer an amendment to correct the numbers. One of the duties of the secretary is to make such corrections when necessary.

282. PARLIAMENTARIAN, DUTIES OF.
The parliamentarian is usually not a regular officer of an organization in the sense that he does not ordinarily hold office for a specified term nor come under the rules usually governing the other officers of the organization. In fact, the parliamentarian may or may not be a member of the society. He may be a professional parliamentarian totally unconnected with the group except in his capacity as parliamentarian.

In any case, he should have certain qualifications.

1. He should know parliamentary law and be able to answer questions and make rulings. Usually this must be done quickly and decisively.

2. He should be familiar with the constitution, by-laws and other rules of the organization which he serves.

3. He should carry authority enough so his rulings are accepted without question.

4. Like an umpire in a baseball game, he should be able to make decisions in such a way that there will be no question about his rulings.

5. He should be totally impartial, being governed entirely by the law and not in any way allowing his partisanship to color his decisions.

The parliamentarian is responsible for the proper conduct of the meeting, therefore, he has two responsibilities.

1. He must answer all questions concerning the rules of parliamentary procedure whether the point in question is concerned with the general rules of parliamentary law or whether it is concerned with the specific rules of the society.

2. He should interrupt the proceedings if the organization is unwittingly violating any of these rules.

283. PARLIAMENTARY AUTHORITY. Every organization which expects to conduct its meetings in an orderly and business-like manner should adopt a parliamentary authority. The society should adopt in its by-laws or rules of order, a rule as follows: "The rules contained in (name the parliamentary authority) shall govern this society in all cases not covered by the rules of the society." If this is done, the society can then adopt only a minimum of special rules that may be needed to supplement the parliamentary authority. In adopting a parliamentary authority, three factors should be considered.

1. The work should be standard. It should contain all the rules used in the ordinary society and should not be a special work prepared for a particular society.

2. It should be authoritative. It should be a work prepared by an authority in the field.

3. It should be easy to use. The ease and quickness with which a specific rule can be found is an important consideration in using a parliamentary authority.

One other fact should be noted. The society should possess a copy of the adopted authority. Frequently a club will adopt a parliamentary authority and then not even have it available to use. Better still, just as every member should possess a copy of the constitution, by-laws and rules of order of the society, so also, every member should own a copy of the adopted parliamentary authority and should have it available to use in meetings. If this is done, meetings can be conducted with much greater efficiency and less waste of time.

284. PARLIAMENTARY INQUIRY. A member who seeks information concerning parliamentary law may make a parliamentary inquiry as follows, "Mr. Chairman, I rise to a point of parliamentary inquiry." He does not wait to be recognized after he says, "Mr. Chairman." The chair then directs him to state his point and the chair answers the inquiry. If the point is one that requires immediate attention, it may interrupt a speaker. If the inquiry is made when another has the floor but the chair believes it is not pertinent enough to require immediate attention, he may defer his answer until the speaker has finished. If the society has a parliamentarian, the chair may refer the point to him for answer.

285. PENDING QUESTION, MEANING OF. A pending question is any matter that is before the assembly for consideration. If a matter has been stated by the chair and has not been disposed of, it is a pending question; sometimes several motions are before the assembly at the same time. In this case, all are pending and the last one stated by the chair is called the immediately pending question because it must be the first one to be considered by the assembly.

286. PERMANENT SOCIETY, HOW TO ORGANIZE. A permanent society is one that is organized with the intent of continuing its existence indefinitely and which does not intend to disband after the accomplishment of a single task or series of tasks. When a permanent society is to be organized, the following steps must be taken:

1. The individual group or individual interested in forming the society must first inform all persons who are in sympathy with the idea and whom they wish in the organization, of their intention and call them together by notifying each of them of their intention to hold a meeting.

2. When those who have been notified come together for the first time, the person who has taken the responsibility of calling the meeting (or someone else selected by the organizers) should take the chair and preside.

3. When the meeting has been called to order by the person presiding, the first business is that of securing a temporary chairman. This may be done in either of two ways:

   a. The presiding officer may call for nominations and then may declare the person whose name was first heard by him nominated and may call for a vote on that name. If the name secures a majority vote, he is declared elected and takes the chair as temporary chairman. If he does not secure a majority vote, another name is nominated and voted on until one is elected.

   b. Or the presiding officer may call for nominations and when a number of names have been nominated and the nominations closed in the usual manner, the names are voted on and the name receiving the most votes is declared elected as temporary chairman.

4. The temporary chairman, having taken the chair, then proceeds to secure a temporary secretary in the same manner.

5. The necessary officers now having been elected the chairman appoints a constitution committee whose duty it is to prepare a constitution and by-laws for the organization. It is helpful to this committee to have a rather full discussion of the purposes, intentions and desires of those present as to the nature of the organization in order that they may consider these in formulating the constitution. The constitution committee may be elected, if it is the will of the organization.

6. A motion fixing the time of the next meeting should be passed and the constitution committee instructed to report at that time.

7. The organization then adjourns until the next meeting.

8. The second meeting should be given over to the adoption of the constitution and by-laws which have been prepared by the committee. (see CONSTITUTION, ADOPTION OF.) The by-laws are adopted in the same manner.

9. The next item of business to come before the meeting is the election of officers provided for in the constitution by the method stipulated in the by-laws. Those elected take office at once.

10. The final step in getting the organization under way is the appointment of any standing committees which have been provided for in the constitution and/or by-laws and then the organization is a going concern.

11. Unless there is further business, the second meeting is adjourned.

287. PLURALITY VOTE. The term plurality vote is used only in elections. When there are more than two candidates, the candidate who receives the highest number of votes is said to have a plurality and wins the election even though he has not received a majority of the votes.

288. POINT OF ORDER. One of the basic responsibilities of the presiding officer is to maintain order. This not only refers to preventing disturbances but also to conducting the meeting within the rules of the society and proper parliamentary law as well as preventing the making of illegal motions and the use of improper language. In other words, it is his duty to stop anything that is unparliamentary. However, any chairman is human and therefore, subject to error. Whenever any error is detected by the chairman, he should call the member making the error to order. If the chairman fails to catch the error, it is the responsibility as well as the right of any member to rise to a point (or question) of order. In order to do this, the member rises, addresses the chair and, without waiting to be recognized, says, "I rise to a point (or question) of order." When this is done, any member who has the floor at the time, should take his seat and await the outcome. The chair then says, "State your point of order" which the member does. The chair then rules on the point by either supporting it or disagreeing with it. If he agrees, he says, "Your point is well taken," and orders the proper correction. If he disagrees, he says, "Your point is not well taken," and orders the proceedings to continue. Sometimes the chair is in doubt, in which case, he may refer to the parliamentarian if there is one and if it is a question of parliamentary law or he may refer the matter to the assembly for decision.

Point of order may interrupt a speaker, is undebatable, does not require a second nor recognition by the chair. It may not be amended, reconsidered or renewed. A question of order must be raised at the time the error or breach occurs. If it is allowed to pass unnoticed, it is too late to bring it up after progress in debate or business. The only exception to this is when the error results in a violation of the rules of the assembly or of parliamentary law. In this case, it may be raised at any time, even after the matter to which it applies has been disposed of.

If any member disagrees with the decision of the chair in ruling on a point of order, he may appeal from the decision of the chair.

289. POLLS, CLOSING AND REOPENING. When an assembly is voting by secret ballot and the presiding officer observes that all have voted who intend to do so, he may declare the polls closed after inquiring if all have voted. He may then order the tellers to count the ballots.

Sometimes, though not often in the ordinary society, a formal motion to close the polls is made. Obviously, the chair should not recognize such a motion until he is sure all have voted. The motion requires a second, is undebatable and requires a two-thirds vote. It can have no secondary motions applied to it except that it may be amended as to the time of closing.

Occasionally it is desired to reopen the polls. For example, if members come into the meeting after the polls are closed and desire to vote, a motion to reopen the polls is in order. This motion has the same status as the motion to close the polls except that it requires only a majority vote to pass.

290. POSTPONE INDEFINITELY, MOTION TO. The term "postpone indefinitely" is actually a misnomer because the purpose of this motion is not to postpone but to kill the main question. It is used by the enemies of the main question primarily as a test of strength without risking a vote. If the enemies of the main question can muster enough voting strength to pass the motion to postpone indefinitely, they have succeeded in killing the main motion. On the other hand, if they do not have strength enough to pass the motion to postpone indefinitely, they have not hurt their position and they now know they do not have strength enough to defeat the main question if it comes to a vote. Also, they learn who is in favor and who is opposed to the main motion and whether it is worthwhile to continue the fight against it.

The motion to postpone indefinitely is debatable and since, if passed, it kills the main motion, it actually opens debate on the main question. Therefore, a member who has exhausted his speaking time on the main question can actually speak again under the guise of debating the motion to postpone indefinitely.

The motion to postpone indefinitely takes precedence over the main motion and nothing else. It yields to all other secondary motions and to all privileged and incidental motions. It cannot be amended and the only motions that may be applied to it are the previous question and motions limiting or extending limits of debate. It can be applied only to main motions. It may be reconsidered if passed but not if lost and if lost, it may not be renewed. It requires a majority vote to pass. If the main question is referred to a committee while the motion to postpone indefinitely is pending, the postponing motion does not go to the committee but is simply ignored.

291. POSTPONE TO A CERTAIN TIME OR DEFINITELY. The motion to postpone definitely or to a certain time is for the purpose of setting aside a definite future time for the consideration of a question. It requires a second, is debatable and amendable as to the time set and by making it a special order. It requires a majority vote and may be reconsidered and renewed after progress. It takes precedence over the motions to refer or commit, to amend and to postpone indefinitely. It yields to all privileged and incidental motions and to the previous question, to lay on the table and to all motions concerning the limits of debate. The motion to postpone to a certain time differs from the motion to make a special order of business in two respects.

1. it requires only a majority vote.
2. the question to which it is applied may not interrupt pending business when the time to which it was postponed arrives.

A matter that is postponed to a certain time cannot be taken up before that time except by a two-thirds vote. The time to which a matter is postponed must fall within the same session or the next succeeding session and a question may not be postponed to the next session in societies that meet less frequently than quarterly. When a matter has been postponed to a certain time, it becomes the order of the day for that time.

292. PREAMBLE, FORM OF. The preamble of a constitution is a statement of the aims and purposes of a society. It is placed at the beginning of the constitution before the first article. The best example of a preamble in this country is the preamble to the Constitution of the United States which begins, "We, the people of the United States, in order to form a more perfect union, etc." and ends, "—do ordain and establish this Constitution of the United States of America."

293. PRECEDENCE IN RECOGNITION. The general rule for the guidance of the presiding officer in recognizing members is that the first member who properly asks for the floor should be given it. However, there are a number of exceptions to this rule which should be followed when it is to the best interests of the society to do so.

1. When a debatable motion is immediately pending, the maker of the motion, if he has not already spoken on the motion, should be given the floor even though he addresses the chair slightly after another member. The same is true of a committee member who has made a report as well as a member who has moved to take a matter from the table or to reconsider.

2. When two members seek the floor at about the same time and one has already spoken on the pending question, the nod should be given to the other even though he is not the first to address the chair.

3. When two members seek the floor at the same time and they are of opposing points of view on the pending question, the chair should recognize the one whose views are opposite to the member who spoke immediately before even though he is not the first one up. In other words, the chair should seek to alternate sides in debate as much as possible.

4. When a series of questions are to be considered and one has been disposed of, the chair should give the floor to the member who rises for the purpose of introducing the next question even though another has addressed the chair first. As a matter fact, when a series of questions are to be considered, no other main motion may be introduced until the series is completed. Also, if a matter is laid on the table to make way for another more urgent question, the member who moved to lay on the table should get the floor in order to introduce the urgent business. The same is true of a member who has moved to suspend the rules to make the consideration of a question possible.

5. When no business is pending and a member rises to move to reconsider or to take from the table but is not the first one up, he should be given the floor provided he states his purpose when he asks for the floor.

6. When the motion to refer a matter to a committee has been passed, no new business may be introduced until all matters concerning the referral (such as size of committee, instructions, etc.) have been settled. Therefore, a member who rises after another and who does so to deal with something concerning the referral, should be given the floor over one who rises to make another motion.

If a member does not agree with the decision of the chair in assigning the floor, he may appeal from the decision. If this appeal is seconded, it is handled in the same manner as any other appeal from the decision of the chair.

294. PRECEDENCE OF MOTIONS. The following motions are listed in the order of precedence. Each motion takes precedence over all of the motions below it.

Privileged motions.
1. to fix time to which to adjourn.
2. to adjourn (unqualified).
3. to take a recess.
4. to rise to a question of privilege.
5. to call for the orders of the day.

Incidental motions (These motions have no particular precedence over each other).
6. to suspend the rules.
7. to withdraw a motion.
8. to read papers.
9. to object to consideration.

10. to rise to a point of order.
11. to rise to a point of parliamentary inquiry.
12. to appeal from the decision of the chair.
13. to call for a division of the question.
14. to call for a division of the house.

Subsidiary or secondary motions.

15. to lay on the table.
16. to call for the previous question.
17. to limit, or extend limits of debate.
18. to postpone to a certain time or definitely.
19. to refer to a committee.
20. to amend.
21. to postpone indefinitely.

Main motions.

22. original main motions.
23. incidental main motions (These motions have no particular precedence over each other).
24. reconsider.
25. reconsider and have entered on the minutes.
26. rescind.
27. rescind and expunge.
28. to take from the table.
29. to adjourn (when qualified).
30. to fix time at which to adjourn.

295. PRECEDENCE, ORDER OF. When several orders have been set for the same time so that they are in conflict, certain rules of precedence will determine the order in which they should be considered.

1. A special order always takes precedence over a general order.

2. Among themselves, general orders take precedence according to the time to which they were assigned but if several were assigned to the same time, they take precedence in the order in which they were created.

3. Among themselves, special orders take precedence in the order in which they were created.

4. When a time is set for a recess or adjournment, the recess or adjournment is a special order for that time and takes precedence over all others regardless of the time it was created.

296. PRESIDENT, DUTIES OF. The presiding officer of an organization may be given any one of a great many titles the most common being chairman, president, moderator, chief, director. In addition to these, there are many others, more fantastic and peculiar to the society involved. Regardless of the title, however, the duties of the presiding officer in any group remain essentially the same. They are set forth in the constitution or by-laws. The more unusual duties, peculiar to the society, are listed and the statement usually ends with a phrase similar to the following: " . . . .and such other duties as are usual to the office of president." These "usual" duties may be listed as follows:

1. to open the meeting at the appointed time.
2. to announce the agenda of business for the meeting.
3. to recognize members who wish the floor.
4. to state all motions which are moved.
5. to put to vote all questions and announce the results of votes.
6. to conduct meetings in accordance with the rules of the society and parliamentary law.
7. to protect the society from annoyance by refusing to recognize persons who are being frivolous or who make dilatory motions.
8. to protect the rights of members.
9. to keep the discussion within the bounds of proper debate.
10. to decide points of order or, if in doubt, to submit the decision to the assembly.
11. to answer points of parliamentary inquiry unless a parliamentarian is used for this purpose.
12. to sign necessary papers and documents.
13. to represent the society in dealing with other individuals or groups.
14. to adjourn the meeting without vote in case of riot, fire, disaster or other serious emergency.

297. PREVENTING FINAL ACTION ON A QUESTION. Sometimes it is necessary for a temporary minority to prevent a temporary majority from carrying out an act which it has passed in the absence of a large percent of the members. For example, suppose a club has one hundred members and its by-laws state that twenty-five percent shall constitute a quorum. If a bare quorum of twenty-five is present, it would be possible for thirteen to pass a motion to carry out an action affecting the entire membership. If those who oppose such a motion believe that it would also be opposed by the absentees, if they were present, it may be desirable, in order to protect the absent majority, to prevent the temporary majority from carrying out the action. This can be done by moving to reconsider and have it entered on the minutes. This motion is not voted on at the meeting in which it was made. It is merely entered on the minutes and suspends all action until the next meeting. Thus it prevents the undesirable action from being carried out until the next meeting when the absentee members can be present. The motion to reconsider and have entered on the minutes can be made only by a member who voted with the prevailing side but it may be seconded by anyone. At the next meeting it is taken up as a simple motion to reconsider.

298. PREVIOUS QUESTION. The motion to close debate is called the "previous question." If the motion were properly named, it would be called "the motion to close debate." Previous question is not only a misnomer but is confusing because frequently when a vote is called for on the previous question, many people think they are voting on the pending motion. This is not true. They are simply voting to close debate on the pending motion and must then proceed to vote on this motion. This confusion is due to the fact that in England where the previous question originated (as did most of our parliamentary law) the call for the previous question means something entirely different. Originally in the United States the motion meant the same as it does in England but in this country it has gradually undergone great changes although the original name has been kept. Only its present use in the United States will be considered here.

There are several forms of the previous question. The *informal* form means that when members of the assembly believe the group is ready to vote, they simply call out, "Question," the chairman says, "Question has been called. If there is no objection, we will proceed to vote on the motion before the house which is . . ." (stating the immediately pending motion). This is called "general consent." One objection by a member of the assembly will prevent this action. (see **GENERAL CONSENT**)

The more *formal* unqualified form means that the previous question is stated in the form of a formal motion. A member of the assembly rises, addresses the chair, is recognized and then says, "I call for (or move or demand) the previous question." This motion requires a second, may not interrupt a speaker and requires a two-thirds vote to pass. Obviously, it is undebatable because to debate it would defeat its

208

purpose which is to stop debate. The two-thirds vote is required because it is a violation of the basic parliamentary rule of full and free debate. When this motion is made it applies *only* to the immediately pending motion. Suppose for example, that there is pending a motion, an amendment to the main motion and an amendment to the amendment. If the unqualified form of the previous question is used, it applies only to the immediately pending motion which is the amendment to the amendment. The chairman says, "The previous question has been called for (or moved or demanded) and seconded on the immediately pending question which is . . . (stating the amendment to the amendment). All those in favor of closing debate on this motion make it known by raising your right hand (or rising)." A show of hands or rising vote is easier to determine the count. If the previous question gets the necessary two-thirds vote, the chair immediately proceeds to take a vote on the amendment to the amendment and then opens the floor for debate on the amendment to the main motion which is the next matter to be considered by the assembly.

The *qualified* form of the previous question states the motion to which it is to be applied, "the previous question on all pending business," for instance. Suppose again there is pending a main motion, an amendment to the main motion and an amendment to the amendment. Now suppose a member says, "I call for the previous question *on all pending business.*" If this passes, the chair must call for a vote first on the amendment to the amendment then, without debate, they must vote on the amendment to the main motion and then, again without debate, they must vote on the main motion. Or a member in the example above may say, "I call for the previous question on the amendment to the amendment and on the amendment to the main motion." If this passes, the chair would call for a vote on the two amendments in turn and then open the main motion for further debate.

The previous question takes precedence over all other motions except privileged motions, incidental motions and the motion to lay on the table, to all of which it yields.

299. PRIORITY OF BUSINESS. When several matters are on the docket for consideration at a given meeting and none has priority over another, the chairman is not bound to consider them in any particular order unless a motion is passed to take them up in a certain order. It is wise for the presiding officer to make up an agenda prior to the meeting but such an agenda does not bind the society to follow it in the order listed. In situations where the meeting is likely to be long and the matters to be considered are numerous, an agenda is useful not only as a guide to the chairman, but also to restrain members from attempting to give priority to a favorite item to the detriment of other equally important matters.

300. PRIVILEGED MOTIONS. Privileged motions have the highest rank of any because of their vital importance to the welfare of the society and/or its members. They take precedence over all other motions. The privileged motions are:
1. fix the time to which to adjourn (privileged only when another matter is pending).
2. adjourn (if unqualified and does not dissolve the assembly).
3. take a recess.
4. questions of privilege (privileged but not a motion but rather a request).
5. call for the orders of the day.

301. PRIVILEGED MOTIONS, DISTINCTION BETWEEN QUESTION OF PRIVILEGE AND. Privileged motions are a small group of motions of the highest rank because of their importance. A question of privilege, while it is a request and not actually a motion, is listed as one of the privileged motions. When a member addresses the chair and says, "I rise to a question of personal privilege," and the chair says, "State your question," and the member says, "I request that the window be closed," this is a question of privilege. But when a member addresses the chair, is given the floor, and says, "I move that the window be closed," this is an ordinary main motion with all the rules of a main motion applying to it.

302. PRIVILEGE, QUESTION OF. A question of privilege is any request relating to the rights, privileges or welfare of a society or any of its members. There are two types of questions of privilege.
1. There are those relating to an individual or group of individuals. For example, a member may be cold as the result of an open window. This type is called *personal privilege*. The member rises, addresses the chair and without being or waiting to be recognized, says, "Mr. Chairman, I rise to a question of personal privilege."
2. The other type deals with the welfare of the society. For example, if a private matter is to be discussed or considered, it would

210

be a question of privilege *affecting the assembly* to request that newspaper reporters be ejected. In such cases, the member says, "Mr. Chairman, I rise to a question of privilege affecting the assembly."

Because of their importance, questions of privilege take precedence over everything except the motion to adjourn and the motion to take a recess to which they yield. When a member rises to a question of privilege, the chair requests him to state his question and when he does, the matter is decided by the chair. Such questions may interrupt a speaker if they are urgent enough. Since a question of privilege is a request and not a motion, it does not require a second, is undebatable and cannot be amended. It is decided by the chair, therefore, does not require a vote. It may be withdrawn but cannot be renewed.

303. PROGRAM COMMITTEE.

In the ordinary club or society, the program committee is usually a standing committee whose function is to arrange the programs or entertainment during the term of its office. Many organizations, such as luncheon clubs, church groups, service clubs and women's clubs, devote a part of their meeting time to a business meeting and a part to entertainment. Frequently the program committee adopts a general theme for a year and centers the program for each meeting around this theme.

In conventions, the program committee has a different function. It is its function to prepare a program for the business of the convention which may last over several days. Usually the committee, which should be appointed well in advance of the convention, has the program printed and distributed to the members. When the presiding officer calls for it, the chairman of the program committee makes his report or submits the printed program and moves that it be adopted. This motion is debatable and may be amended. It requires a majority vote for adoption but once adopted, the program cannot be changed or deviated from except by a two-thirds vote or by a majority vote of the entire membership. The report of the program committee is usually called for immediately following the report of the credentials committee.

304. PRO TEM OR TEMPORARY CHAIRMAN.

A person who acts temporarily for the chairman is called a temporary chairman or chairman pro tempore (for the time being). This term, however, does not apply to the vice-president nor to any other officer who succeeds to the chairmanship by virtue of his office. The rules of a society usually provide that in the absence or incapacity of the president, the vice-president shall take over as part of his duty. Also, usually, if the president wishes to relinquish the chair (to make or discuss a motion, for example) he asks the vice-president to take over. The term pro tempore does not apply in this case.

However, if the vice-president or any other officer who would normally succeed the president is not available, then the president may appoint a chairman from among the membership. In this case, he is called the "chairman pro tem." The office of chairman pro tem may be terminated in any one of three ways.

1. the president may elect to resume the chair.
2. adjournment terminates the office.
3. the assembly may choose to elect another chairman and thus terminate the office.

305. PROXY VOTING.

Proxy voting is a method by which a member is granted permission, in writing, to vote for or in the place of another member. An absent member may request another member to vote for him on all questions that come up at a given meeting or he may restrict the proxy to certain matters or to apply to only one question. If a member holds one proxy, it means he may vote twice, once for himself and once for the person whose proxy he holds. In corporations, where the right to vote is determined by the possession of transferable stock, state law permits proxy voting. In the ordinary society, proxy voting is not a good practice. It is never permitted unless specifically provided for in the rules of the society and unless the proxy is given in writing by the absent member.

306. PUNISH MEMBERS, RIGHT OF ASSEMBLY TO.

It is the inherent right of any assembly, organization or society to make its own rules and laws provided these laws do not conflict with the laws of the nation, state or municipality within which the organization operates. The society also has the right to enforce its laws upon its members and to punish any member for disobedience of the law. The most extreme penalty that may be used is expulsion from membership.

If the society deems it necessary for its own protection to publish or give public notice that the person is no longer a member, it may do so. The society does not have the right to go beyond what is necessary for its own protection, however. For example, the society may make a public statement that the party is no longer a member but it may not

212

publish the charges of which he was found guilty and for which he was expelled. The publication of these charges is grounds for libel.

307. PUTTING THE QUESTION. The process of putting the question or motion involves several steps.

1. the chair asks, "Are you ready for the question?" or, "Is there any further discussion?"
2. the chair restates the motion.
3. the chair takes the affirmative vote.
4. the chair takes the negative vote.
5. the chair announces the result of the vote.

When it appears to the chair that the discussion on a motion is over, he asks, "Are you ready for the question?" or "Is there any further discussion?" If no one claims the floor to speak, he restates the motion and puts it to a vote by saying, "The motion is that we do thus and so. All those in favor of the motion make it known by saying 'aye' (or whatever method of voting is to be used). Those opposed 'no' " He then announces the result by saying "The motion is carried" or "The motion is lost." This whole process is called putting the question because it puts the motion to a vote.

308. QUASI COMMITTEE OF THE WHOLE. The word quasi means "as if in" so the term quasi committee of the whole means "as if in committee of the whole." When it is desired to use this informal method of considering a matter, someone moves as follows: "I move that this matter be considered as if in committee of the whole." When this motion is passed, the society automatically goes into quasi committee of the whole. The presiding officer of the society becomes the chairman of the committee and the secretary of the society becomes the secretary of the committee. A quasi committee of the whole operates in much the same manner as a regular committee of the whole except that it cannot make any motions except the motion to amend. It may debate and amend the motion referred to it but may make no other motions. The secretary should keep minutes but they are temporary and should not be made part of the regular minutes of the society. When the committee has finished debating and amending the matter referred to it, the chairman announces that the assembly has had the matter under consideration as if in committee of the whole and he reports what has been done. The assembly then acts on this report in the same manner as if it were a report from a committee of the whole. The motion to rise is not necessary to discontinue a quasi committee of the whole.

309. QUESTION, ALWAYS KEEP, CLEAR BEFORE ASSEMBLY BY CHAIR. One of the very important responsibilities of the chair is to never allow confusion to arise as to what is the pending question. Much confusion can be avoided, if the chair will repeat the question at every opportunity. For example, it is moved, "That we do thus and so." The chair says, "It has been moved that we do thus and so. Is there a second?" The motion is seconded and the chair says, "It has been moved and seconded that we do thus and so. Is there any discussion on the motion?" After debate appears to be completed, the chair says, "Is there any further discussion? If not, the question is that we do thus and so. Are you ready for the question? All those in favor of the motion that we do thus and so make it known by raising your right hand. Down hands. All those opposed to doing thus and so raise your right hand. Down hands. The motion that we do thus and so is carried (or lost)." In doing this the chair has repeated the question at every step of the way and has prevented any doubt from arising in the minds of the members.

310. QUESTION, CALL FOR THE. When the members of a society wish to close debate and proceed to a vote on the pending question, they may do so informally by calling out "Question, question." This is an informal way of moving (or calling for) the previous question. If no member has or is seeking the floor, the chair upon hearing the call, "Question", says, "The question has been called for. Are you ready for the question?" If no one claims the floor, the chair proceeds to put the pending motion to a vote. The fact that no member claims the floor indicates that debate has been closed by general consent. If a member does claim the floor general consent is not given and debate continues.

311. QUESTION, CALL FOR, TO BE SUPPRESSED. When the members of a society wish to close debate and proceed to a vote on the matter before them, they may do so informally by calling out, "Question, question." This procedure must not be misused, however; it should never be done when another has the floor or is seeking the floor. It is the duty of the presiding officer to suppress the call for the question and protect the member who has or is seeking the floor.

312. QUESTION, DIVISION OF. When a motion or resolution consists of two or more independent or semi-independent parts, it may be wise to divide the question in order to allow the assembly to consider each part separately. This can be done only if the parts are independent enough so each can stand as a separate motion. For example, a motion, "That this club hold a picnic and that hot dogs be served as refreshment" could not be divided because the second part is entirely dependent on the first. Thus, if the part "to hold a picnic" fails, the second part "to serve hot dogs" becomes foolish. On the other hand, a motion "That this club hold a picnic on Saturday afternoon and a dance on Saturday evening" could be divided because either part of the motion could be carried out without the other.

The proper form of this motion is, "I move that this question be divided into two parts, the first part that . . . ., and the second part that . . . ." Or it may be stated, "I move that the pending question be divided as follows . . . ." The motion to divide takes precedence over the pending question, the motion to amend and to postpone indefinitely. It yields to all other secondary motions and to all privileged and incidental motions. It requires a second, is not debatable, may interrupt a speaker and may be reconsidered. It may be amended only with respect to the method of division and requires a majority vote, if necessary, but is usually adopted by general consent.

Each part of the divided question is debated and voted on separately but it is not necessary to move the adoption of each since the original main motion to adopt covers all the parts.

313. QUESTION OF ORDER. One of the basic responsibilities of the presiding officer is to maintain order. This not only refers to preventing disturbances but to conducting the meeting within the rules of the society and proper parliamentary law as well as preventing the making of illegal motions and the use of improper language. In other words, it is his duty to stop anything that is unparliamentary. However, any chairman is human and therefore, subject to error. Whenever any error is detected by the chairman, he should call the member making the error to order. If the chairman fails to catch the error, it is the responsibility as well as the right of any member to rise to a point (or question) of order. In order to do this, the member rises, addresses the chair and, without waiting to be recognized, says, "I rise to a point (or question) of order." When this is done, any member who has the floor at the time, should take his seat and await the outcome. The chair then says, "State your point of order" which the member does. The chair then rules on the point by either supporting it or disagreeing with it. If he agrees, he says, "Your point is well taken," and orders the proper correction. If he disagrees, he says, "Your point is not well taken," and orders the proceedings to continue. Sometimes the chair is in doubt, in which case he may refer to the parliamentarian if there is one and if it is a question of parliamentary law or he may refer the matter to the assembly for decision.

Point of order may interrupt a speaker, is undebatable, does not require a second nor recognition by the chair. It may not be amended, reconsidered or renewed. A question of order must be raised at the time the error or breach occurs. If it is allowed to pass unnoticed, it is too late to bring it up after progress in debate or business. The only exception to this is when the error results in a violation of the rules of the assembly or of parliamentary law. In this case, it may be raised at any time, even after the matter to which it applies has been disposed of.

If any member disagrees with the decision of the chair in ruling on a point of order, he may appeal from the decision of the chair.

314. QUESTION, STATING THE. A motion may not be debated until it has been made, seconded and stated by the chair. When a motion has been properly made and seconded, the chair repeats the motion and calls for discussion in the following manner: "It has been moved and seconded that we do thus and so. Is there any discussion?" This is called "stating the question" and has the effect of bringing it before the assembly for debate.

315. QUESTION, TO CONSIDER A SECOND TIME. A question can be brought before the assembly for consideration a second time in various ways depending upon what disposition was made of it when it was considered the first time.

1. If the question was referred to a committee, it can be considered a second time when the committee reports it back to the assembly.

2. If the motion has been laid on the table, it can be considered a second time by passing the motion to take from the table.

3. If it has been postponed to a certain time or made a special order for a certain time, it may be considered again by calling for the orders of the day when the time arrives.

4. If the question has been passed, rejected or postponed indefinitely, any member, who voted with the prevailing side, may move to reconsider. If passed, this motion reopens the question for consideration a second time.

5. If the motion to reconsider is not available because no one is both willing and able to move it, the motion may be made to rescind the vote which adopted, rejected or postponed indefinitely. If the rescinding motion is passed, the question which was adopted, rejected or postponed indefinitely is reopened for consideration.

6. In some instances, a motion may be brought before the assembly for consideration a second time by renewing it. This is accomplished by simply proposing the motion again.

316. QUESTION, TO MODIFY THE. When a motion is poorly worded, the chair may request the maker to reword or modify his motion. Or the chairman himself may re-phrase the motion with the permission of the proposer. When a motion is not exactly to the liking of the assembly, it may be modified by amendment.

317. QUESTION, TO SUPPRESS THE. It usually requires a two-thirds vote to suppress without debate a motion that is legally made. If two-thirds of the assembly wish to suppress a question, it may be done by any of the following methods:

1. objection to consideration.
2. call for the previous question and then vote down the motion to be suppressed.
3. postpone indefinitely. (majority vote only)
4. lay on the table. (majority vote only)

Each of these motions is discussed under its own heading. The use of the motion to lay on the table to suppress a question is unfair because it does not require a two-thirds vote. Also, it is dangerous because the friends of the suppressed motion may later find themselves in the majority and may take it from the table and pass it.

318. QUORUM. The term quorum is defined as the number of members of a society required to be present to transact business legally. Parliamentary law provides that, unless otherwise specified by the rules of the society, a majority of the members shall constitute a quorum. If any number, other than a majority, is desired, it should be so specified in the rules. The number required for a quorum will vary widely according to the nature of the society. In a mass meeting, the number present is a quorum since they constitute the membership. A small organization the members of which live in close proximity, such as the active members of a college sorority or fraternity, may require a very high percent of members to be present to conduct business. On the other hand, a society with a widely scattered membership, such as a national association which meets only once a year in convention, must make its quorum small. Also, some organizations, such as a church or a fraternal society, must keep the quorum requirement small because the register of membership is unreliable and members become widely scattered. The best guide in setting a quorum is the maximum number that can be reasonably depended upon to attend meetings under normal conditions. The quorum may be expressed in percentages, such as fifty percent of the active members or it may be stated in terms of a specific number.

319. QUORUM, BOARDS CANNOT DECIDE UPON. In regard to what constitutes a quorum, boards, executive committees, etc. are on the same basis as ordinary committees. Since their power is delegated to them by the parent body, the number that must be present at a meeting in order to conduct business, which is called a quorum, is determined by the parent body unless the power is delegated to the committee.

320. QUORUM IN COMMITTEES. A committee is the creation of the parent organization, therefore, it has no powers except these delegated to it by its creator. This includes determining the number constituting a quorum. The society may state the number necessary for a quorum or it may specifically delegate this right to the committee. If there is no statement to the contrary, a majority of the committee constitutes a quorum and is the number which must be present to conduct business. For example, in a committee of seven, a quorum of four could officially conduct business.

321. RATIFY. The term ratify means to confirm by expressing consent, approval or formal sanction. An amendment to the constitution of the United States must be "Ratified" by three-fourths of the legislatures of the states. In the ordinary society, the motion is seldom used, but when needed, no other will take its place. It is used to confirm or approve some action of an officer, delegate or committee which requires the approval of the society and which the society has the right to authorize. The society cannot ratify an act which it does not have the right to authorize in advance. It cannot ratify an act done in violation of any law or rule either of government or the society itself. The motion to ratify is a main motion; it is debatable and amendable and requires a majority vote.

322. READER, DUTIES OF. The office of official reader is not common since the secretary usually has the responsibility of reading communications, papers, and resolutions. In large conventions, however, where the other duties of the secretary are heavy, an official reader may be used. He should be a good oral reader with an effective voice. It is his duty to read aloud any matters referred to him for that purpose.

323. READING OF PAPERS. A member does not have the right to read nor cause the secretary to read from any book or paper as a part of his speech if any member objects. Permission may be granted, upon request or motion, by either general consent or majority vote. When permission is requested, the chair asks if there is any objection and if there is none, it is granted. If there is objection, the matter is put to a vote. The request or motion to grant leave to read papers yields to all privileged motions, cannot be debated or amended or have any secondary motions applied to it.

When papers are placed before the assembly, any member may demand that they be read once and if they have been amended or the debate on them has been lengthy, he cannot be compelled to vote on them until they have been read again if he wishes. If it is obvious that the request is for information and not delay, the chair should direct them to be read. If there is objection, however, permission must be granted by a vote of the assembly. A member who was not present when a paper was read cannot demand that it be reread.

324. RECEPTION OF COMMITTEE REPORTS. Many organizations adopt a standard agenda or order of business which they follow in all meetings. When this is done, there is usually a place provided for reports of committees. When the time for reports arrives, the chair calls for reports of special committees in the order in which they were appointed. When a report is called for, the reporting member (usually, but not necessarily the chairman of the committee) obtains the floor in the usual manner, reads the report and hands it to the chairman or secretary. If the report requires action by the society, the reporting member (or some other member of the society) moves that the report be accepted or adopted, whichever is appropriate.

If there is no provision in the order of business for committee reports, the report may be made at any time the committee is ready, provided no business is pending and the society is willing to receive the report. The reporting member obtains the floor and states that the committee has agreed upon a report and is ready to present it. The chair may then direct him to make the report if he believes the assembly is ready to receive it. The report is read, handed to the chair or secretary and the appropriate motion is made for its adoption or acceptance. If the chair is not sure whether the society is ready to receive a report, he should put it to a vote. If a majority are in favor, the report is received. The motion to receive a report is undebatable. If a majority are opposed to receiving the report, a time should be set for its reception.

325. RECESS IN ORDER WHEN NO QUORUM IS PRESENT. If a meeting is called to order and a quorum is not present, it is in order to move to take a recess. This is done if it is believed that enough members to make a quorum will arrive later or if the assembly has voted to take measure to secure a quorum. These two motions and two others, to fix the time to which to adjourn and to adjourn are the only ones that can be made when no quorum is present.

326. RECESS, TO TAKE A. The motion to take a recess is a high ranking privileged motion taking precedence over all motions except to fix the time to which to adjourn and to adjourn to both of which it yields. If it is made when no business is before the assembly, it loses its privilege and becomes a regular main motion. When privileged, it is undebatable and can be amended only as to the length of the recess. It can have no other secondary motions applied to it. At the end of the recess, the chair re-convenes the assembly and business is resumed at the point where it was broken off.

327. RECOGNITION, PRECEDENCE IN. The general rule for the guidance of the presiding officer in recognizing members is that the first member who properly asks for the floor should be given it. However, there are a number of exceptions to this rule which should be followed when it is to the best interests of the society to do so.

1. When a debatable motion is immediately pending, the maker of the motion, if he has not already spoken on the motion, should be given the floor even though he addresses the chair slightly after another member. The same is true of a committee member who has made a report as well as a member who has moved to take a matter from the table or to reconsider.

2. When two members seek the floor at about the same time and one has already spoken on the pending matter, the nod should be given to the other even though he is not the first to address the chair.

3. When two members seek the floor at about the same time, and they are of opposing points of view on the pending question, the chair should recognize the one whose views are opposite to the member who spoke immediately before even though he is not the first one up. In other words, the chair should seek to alternate sides in debate as much as possible.

4. When a series of questions are to be considered and one has been disposed of, the chair should give the floor to the member who rises for the purpose of introducing the next question even though another has addressed the chair first. As a matter of fact, when a series of questions are to be considered, no other main motion may be introduced until the series is completed. Also, if a matter is laid on the table in order to make way for another more urgent question, the member who moved to lay on the table should get the floor in order to introduce the urgent business. The same is true of a member who has moved to suspend the rules to make the consideration of a question possible.

5. When no business is pending and a member rises to reconsider or to take from the table, but is not the first one up, he should be given the floor provided he states his purposes when he asks for the floor.

6. When the motion to refer a matter to a committee has been passed, no new business may be introduced until all matters concerning the referral (such as size of committee, instructions etc.) have been

settled. Therefore, a member who rises after another and who does so to deal with something concerning the referral, should be given the floor over one who rises to make another motion.

If a member does not agree with the decision of the chair in assigning the floor, he may appeal from the decision. If this appeal is seconded, it is handled in the same manner as any other appeal from the decision of the chair.

328. RECOMMIT, MOTION TO.

When a committee reports upon a matter referred to it, if the society is dissatisifed with the report or wishes the committee to do further work on the matter, the motion to recommit is made. This motion has the same status as the motion to commit. It is a secondary motion, requires a second, is debatable if the matter being recommitted is debatable and may be amended. The proper form is; "I move this matter be recommitted to the committee." If the committee is a special one which would be discharged after its report is made, the motion to recommit revives the committee.

329. RECONSIDER, AND HAVE ENTERED ON THE MINUTES.

The motion to reconsider and have entered on the minutes says, in effect; "I move that the motion to reconsider this matter be entered on the minutes and be taken up at the next meeting." The motion to reconsider and enter on the minutes is applied only to matters which have been passed, rejected or postponed indefinitely. It is used to protect the society from a temporary, but unrepresentative majority by preventing it from carrying out an act which is opposed by the real majority. For example, suppose a club has one hundred members and its by-laws state that twenty-five percent shall constitute a quorum. If a bare quorum of twenty-five is present, it would be possible for thirteen to pass a motion to carry out an action affecting the entire membership. If those who oppose such a motion believe that it would also be opposed by the absentees, if they were present, it may be desirable, in order to protect the absent majority, to prevent the temporary majority from carrying out the action. This can be done by moving to reconsider and have it entered on the minutes. This motion is not voted on at the meeting in which it is made. It is merely entered on the minutes and suspends all action until the next meeting. Thus it prevents the undesirable action from being carried out until the next meeting when the absent members can be present to reconsider and vote down the undesirable matter. The motion to reconsider and have entered on the minutes can be made only by a member who voted with the prevailing side, but it may be seconded by anyone. At the next meeting it is taken up as a simple motion to reconsider.

330. RECONSIDER, EFFECT OF ADOPTING MOTION TO. If the motion to reconsider is passed or adopted, the matter to which it applies is back on the floor in the same position it was before the original vote on it was taken. This has several implications:

1. If the motion to reconsider a question is passed on the same day the question was voted on and there was a limit on debate on the question and a member had exhausted his right to speak, he does not have the right to speak again on the motion being reconsidered.

2. If the motion to reconsider is passed on the next day after the question to be reconsidered was voted on, the member who had previously exhausted his right to speak, is entitled to speak again.

3. If the original motion was voted on while the previous question was in effect, the previous question does not apply when it is reconsidered.

331. RECONSIDER, EFFECT OF MAKING MOTION TO. From the time the motion to reconsider has been properly made and seconded until it has been disposed of, it has the effect of preventing the execution or carrying out of the matter to which it is applied. For example, suppose the motion to read a paper has been passed. Suppose further, that the motion to reconsider this motion has been made and seconded before the paper is read. The effect would be to prevent the reading of the paper until the motion to reconsider has been disposed of. In other words, action on the reading of the paper is suspended as long as the motion to reconsider reading it is pending.

332. RECONSIDER IN COMMITTEE. The motion to reconsider cannot be made in committee of the whole or quasi committee of the whole. In standing and special committees a vote can be reconsidered at any time, regardless of the time elapsed, provided the motion to reconsider is made by a member who voted with the prevailing side on the motion to which it is applied. The motion to reconsider cannot be made in committees at a meeting subsequent to the one in which the motion to which it is applied was passed unless all members of the committee who voted with the prevailing side are present or have been notified that the motion to reconsider is going to be proposed.

333. RECONSIDER, MOTION TO. The purpose of the motion to reconsider is to bring before the assembly a matter that has already been disposed of by being passed or rejected. It is a special main motion, but holds a high rank because it can be made while another motion is pending, while another has the floor if he is not speaking or even after the motion to adjourn has been passed as long as the chair has not declared the meeting adjourned. However, it must be made only by a member who voted with the prevailing side when the matter to which it is applied was voted on. It may be seconded by anyone. In debate, it holds the same rank as the motion to which it applies. The motion to reconsider cannot be amended, reconsidered or postponed indefinitely. It cannot be renewed except by general consent and it cannot be applied to any motion that may be renewed reasonably soon. It must be made on the same day or the next day following the vote that is to be reconsidered was taken. Sundays, recesses and holidays do not count as days. It takes a majority vote and can be applied to amendments as well as main motions.

334. RECONSIDERED, MOTIONS THAT CANNOT BE. No motion that can be renewed within a reasonable time can be reconsidered nor can any motion when the same result can be attained in some other way. Any action that has been partially or completely carried out cannot be reconsidered (except the motion to limit debate). The following motions cannot be reconsidered:

1. Any action which the assembly cannot undo.
2. An affirmative vote on a contract when the other party has been notified.
3. Reconsider.
4. Adjourn.
5. Take a recess.
6. Lay on the table.
7. Take from the table.
8. Suspend the rules.
9. Suspend the order of business.
10. Affirmative vote on the orders of the day.
11. Affirmative vote to adopt, amend, repeal or rescind any rule or set of rules of the society such as the constitution, by-laws and rules of order, if previous notice is required.
12. Elect to membership if the person affected has been notified and has not declined.

13. Affirmative vote to elect to office if the member has been notified and has not declined.

14. Affirmative vote to reopen nominations.

15. Negative vote to postpone indefinitely.

16. Affirmative vote to commit or refer if the committee has taken up the matter referred.

17. Approval of the minutes.

335. RECORDING SECRETARY. When a society has an officer whose title is Recording Secretary, it implies that there also is a corresponding secretary. In this case, the duties of the recording secretary are the same as those of the secretary, scribe, recorder or clerk except that he is not responsible for carrying on the correspondence of the society. (see **SECRETARY, DUTIES OF**)

336. RECORDS, ACCESS TO. All records and papers, including the minutes of meetings, belonging to a society are in the custody of the secretary unless otherwise assigned. Some exceptions are the treasurer's books which are the responsibility of the treasurer and papers placed in the charge of an archivist or librarian. All records must be available to all members at all reasonable times. If records are needed by a committee, they are turned over to its chairman, but must be returned when no longer needed. The records of a committee are the property of that committee and must be available to any member of it, but need not be made available to any other member of the society.

337. REFER, MOTION TO. The motion to commit or refer is a motion to refer a matter to a committee. If the matter to be committed or referred is pending, that is, if it is on the floor or before the assembly, the motion to commit is a secondary motion. Suppose the society is considering the question of building a clubhouse and it is moved to refer the matter to a committee, then this motion is a secondary motion. On the other hand, if the matter is not before the assembly, and a motion is made to refer it to a committee, then the motion to commit is a main motion. For example, a member moves that a committee be appointed to investigate the possibilities of building a clubhouse.

The motion to refer cannot be applied to secondary motions. It cannot be laid on the table nor postponed, but both these motions take precedence over it and if either is applied to the main motion and is passed while the motion to commit is pending then the motion to refer goes with the main motion. Such motions as the previous question, to limit debate, to extend limits of debate, and to amend may be applied to it and not affect the main motion. For example, if a matter is before the assembly and the motion is made to refer it to a committee and then the motion is made to limit debate to ten minutes, this does not limit debate on the main motion, but only on the motion to refer. This indicates that the motion to commit is debatable which is true, but the debate must be confined to the matter of referring to a committee and cannot include debate on the main motion. In the United States Congress the motion to refer or commit is not debatable.

When an amendment is pending and the motion is made to refer the main motion to a committee, the amendment goes to the committee with the main motion. If a committee has begun consideration of a matter referred to it, it is too late to reconsider the motion to commit. Prior to that time, however, the motion to reconsider may be applied to it.

The motion to commit or refer is used also when it is desired to go into committee of the whole and when it is desired to consider a matter informally. For committee of the whole the proper form is: "I move that the assembly resolve itself into a committee of the whole to consider . . . ." (name the matter). For informal consideration the proper motion is: "I move that . . . . (name the subject) be considered informally." Both these motions have the same status as the motion to refer to a committee.

338. REGISTRATION OF DELEGATES. The registration of delegates or members of a convention is an important and often complicated procedure. The job is usually handled by a registration committee and in large conventions requires the assistance of considerable clerical help. The machinery for registration should be set up well in advance and should be in full operation a day or two before the opening of the convention. The work not only involves getting the names and addresses of the delegates, but may include issuing badges, getting addresses or hotel room numbers of out of town delegates, collecting dues or registration fees, distributing programs, giving out information and serving as a general clearing house for the members of the convention.

339. RENEWAL OF A MOTION. When a main motion has been rejected, postponed indefinitely or objection to its consideration has been passed, it cannot be renewed at the same session, but it may be reintroduced at any future session. The process of renewing a matter is simple. It is merely proposed again. Some motions may be renewed at the same session while others must wait for a future session to be reintroduced. In no case can a motion be renewed until there has been progress in debate or some other business has been transacted. The following motions may be renewed at the same session:

1. to adjourn.
2. to commit or refer to a committee.
3. to close debate (call for the previous question).
4. to fix the time to adjourn.
5. to lay on the table.
6. to make a special order.
7. to call for the orders of the day.
8. to postpone to a certain time.
9. to rise to a question of privilege.
10. to take a recess.
11. to take from the table.
12. to withdraw a motion.
13. to limit (or extend limits of) debate.
14. to call for a division of the question.

In no case should the chair allow a motion to be renewed for the purpose of wasting time or delaying progress or preventing action on or consideration of another matter because it then becomes a dilatory motion.

340. RENEWED, MOTIONS THAT CANNOT BE. If a motion has been withdrawn by the maker, the matter has the same status as though it had never been made, therefore, any withdrawn motion may be reintroduced and the rules on renewal do not apply. With this exception, the following motions cannot be renewed:

1. to adopt an original main motion.
2. to postpone indefinitely.
3. to reconsider.
4. to object to consideration.
5. to fix time to which to adjourn for the same time.
6. to suspend the rules for the same purpose at the same meeting.
7. to amend.

8. to amend an amendment.
9. appeal from the decision of the chair.
10. division of the house.
11. main motion at the same session.
12. to reopen nominations.
13. to rescind.
14. point of order.
15. parliamentary inquiry.

341. REOPENING NOMINATIONS. If it is desired to reopen nominations after they have been closed, it may be done by a motion to that effect. This motion requires a second, is undebatable and can have no secondary motions applied to it except that it can be amended as to the time of reopening. It yields to privileged motions and requires a majority vote to pass.

342. REPEAL, MOTION TO. The purpose of the motion to annul, repeal or rescind is to undo an act already passed. This can be done if no action has been taken to carry out the act and no commitments have been made. However, if any action has been taken, the motion to annul, repeal or rescind is out of order. It is a special main motion and therefore cannot interrupt anything that is on the floor. It is not in order during the same meeting at which the action to which it is applied was passed and it may be applied only to business that has been passed since it is obvious that it is impossible to repeal something that is not in effect. Since it is a main motion, it requires a second, is debatable and may have applied to it any motion that would apply to any other main motion.

If no previous notice of intent to make the motion to annul, repeal or rescind is given, the motion requires a two-thirds vote to pass. However, if proper notice has been given either at the previous meeting or in the notice of the meeting, then it requires only a majority vote. This notice may interrupt business, but may not interrupt a speaker who has the floor.

343. REPORTS, ERRORS IN ACTING UPON. After a committee report has been presented, it is common to move that it be received. This is an error. Receiving a report means allowing it to be presented. Therefore, the motion to receive should be made (if at all since it is usually done by general consent) only to determine whether the assembly wishes the report to be presented. To move to "receive" is the same as moving to "hear" the report or the motion that the report be presented.

Another common error is to move to "adopt" when the report contains only facts and there is no recommendation for action. The motion in this case, should be to "accept" although no motion is actually necessary. Also, the motion to "accept" should not be applied to a motion recommending action. The motion in this case should be to "adopt."

344. REPORTS OF COMMITTEES, AMENDMENT OF. When the report of a committee includes a recommendation for action it should be accompanied by a motion to adopt the report. When this is done, the motion to adopt becomes an ordinary main motion and may be treated as such. This being the case, the recommendation may be amended in the same manner as any other regular motion. It should be pointed out, however, that if the matter was referred to the committee in the first place, objection to consideration of the motion to adopt may not be made since the matter was previously considered at the time it was referred. Also it should be made clear that any amendments which are applied or attached to the recommendation are acts of the assembly and are not a part of the committee's recommendation. The assembly has no right to change the report of the committee in any way although it does have the right to alter what it adopts. Thus if the picnic committee recommends that the society hold a picnic on July fourth at three o'clock in the afternoon and this recommendation is amended to change the time to one o'clock in the afternoon, the minutes should clearly indicate that the recommendation of the committee was three o'clock because the recommendation of the committee cannot be altered by the society. Since the time was changed to one o'clock by the society, this should be indicated as an act of the society not as the recommendation of the committee. The committee's report should be recorded exactly as it was made and any alterations in it made by the assembly should be indicated as such.

345. REQUEST FOR INFORMATION. During debate on a question, it often occurs that a member may wish to get information or clarification of a point by asking a question. He may seek this information from the chairman or from the speaker if another member has the floor or from another member if no one has the floor. The inquirer rises and says, "Mr. Chairman, I rise for information," or "I rise to a point of information." The chair then directs him to state his point which he does. If the question is directed to the chair, it is answered by him. If the question is directed to another member, the chair requests that person to answer. If the question is directed to the speaker, the chair asks if he will yield to a question and if he consents, the inquirer addresses his question to the chair and the speaker by saying, "Mr. Chairman, I should like to ask the gentleman . . . ." The reply of the speaker is made the same way, that is through the chair who, however, remains silent during the conversation. The time consumed by the inquiry and answer is charged against the time of the speaker.

346. REQUEST FOR PRIVILEGE. A question of privilege is any request relating to the rights, privileges or welfare of a society or any of its members. There are two types of questions of privilege. (1) there are those relating to an individual or group of individuals. For example, a member may be cold as the result of an open window. This type is called personal privilege. The member rises, addresses the chair and without waiting to be recognized, says, "I rise to a question of personal privilege." (2) The other type deals with the welfare of the society. For example, if a private matter is to be considered, it would be a question of privilege affecting the assembly to request that newspaper reporters be ejected. In such cases, the member says, "Mr. Chairman, I rise to a question of privilege affecting the assembly."

Because of their importance, questions of privilege take precedence over everything except the motion to adjourn and the motion to take a recess to which they yield. When a member rises to a question of privilege, the chair requests him to state his question and when he does, the matter is decided by the chair. Such questions may interrupt a speaker if they are urgent enough. Since a question of privilege is a request and not a motion, it does not require a second, is undebatable and cannot be amended. It is decided by the chair, therefore, does not require a vote; it may be withdrawn, but cannot be renewed.

347. REQUEST TO BE EXCUSED FROM DUTY. When an individual joins an organization or society, he usually assumes certain obligations and responsibilities. These should be clearly stated in the rules and must be made clear to the member. Beyond these responsibilities, however, a member cannot be required to perform tasks which he is unable or unwilling to perform.

If a member is nominated for an office or appointed on a committee and is unable or unwilling to serve, he should make this fact known before the election or before the appointment goes into effect. This assumes that he is present at the time. If he fails to decline immediately, he has, by his silence, accepted the duty and is obligated to perform it until there has been reasonable time for the society to accept his resignation. If the member was not present at the time of the election or appointment, he should resign as soon as he learns of the appointment or election. A society has no right to force an office on an unwilling member, therefore, it is not good policy to refuse to accept a resignation. Usually resignations are presented to and accepted by the presiding officer, but if a motion is made, it is an ordinary main motion. It yields to incidental and privileged motions, is debatable, requires a second and a majority vote and may have secondary motions applied to it.

A good method in common practice to avoid misunderstanding is to approach the member in advance and secure his acceptance to serve before his name is proposed for duty or office. This is almost always done when a nominating committee is used.

348. REQUESTS OF ANY KIND. Members are entitled to make certain requests if they are pertinent to the business before the assembly or are desirable for the welfare of the assembly or any of its members. The following are legitimate requests:

1. parliamentary inquiry.
2. request for information.
3. request leave to withdraw or modify a motion.
4. request leave to read a paper.
5. request to be excused from duty.
6. any question of privilege.

349. RESCIND AND EXPUNGE, MOTION TO. The motion to expunge is very rarely used, only once in the entire history of the United States Congress, for example. The effect of this motion is to express very strong disapproval of a motion or portion of a motion that has been previously passed. It is usually used in conjunction with the motion to rescind, thus, "I move to rescind and expunge from the minutes . . . ." It is debatable and may be amended. It can be reconsidered only if it has failed to pass. It always requires a two-thirds vote. A matter is expunged by drawing a line around the part to be expunged and writing across it the words, "expunged by order of the assembly." This should be dated and signed by the secretary. To expunge does not mean to erase or eliminate the matter from the minutes, but only to express disapproval by indicating that it has been rescinded and expunged. The matter should not be so blotted that it cannot be read.

350. RESCIND, MOTION TO. The purpose of the motion to annul, repeal or rescind, is to undo an act already passed. This can be done if no action has been taken to carry out the act and no commitments have been made. However, if any action has been taken, the motion to annul, repeal, or rescind is out of order. It is a special main motion and therefore cannot interrupt anything that is on the floor. It is not in order during the same meeting at which the action to which it is applied was passed and it may be applied only to business that has been passed since it is obvious that it is impossible to repeal something that is not in effect. Since it is a main motion, it requires a second, is debatable and may have applied to it any motion that would apply to any other main motion.

If no previous notice of intent to make the motion to annul, repeal or rescind is given, the motion requires a two-thirds vote to pass. However, if proper notice has been given either at the previous meeting or in the notice of this meeting, then it requires only a majority vote. This notice may interrupt business, but may not interrupt a speaker who has the floor.

351. RESCINDED, VOTES THAT CANNOT BE. No vote can be rescinded if it has resulted in anything being done that cannot be undone. Thus, if a contract has been favorably voted on and the other party notified, it is too late to rescind. If a resignation, either from office or from the society, has been accepted and the member notified, the acceptance cannot be rescinded, but the member may be reelected if both the member and the society agree. If an individual is elected to membership in the society and notified of the fact, his election cannot be rescinded.

352. RESIGNATIONS. Resignations should be presented in writing and addressed to the secretary of the society if the resignation is from membership or elected office. If the resignation is from an appointed office, it should be addressed to the person who made the appointment;

resignations are accepted by the appointing member in case of appointed offices. In all other cases, they are accepted by vote of the assembly.

353. RESOLUTIONS, ADOPTION OF. Since a resolution is an ordinary main motion, it has the same status as any other main motion. It may not interrupt a speaker, it must be seconded and the maker must be recognized by the chair. It is debatable, amendable, may be reconsidered and requires a majority vote. It may not be renewed at the same session. Because of its complicated nature, the chair should order it reread by the secretary before a vote is taken. The resolution proper should be considered first and then the preamble because changes in the preamble may be made necessary by amendments made to the resolution proper. The adoption of the entire resolution is voted on at the same time.

354. RESOLUTIONS, AMENDMENT OF. The process of amending a resolution is not basically different from that of amending an ordinary motion since a resolution is merely a somewhat different form of a main motion. When the motion to adopt a resolution has been properly made, seconded and stated (by the chair), it is ready for debate. If a member wishes to amend it, he rises, obtains the floor and states his amendment. The chair then calls for a second and if seconded, declares the amendment open for debate which must be confined to the amendment. When debate is completed, the chair proceeds to a vote on the amendment and declares it passed or failed as the case may be. He then calls for further discussion on the resolution (if the amendment failed) or on the resolution as amended (if the amendment passed). A resolution, like any main motion, may be amended any number of times as long as the amendments are proposed and considered one at a time. An amendment to a resolution must be germane to the resolution. An amendment may not be made to strike out the words "resolved" from a resolution. An amendment to an amendment of a resolution is in order since it is an amendment of the second degree.

355. RESOLUTIONS, COMMITTEE ON. Resolutions may be offerred for the consideration of an assembly in either of two ways. (1) Any member may offer a resolution in the same manner as he would offer any main motion. (2) Or a resolutions committee may be charged with the responsibility of drawing up resolutions for the society. A resolutions committee is more frequently used in mass meetings and conventions. It is less common in a society which meets regularly and frequently. A resolutions committee may be provided for in the rules of the society in which case it is usually appointed well in advance of the meeting and prepares resolutions at its convenience. If no provision for such a committee exists in the rules, a committee on resolutions may be created in the same manner as any other committee.

When the resolutions committee has been appointed or elected, it should retire from the meeting and draft whatever resolutions are desired. When the committee returns, it should be prepared to report as soon as the pending business on the floor at the time is disposed of. The chairman of the committee (or the reporting member if other than the chairman) obtains the floor, reads the resolutions, moves their adoption and hands them to the presiding officer or the secretary. They are then acted upon by the assembly. Resolutions may be amended, debated and in general, dealt with in the same manner as any other committee report.

356. RESOLUTIONS CONTAINING SEVERAL PARAGRAPHS, ACTING ON.

When a resolutions committee reports a series of resolutions that cannot be considered separately or when a single resolution contains several parts, it is considered by paragraph. The term "paragraph" is used to designate natural subdivisions. For example, in a set of by-laws each separate by-law is considered as a paragraph. The same is true of each article of a constitution and in the case of a series of related resolutions, each resolution is called a paragraph.

The procedure in considering by paragraph is the same as in adopting a constitution or set of by-laws. A motion is made to adopt the entire matter, then each "paragraph" is considered in turn. It is debated and amended, if desired, but is not adopted. When all paragraphs have been considered in this manner, another opportunity is given to make further amendments and finally the motion to adopt (which was previously made) is passed.

357. RESOLUTIONS, FORM OF.

A resolution is always a main motion. When a motion is long and complicated it is placed in the form of a resolution. (1) The preamble states the reasons for the recommended action and (2) the resolution proper contains the recommended action. Each paragraph of the preamble should begin with the word "Whereas" which should be capitalized and followed by a comma. The first word following "Whereas" should be capitalized. Each paragraph should end with the word "and" except the last, which should end with the words "therefore be it." Each paragraph of the resolution proper should begin with the words "Resolved, That" with both words capitalized and a comma between them. Each paragraph should end with the word "and" except the last which should be ended with a period. The following example will illustrate the proper form of a resolution.

"Whereas, It is the avowed policy of this society to support its members whenever possible in their legal undertakings, and

Whereas, One of our members, Joe Smith, is a candidate for membership on the School Board of this city, and

Whereas, The beliefs of this society concerning the operation of our schools are the same as those expressed by Joe Smith in his campaign; Therefore be it

1. Resolved, That this society contribute the sum of one hundred ($100.00) dollars to the campaign fund of Joe Smith, and
2. Resolved, That each member of this society actively campaign for the election of Joe Smith, and
3. Resolved, That each member of this society pledge his vote to Joe Smith in the forthcoming election."

358. RESOLUTIONS, HOW TO MAKE. When a member wishes to propose a resolution, he should write it out in exactly the form in which he wishes it adopted. Since it is a main motion, he should wait until such a motion is in order and then, after obtaining the floor in the usual manner, he should say, "I move the adoption of the following resolution." He should then read the resolution and present a copy of it to the secretary of the society. If it is seconded, it is open to discussion and amendment and handled in the same manner as any main motion.

359. RESOLUTIONS SHOULD BE IN WRITING. A resolution is used in place of an ordinary motion because of the complicated or involved nature of the subject. For this same reason, a resolution should *always* be presented in writing so the secretary can place it in the minutes exactly as proposed and so the chairman or secretary can reread it to the society during debate, if necessary.

360. RESOLUTIONS, WHEN NOT IN ORDER. Just like any other main motion, a resolution is not in order if it conflicts with any governmental law of the community in which the society is located. In the United States, this includes federal, state and local laws. Also, it cannot conflict with any rule of the society in which it is made nor with any rule of a society which has jurisdiction over the society in which it is made.

361. RESPECTFULLY SUBMITTED, NO LONGER USED. The expression "Respectfully submitted" is no longer used in connection with the signature of the secretary in submitting his minutes nor preceding the signatures of the members of a committee in submitting a report. The word "Signed" followed by a comma is used in both cases.

362. RESTORE TO MEMBERSHIP OR OFFICE. When a member has been expelled from membership or office or his resignation from either has been accepted and it is desired to restore him to the office or to membership, it must be done in the same manner in which he secured the position in the first place. He must be re-elected in the manner prescribed by the rules of the society which governed his original election.

363. REVISION OF CONSTITUTION AND BY-LAWS. Every constitution, set of by-laws and set of standing rules should contain an article providing a method by which they may be amended at any regular (but not special) meeting of the society by a majority vote of the *entire* membership. If a copy of the proposed amendment was submitted in writing, at the immediately preceding regular meeting, then they may be amended by a two-thirds vote of *those voting* if a quorum is present. The above is the basic parliamentary rule for amending these documents. Beyond this rule, each organization may and should set up its own rules. (For more specific details see **AMENDMENT OF CONSTITUTION, BY-LAWS AND RULES OF ORDER.**)

364. RIGHT OF ASSEMBLY TO EJECT PERSONS. Every organization, society or assembly has the right to determine who may and who may not attend its meetings. This determination may be made in the constitution, by-laws or standing rules of the society. Or it may be made by a vote of the assembly. Thus by either a rule or by a vote the society may decide to eject a person or persons. When this decision is made it is the responsibility of the presiding officer to carry out the decision and he may use whatever force necessary to see that it is done.

If a society has a sergeant-at-arms, he may be called on by the presiding officer to eject the unwelcome person and he may request whatever assistance necessary to carry out the order. If there is no sergeant-at-arms, the chairman may appoint members to do the evicting.

Force may be used to eject a party, but care should be exercised because if the members should be unnecessarily forceful, they may be liable for damages. This liability applies only to the ejecting persons and does not apply to the presiding officer nor to the society because they did not exceed their legal rights in ordering the ejection.

365. RIGHT OF ASSEMBLY TO PUNISH MEMBERS. It is the inherent right of any assembly, organization or society to make its own rules and laws provided these laws do not conflict with the laws of the nation, state or municipality within which the organization operates. The society also has the right to enforce its laws upon its members and to punish any member for disobedience of the law. The most extreme penalty that may be used is expulsion from membership.

If the society deems it necessary for its own protection to publish or give public notice that the person is no longer a member, it may do so. The society does not have the right to go beyond what is necessary for its protection however. For example, the society may make a public statement that the party is no longer a member, but it may not publish the charges of which he was found guilty and for which he was expelled. The publication of these charges is grounds for libel.

366. RIGHTS OF ASSEMBLIES. The following are the inherent rights of any legal society, club or organization:

1. Right to make its own rules and laws provided they do not conflict with any higher society of which it is a part nor with the laws of any governmental body under whose jurisdiction or within whose territory it operates.

2. Right to enforce its rules and laws.

3. Right to punish members, the most extreme penalty being expulsion from the society.

4. Right to protect itself by publishing the fact that an expelled person is no longer a member of the society, but not the right to publish the reasons for his expulsion.

5. Right to incorporate in accordance with the laws of the state in which it operates.

6. Right to determine who shall be present at meetings.

7. Right to forcibly eject undesirable persons using sufficient force to effect his removal, but no more.

8. Right to assistance by the police in ejecting undesirable persons or in maintaining order.

9. Right to impeach any of its officers and to remove them from office.

367. RISE, MOTION TO, IN COMMITTEES MEANS ADJOURN WITHOUT DAY. Committee meetings are at the call of the chairman, therefore, it is unnecessary to set a time for further meeting although this is not prohibited. When a committee uses the motion to adjourn to terminate a meeting, it means that the committee is not ready to report and expects to hold other meetings. When a committee is ready to terminate its last meeting and report, it uses the motion "to rise" or to "rise and report." The motion to rise in committees is the same as the motion to adjourn without day or sine die when used in a regular society. It means to adjourn without plans for a future meeting.

368. RISING VOTE. Standing or rising vote is one of the common methods of voting. Because it is more accurate than voting by voice or even a show of hands, it is used if the vote is likely to be close or when it is desired to record the exact number of votes on each side. This frequently happens when a motion requires a two-thirds vote. If the chair has taken a vote by voice and he is in doubt concerning the outcome, he says, "The chair is in doubt," and then order a vote either by standing or by a show of hands. When division of the assembly is demanded, the vote is by rising. The proper procedure in taking a standing vote is as follows; the chair says "all those in favor of the motion make it known by rising." He then counts those standing and says, "Be seated. All those opposed please rise." After counting the negative vote, he says, "Be seated," and announces the result.

369. ROLL CALL, VOTE BY. Voting by yeas and nays or roll call as it is more commonly called, is one of the most time-consuming and least used methods of voting. Since it is not common practice, it is usual to use it only upon demand. The motion to vote by roll call requires a second and a majority vote. Roll call vote is used more frequently in representative bodies because the members represent a constituency which has the right to know how their representative voted especially on issues directly concerning them.

When a roll call vote has been ordered, the chair says, "When your name is called, those in favor of the motion will answer 'yes' (or yea and those opposed will answer 'no' Nay)." He then orders the secretary to call the roll. The names are called in alphabetical order except the chair whose name is called last (provided he has the right to vote). A member may vote yes or no or he may answer "present" if he does not wish to vote. The secretary records the vote beside each name, usually in a separate column for each possible answer. In order to eliminate any possible error, when the vote is completed, the secretary re-reads the roll and repeats the vote recorded beside each name. The result is given to the chair who announces the outcome of the vote. The roll sheet upon which the vote was recorded becomes a part of the minutes of the meeting.

Roll call vote cannot be ordered in committee of the whole.

370. RULES OF ORDER, AMENDMENT OF. If a society has adopted a set of rules of order, it should contain a provision for its amendment. This provision should stipulate the same procedure as is required for amending the constitution and by-laws of the society. The general rules of parliamentary law provide the same method for amending rules of order as is required for amending a constitution or a set of by-laws. (see **CONSTITUTION, AMENDMENT OF.**)

371. RULES OF ORDER, CONTENTS OF. Rules of order are those rules adopted by a society which pertain to the orderly conducting of business. Parliamentary law is actually a set of rules of order which are in common use in most societies. If a society has adopted a parliamentary authority as its guide in conducting business, it may be unnecessary for it to adopt any special rules of order unless its business is of such a nature that special rules peculiar to that society are necessary. For most societies, the regular rules of parliamentary law are sufficient.

372. RULES, SUSPENSION OF. Rules are adopted for the welfare and protection of a society and its members and to facilitate the orderly conducting of business. Because this is true, rules should not be suspended unless there is a real reason for doing so. The laws contained in the constitution can never be suspended. The by-laws may be suspended only if they contain an article providing for it. This provision should require previous notice and a two-thirds vote. Rules of order may be suspended by a two-thirds vote provided it is not a rule that protects absentees or a minority of less than one-third of the members. Since standing rules may be adopted by a majority vote, they may be suspended by the same vote. One difficulty lies in the fact that frequently societies are not clear in making their rules. Thus by-laws may contain articles that should be in the standing rules or rules of order are placed in the standing rules. In the preparation and adoption of rules, a society should clearly understand the difference in the functions of these sets of rules and should place them where they belong.

The purpose of the motion to suspend the rules is to temporarily set aside a rule in order to consider a matter not permitted by that rule. This includes taking up a matter out of its regular order, matters relating to business procedure and priority of business. If it is desired to do something that violates a rule of the society, but is not in violation of its constitution or by-laws and is not contrary to parliamentary law, the rule may be suspended. When it is moved to suspend a rule, the reason must be stated and the suspension cannot be used for other purposes. As soon as the matter for which the rule was suspended is accomplished, the rule goes back into effect. The proper form of the motion, "I move to suspend the rule which interferes with . . ." When a question is pending, the motion to suspend the rules cannot be made unless it has to do with the pending question. The motion to suspend the rules is undebatable and unamendable and requires either a two-thirds or a majority vote depending upon the rule to be suspended. It yields to all privileged motions except orders of the day and to all incidental motions which are concerned with it. Also it yields to the motion to lay on the table.

373. SECOND, MOTIONS REQUIRING. The following motions require a second in order to be considered.

1. adjourn.
2. adopt, accept, agree to.
3. adopt any rule or law.
4. amend a motion or amendment.
5. amend any rule.
6. appeal from the decision of the chair.
7. commit or refer to a committee.
8. limit or extend limits of debate.
9. division of the question.
10. fix time at which to adjourn.
11. fix time to which to adjourn.
12. consider informally.
13. lay on the table.
14. main motions.
15. close nominations.
16. reopen nominations.
17. make a special order.
18. postpone to a certain time.
19. postpone indefinitely.
20. previous question.
21. take a recess.
22. reconsider.
23. rescind, repeal or annul.
24. suspend the rules.
25. take from the table.

374. SECOND, WHEN NOT REQUIRED. The following motions do not require a second:

1. rise to a question of privilege.
2. rise to a point of order.
3. objection to consideration.
4. call for the orders of the day.
5. call for a division of the house.
6. call up motion to reconsider.
7. filling blanks.
8. nominations.
9. leave to withdraw a motion.

242

10. rise to a point of parliamentary inquiry.
11. rise to a point of inquiry (for information).

375. SECONDARY MOTIONS. A certain class of motions are used to assist in the proper disposition of main motions. Since these motions apply to the main motion, they are appropriately called secondary or subsidiary motions. They take precedence over the main motion and yield to all privileged and incidental motions. The secondary motions are:

1. to lay on the table.
2. previous question.
3. limit debate.
4. extend limits of debate.
5. postpone to a certain time.
6. make a special order of business.
7. refer to a committee (commit or re-commit).
8. amend.
9. postpone indefinitely.

376. SECONDING MOTIONS. With a few exceptions, all motions require a second. This is to prevent wasting time on a matter that is favored by only one member. It is possible for the chair, when he is certain that a motion is favored by several, to ignore the fact that the motion has not been seconded, but this is not good policy because any member can rise to a point of order and waste more time than would be consumed in seconding the motion.

The procedure in seconding a motion is very simple. A member makes a motion, "That we do thus and so." The chair says, "It has been moved that we do thus and so. Do I hear a second?" Or "Is there a second?" Another member then rises and says, "I second the motion" or "I second it." In fact, it is not necessary to rise, but it is better especially in large assemblies or if there are non-members present. Frequently, especially in small groups, a member will simply call, "Second." It is unnecessary to obtain the floor to second a motion. When the chair hears a second, he says, "It has been moved and seconded that we do thus and so. Is there any discussion?" The motion is then ready for debate. It is wise for the chair to repeat the motion both after it is made and after it is seconded so there is or can be no doubt as to what the motion is that is pending.

If there is no response when the chair calls for a second, the chair says, "The motion dies for want of a second. Is there any further business?"

377. SECONDING NOMINATIONS. It is unnecessary to second nominations from the floor, but it is not prohibited. When a nomination is made it is in order to second it and to even make a seconding speech, but it is not necessary. It is usually done in political conventions, but is not usually done in the ordinary society.

378. SECONDING, UNNECESSARY TO OBTAIN THE FLOOR FOR. When a motion requiring a second is made, the chair repeats the motion and calls for a second. Since it is unnecessary to be recognized in order to second a motion, a member rises and says, "I second the motion." It is not necessary even to rise, but in large assemblies it is better. Frequently, the member will simply call, "Second" from his seat.

379. SECRETARY, CORRESPONDING. Small organizations usually have only one secretary whose title is "secretary" and whose duty, among other things, is to carry on any correspondence of the organization including sending out notices of meetings. When an organization is large or has a large amount of correspondence due to its nature, it is desirable to have a corresponding secretary. It is his duty to send out notices of meetings, write and receive all correspondence and report any correspondence which may require action by the society. He may be assigned other duties, but if so, they should be specified always in the rules of the society. The word "corresponding" should always be used when referring to this officer because the word "secretary" when used alone always refers to the recording secretary.

380. SECRETARY, DUTIES OF. There are several titles by which the recording officer may be called. Some of these are secretary, clerk, recording secretary (if there is also a corresponding secretary), recorder, and scribe. The main function of the recording secretary is to take notes during meetings and to transcribe these notes into the minutes or record of the meeting. Some of his other duties are to carry on the correspondence of the society (unless there is a corresponding secretary); to serve as custodian of all records such as minutes, official documents and other papers except those placed in the custody of an archivist or historian; to furnish all papers and documents to members and committees when they are entitled to them; to keep a book containing the constitution, by-laws, standing rules, rules of order and all other laws of the society, and to add any amendments to these laws when they are made; to keep the presiding officer informed of the agenda of meetings and pending business; to read back to the society, upon request, any pending motions or papers; to send out notices of all meetings, regular and special (unless there is a corresponding secretary); to call roll when requested; to have at each meeting a list of all committees, both special and standing; to assist the presiding officer in taking notes, when requested; to call roll and record votes in a roll call vote; to open meetings and conduct the election of a temporary chairman in the absence of the president and vice-president. In addition to these ordinary duties, the by-laws may prescribe others such as signing, with the president, orders to the treasurer for the payment of bills. Just like the other officers, except the presiding officer, the secretary has the right to make motions, debate and vote.

381. SECRETARY, EXECUTIVE. An executive secretary is not ordinarily necessary in a small club or organization. On the other hand, large local societies as well as state and national organizations usually make use of one. He is usually a paid official who devotes much or all of his time to the job. He may be a member of the organization, but often is not. He must be a good organizer and administrator. He serves under the direction of the executive committee and is usually hired by them. The executive secretary serves as assistant to the officers and executive committee, carries on the business of the society, heads the business office and maintains continuity of policy.

382. SECRETARY, RECORDING. When a society has an officer whose title is recording secretary, it implies that there also is a corresponding secretary. In this case, the duties of the recording secretary are the same as those of the secretary, scribe, recorder, or clerk except that he is not responsible for carrying on the correspondence of the society. (see **SECRETARY, DUTIES OF.**)

383. SERGEANT-AT-ARMS, DUTIES OF. The sergeant-at-arms is responsible for the comfort and welfare of the members of the society. He has charge of the seating arrangment, public address system and such matters as heating, lighting, and ventilation. He assists the chairman in maintaining order, conducts undesirable persons from the room when ordered to do so and carries out directions given him by the presiding officer. He has charge of keeping (guarding) the door. He is custodian of all property of the society except such things as papers and documents that are assigned to other officers.

384. SERIATIM CONSIDERATION. When a number of closely related items are submitted under one motion to adopt, such as a set of rules, a set of by-laws or a series of resolutions, it is not desirable to adopt each one separately because as soon as one is adopted it goes into effect immediately and may affect a later one. Also it may be necessary, as the result of a later item, to change an earlier one that has already been considered and if the earlier one has been adopted, it can only be changed by a motion to reconsider. A much better method is to consider each one separately, but not vote on it until all have been considered and then to vote on all of them at once. This procedure is called "consideration by paragraph" or "consideration by seriatim." The proper form of this motion is: "I move that this matter be considered by paragraph (or seriatim)." The word article, resolution, or section may be substituted for the word paragraph if it is more appropriate. While considering each separate paragraph, amendments may be offered and these amendments may be adopted. Also it is possible to return to a previously considered paragraph and make other changes if it is desired. This cannot be done if each paragraph is voted on separately at the time it is considered.

385. SESSION AND MEETING, DISTINCTION BETWEEN. The term meeting is used to mean the coming together of the members of a society in a single assembly during which they do not separate except to recess and which is terminated by adjournment. Thus, if an organization starts a meeting in the morning, takes a recess for lunch and reconvenes again in the afternoon, it is the same meeting and they take up after lunch exactly where they left off in the morning. On the other hand, if they meet in the morning, adjourn at twelve o'clock, eat lunch and meet again at one o'clock, it constitutes two separate meetings, but only one session.

The term session may apply to a single meeting as in the case of a society that meets regularly once a week or once a month or some stated period. Each meeting constitutes a session. On the other hand, a session may constitute a whole series of meetings, as a session of Congress. A series of meetings held over a period of several days in a convention would make up one session. A session is terminated by the adjournment of a meeting without providing for another meeting. Also in a society holding regular meetings, a session is terminated by the adjournment of a meeting until the next regular meeting.

386. SINE DIE, ADJOURN. There is no such motion "to adjourn sine die." Sine die is a Latin term meaning "without day" and refers to the effect of adjournment on the future status of the society. If the simple, unqualified motion to adjourn is passed and if the organization has made no provision for a future meeting, then it is said to have "adjourned sine die" and the effect is to dissolve the organization since a society which adjourns without any provision for another meeting has actually adjourned itself out of existence but if provision has been made for a future meeting to be held, its effect is merely to close the session.

387. SOCIETY, MEANING OF. The word society, as it is used in parliamentary language, is a general term which is applied to any group of persons organized for the purpose of conducting business for their mutual benefit or pleasure or for the benefit or pleasure of other persons whom they represent. Some societies, such as the United States Senate, are required by law, others are authorized, but not required, such as incorporated societies and still others entirely voluntary. As used in this sense, the word society is synonymous with such terms as organization, club and assembly.

388. SPEAKER, CALL TO ORDER. A speaker may be called to order if he violates any rule of the assembly or of parliamentary law or if he is guilty of any indecorum or uses improper language in debate. If it is a simple matter of indecorum or language, the call to order must be made at the time the breech of order occurs, but if it is a matter of an unlawful act, he may be called to order at any time. For example, if a motion is made which violates any of the rules of the assembly, it is never too late to raise a point of order.

The chairman has the right to call a speaker to order or any member may say, "Mr. Chairman, I call the speaker to order." This may interrupt the speaker, does not require a second and is neither debatable nor amendable. It does not require a vote since it is decided by the chair. If the chair is in doubt, he may refer it to the assembly in which case, the matter is decided by a majority vote.

389. SPECIAL COMMITTEES. Special committees are chosen to do a particular job and are dismissed when the job is completed and a report made. Special committees are usually appointed by the presiding officer, but may be elected or may be named by the maker of a qualified motion to refer or commit. In small committees, the chairman generally acts as secretary and keeps notes of the proceedings and actions taken. If the work is complicated or the committee large, a secretary is frequently elected. A special committee may hold several meetings, in which case it adjourns at the end of each meeting except the last when the motion is made to "rise" or to "Rise and report." To adjourn assumes that the committee will meet again at the call of the chairman, therefore to adjourn without fixing a time for the next meeting does not disband the committee and all of the meetings are considered as one session. When the motion is made to "rise" or to "rise and report," it is assumed that the committee has completed its work and this will be the last meeting. Meetings may be called by the chairman at any time or if he fails to call meetings, they may be called by any two members if they notify all the other members. A special committee may be discharged by a two-thirds vote of the society, but unless this happens, it continues to exist until the work assigned to it is completed.

When a special committee has completed its work it prepares a report and passes the motion to "rise" or to "rise and report." The report is usually made by the chairman, but not necessarily. A committee may disagree on the report, in which case two reports are made, a majority report and a minority report, the chairman making the report with which he agrees. A special committee may not consider any business of the society except that assigned to it. All papers and documents given to it and belonging to the society must be returned to the society, but papers belonging to the committee, including minutes of its proceedings, may be retained or destroyed by the committee.

390. SPECIAL MEETINGS. Most permanent organizations provide in their rules for the calling of special meetings. A special meeting is one that is called in addition to and at a different time from regular meetings. They do not follow the regular order of business because they are usually called for the purpose of handling an emergency problem or some matter that cannot wait for a regular meeting. Only definitely specified business is transacted at special meetings. Provision for the calling of special meetings must appear in the rules (usually the by-laws) of the society. If not any such provision is made, special meetings cannot be called. The usual provision is that special meetings may be called by the president on his own initiative or by the executive committee or by the president, if requested by a certain percent of the members. When a special meeting is called, all members must be notified and the notice must state the specific business to be considered. A copy of the call should appear in the minutes of the special meeting. No business may be conducted except that which was stated in the call. If a member is intentionally not notified of a special meeting, the business transacted at the meeting is illegal.

391. SPECIAL ORDER. A special order is any matter that has been assigned to a certain time for consideration. It should be noted that there is a slight difference between the motion to postpone to a certain time and the motion to make a special order for a certain time. The difference is that when the time arrives, the special order may interrupt any business pending at that time except other special orders made before it, questions of privilege and motions relating to a recess or adjournment. On the other hand, a matter that has been postponed to a certain time may not interrupt pending business, but must be considered as soon as the pending business is completed. A special order may not be considered before the time assigned to it except by a two-thirds vote. It requires a two-thirds vote to create a special order and no special order may be made so that it interferes with another special order. If the motion to make a special order is applied to a pending question, it is a secondary motion and is debatable and amendable. If there is no motion pending and the motion to make a special order is applied to a matter introduced at the same time, then the motion to create a special order is a main motion. If a matter that was made a special order is not called up at the time specified, it loses its privilege and is taken up as unfinished business.

392. SPECIAL ORDER OF BUSINESS, MOTION TO MAKE. The purpose of the motion to make a question a special order of business for a certain meeting or a certain time is to postpone the question to that time and to guarantee that it will be taken up at that time regardless of what is on the floor or pending. In this sense it is different from the motion to postpone to a certain time because the later cannot

249

interrupt pending business when the time comes, while special orders can. If the motion is applied to a question that is before the assembly at the time, it is a secondary motion and should be stated in the following manner: "I move that this matter be made a special order of business for such and such a time." If the matter to which it is applied is not before the assembly, the motion to make a special order is a main motion and is stated as follows: "I move that the matter of thus and so be made a special order of business for such and such a time." In either case it requires a second, is debatable and amendable and requires a two-thirds vote. Also it may be reconsidered and renewed.

393. SPECIAL ORDERS, SERIES OF, MADE BY A SINGLE VOTE. A series of special orders may be created by a single vote by moving that each item be a special order following the one before it. The motion is made as follows: "I move that the following questions be made successive special orders of business for two o'clock next Friday." (name the questions in the order that it is desired to take them up.) In such a case, the series is treated the same as a program and nothing can interrupt until the entire series has been taken up except by a two-thirds vote.

394. SPEECHES, NUMBER AND LENGTH OF, ALLOWED IN DEBATE. Originally in parliamentary law, a member was entitled to speak as long and as many times as he could obtain the floor. The only restriction was that his remarks must be germane and he could not read, repeat nor speak with undue slowness.

In modern parliamentary procedure, it has been found desirable to place some restrictions on the number and length of speeches that may be made by any one member on a given question. Any society may make its own rules concerning debate and these rules may be changed by a two-thirds vote of those voting. If the society has no rules concerning debate and if no restrictions have been placed on a given motion by the assembly, parliamentary practice dictates that no member shall speak more than ten minutes at a time nor more than twice on a given motion. Also a member should not be allowed to speak a second time as long as members who have not spoken wish to do so. The maker of a motion should be allowed to speak first if he wishes and also to close the debate if he has not exhausted his twenty minutes.

If a member, while speaking, yields the floor to another, the time is charged against the speaker just as though he had continued speaking.

On the other hand, if the speaker is interrupted by a point of order or other matter that may interrupt a speaker, the time taken by the interruption is not charged against his time.

395. STANDING COMMITTEES. Standing committees are permanent in nature, may be either elected or appointed, are provided for in the rules of the society and their duties and powers are generally specified. Even though the rules do not provide for them, standing committees may be established by custom or common practice. Usually the term of office of members of standing committees coincides with the term of office of the officers of the society, but frequently the term of office of the committee is longer and staggered so that only a part of the committee goes out of office at a time. This is especially true when it is considered wise to have a nucleus of experienced persons on the committee. Standing committees are often called permanent committees. They do all the work of a particular kind assigned to them and, unlike special committees, often work independently of the parent organization. They may make reports from time to time as called for by the society and usually prepares an annual report which is adopted or accepted by a vote of the society. Acceptance of a report by the society does not disband a standing committee as it does in the case of a special committee. Examples of standing committees are; Finance Committee, Membership Committee, Program Committee, Flower Committee, Entertainment Committee, Social Committee and Publicity Committee.

396. STANDING OUT OF ORDER WHEN ANOTHER HAS THE FLOOR. Courtesy is a basic principle of parliamentary law and many of its rules are designed to guarantee that courtesy will prevail. This is the reason for the rule which prohibits a member from standing when another has the floor. Not only is it a breach of etiquette to stand, move about, talk or otherwise create a disturbance, it is unparliamentary. If a member is concerned with a matter of such importance that parliamentary law permits it to interrupt a speaker, he has the right to stand to present it. Otherwise, the speaker is entitled to the right to speak without interruption or disturbance.

397. STANDING RULES. Standing rules deal with the business of the organization. They are the rules which govern the ordinary operation or activity, but which are not of such importance that they should be included in the constitution or by-laws. They should be easily adapted to the immediate needs of the moment, but which serve as a general guide for procedure. Standing rules may be adopted without previous notice and by a majority vote and may be suspended or rescinded by the same vote. They may be amended without previous notice and by a two-thirds vote. They do not interfere with the freedom of operation of the society because a majority vote will suspend them if previous notice is given. Of course, it goes without saying that the standing rules must not be conflict with the constitution, by-laws or rules of order.

398. STANDING RULES, AMENDMENT OF. Standing rules deal with the business of the organization. They are the rules which govern the ordinary operation or activity, but which are not of such importance that they should be included in the constitution or by-laws. They should be easily adapted to the immediate needs of the moment, but should serve as a general guide for procedure. Standing rules may be adopted without previous notice and by a majority vote and may be suspended or rescinded by the same vote. They may be amended without previous notice and by a two-thirds vote. They do not interfere with the freedom of operation of the society because a majority vote will suspend them. Of course, it goes without saying that the standing rules must not be in conflict with the constitution, by-laws, or rules of order.

399. STANDING VOTE. Standing or rising vote is one of the common methods of voting. Because it is more accurate than voting by voice or even a show of hands, it is used if the vote is likely to be close or when it is desired to record the exact number of votes on each side. This frequently happens when a motion requires a two-thirds vote. If the chair has taken a vote by voice and he is in doubt concerning the outcome, he says, "The chair is in doubt," and then orders a vote either by standing or by a show of hands. When division of the assembly is demanded, the vote is by rising. The proper procedure in taking a standing vote is as follows: The chair says, "All those in favor of the motion make it known by rising." He then counts those standing and says, "Be seated. All those opposed please rise." After counting the negative vote, he says, "Be seated" and announces the result.

400. STATING THE QUESTION, FORM OF. A motion may not be debated until it has been made, seconded and stated by the chairman.

When a motion has been properly made and seconded, the chair repeats the motion and calls for discussion in the following manner: "It has been moved and seconded that we do thus and so. Is there any discussion?" This is called, "stating the question" and has the effect of bringing it before the assembly for debate.

401. STRIKING OUT AND INSERTING WORDS, AMENDMENTS BY. The amendment to "strike out and insert words" is sometimes called "amendment by substitution" and is a combination of the amendment "to strike out words" and the amendment "to insert or add words." It will be noticed that this amendment has two parts, "to strike out" and "to insert." Therefore, if second degree amendments are to be applied to it, those affecting the strike out part should be considered first and then those applying to the insert part. After this the question is put on the amendment "to strike out and insert."

Once passed, the inserted words cannot be struck out nor the stricken words reinserted unless they are so changed as to make a new question. If lost, it does not preclude the amendment to strike out the same words nor the amendment to insert the same words. Nor does it prevent another amendment to "strike out and insert" provided either the words to be struck out or inserted are enough different so that the motions are not identical. If the words to be struck out are separated, an amendment may be offered to strike out as much of the motion as is necessary to include all the words to be struck out and to insert the desired revision including the words to be inserted. If it is desired to insert words in a different place from those to be struck out, then the inserted words must be materially the same as those struck out. On the other hand, if the words to be inserted are to occupy the same places as the eliminated words, they may, in fact should, differ from the words struck out, but they must be germane to the rest of the motion. The amendment to strike out words in one place and to insert different words in a different place is not in order. Either the words must be the same and the place changed or the place must be the same and the words changed. If it is desired to make several changes in a motion, it is better to reword the whole motion and offer it as a "substitute motion."

402. STRIKING OUT WORDS, AMENDMENT BY. An amendment made for the purpose of deleting words from a motion can be applied only to consecutive words as they appear in the original motion. If it is

253

desired to strike out words which are separated by other words, it is necessary to use separate amendments for each group of words or else to amend by substituting a whole new clause or sentence for the one containing the words. For example, if the motion "That we have a *pot-luck* picnic with a *formal* program on Friday afternoon" is before the organization and it is desired to strike out the *underlined* words, it requires one amendment to eliminate the word "pot-luck" and another amendment for the word "formal." Or it can be amended by substituting the words "a picnic with a program." Both the underlined words above cannot be eliminated by one amendment to strike out because they are separated by the words "picnic with a."

The amendment to strike out words, if it is of the first degree, may be amended only by striking out words. The effect of such an amendment to the amendment is to leave the words in the original motion. For instance, in the motion above, "That we have a *pot-luck picnic with a* formal program on Friday afternoon," suppose the amendment is made to strike out the underlined words "pot-luck picnic with a." If this were passed, the motion as amended would read: "That we have a formal program on Friday afternoon." But suppose an amendment to the amendment to strike out the words "picnic with a" to the original motion so it would read "That we have a picnic with a formal program." Thus only the word "pot-luck" would have been deleted.

If the amendment to strike out certain words is passed, the words thus eliminated cannot be reinstated or reinserted unless the wording is so changed as to make it a different motion. On the other hand, if the amendment to strike out certain words fails, it does not prevent the following amendments from being made concerning the same words:

1. to strike out the same words and insert other words.
2. to strike out a part of the same words.
3. to strike out a part of the same words and insert other words.
4. to strike out those words along with other words.
5. to strike out those words with others and insert words.

403. SUBSIDIARY MOTION. A certain class of motions are used to assist in the proper disposition of main motions. Since these motions apply to the main motion, they are appropriately called secondary or subsidiary motions. They take precedence over the main motion and yield to all privileged and incidental motions. The secondary motions are:

1. to lay on the table.
2. previous question.
3. limit debate.
4. extend limits of debate.
5. postpone to a certain time.
6. make a special order of business.
7. refer to a committee (commit or re-commit).
8. amend.
9. postpone indefinitely.

404. SUBSTITUTE MOTION. The motion to substitute one motion for another motion is, in reality, a method of amending. However, because of the peculiar nature of this type of amendment, it is handled in a different manner from an ordinary amendment. The chair should entertain second degree amendments to the original motion and after it has been perfected by its supporters, the chair should call for second degree amendments to the substitute motion. When this is done and both motions have been perfected, the organization is ready to vote on the amendment to substitute one motion for the other. If the substitution is adopted, it is still necessary to vote on the main motion as amended because it has only been voted to substitute not to adopt. If the amendment to substitute is lost, the society has only decided that that particular substitution shall not be made, therefore, the original motion must still be voted on. When a substitute motion is offered by a committee, it is handled in the same manner.

405. SUBSTITUTING ONE PARAGRAPH FOR ANOTHER, AMENDMENT BY. There are three methods of amending a motion or resolution when the change affects an entire paragraph. An amendment may be made "to strike out" a paragraph, or "to add or insert" a paragraph, or "to substitute one paragraph for another." This last is a combination of the first two. Since the debate, if any, will resolve itself around the question of which paragraph to include in the main motion, the chair should first entertain second degree amendments to the original paragraph and after it has been perfected by its supporters the chair should call for second degree amendments to the proposed paragraph. When this is done and both paragraphs have been perfected, the organization is then ready to vote on the amendment to substitute one paragraph for the other.

Sometimes the substitution includes the entire motion or resolution. It is then called a "substitute motion." In this case and if the substitution is adopted it is still necessary to vote on the main motion as amended because it has only been voted to substitute not to adopt. When one paragraph has been substituted for another, it cannot be amended by adding to it. Also the eliminated paragraph cannot be reinserted unless it has been changed enough to make it a new paragraph.

If the amendment to substitute is lost, the organization has only decided that that particular paragraph shall not replace the original, therefore, it is in order to offer it as a substitution for some other paragraph, or it may be inserted without replacing any paragraph. Also the retained paragraph may be amended in any way desired including the amendment "to strike out." No amendment is in order that presents a question that has already been decided.

It is not correct parliamentary language to speak of substituting one word or part of a paragraph for another. The word "substitute" is applied only to an entire paragraph. However, when a motion or resolution is being considered by sections, it is in order to "substitute" one section for another. One cannot move to substitute one entire resolution or report for another until all sections have been considered and the entire resolution or report has been opened by the chair for amendment.

When a motion or resolution is referred to a committee and at the time of referral has first and second degree amendments pending, they may report it back with a substitute motion or resolution which they recommend. In this case, the chair should first take up the pending amendment, then the substitute motion recommended by the committee which is handled exactly the same way as any other amendment to substitute.

406. SUPPRESS A QUESTION, TO. It requires a two-thirds vote to suppress without debate a motion that is legally made. If two-thirds of the assembly wish to suppress a question, it may be done by any of the following methods:

1. objection to consideration.
2. call for the previous question and then vote down the motion to be suppressed.

3. postpone indefinitely.
4. lay on the table.

Each of these motions is discussed under its own heading. The use of the motion to lay on the table to suppress a question is unfair because it does not require a two-thirds vote. Also, it is dangerous because the friends of the suppressed motion may take it from the table and pass it.

407. SUSPENSION OF RULES. Rules are adopted for the welfare and protection of a society and its members and to facilitate the orderly conducting of business. Because this is true, rules should not be suspended unless there is a real reason for doing so. The laws contained in the constitution can never be suspended. The by-laws may be suspended only if they contain an article providing for it. This provision should require previous notice and a two-thirds vote. Rules of order may be suspended by a two-thirds vote provided it is not a rule that protects absentees or a minority of less than one-third of the members. Since standing rules may be adopted by a majority vote, they may be suspended by the same vote. One difficulty lies in the fact that frequently societies are not clear in making their rules. Thus by-laws may contain articles that should be in the standing rules or rules of order are placed in the standing rules. In the preparation and adoption of rules, a society should clearly understand the difference in the functions of those sets of rules and should place them where they belong.

The purpose of the motion to suspend the rules is to temporarily set aside a rule in order to consider a matter not permitted by that rule. This includes taking up a matter out of its regular order, matters relating to business procedure and priority of business. If it is desired to do something that violates a rule of the society, but is not in violation of its constitution or by-laws and is not contrary to parliamentary law, the rule may be suspended. When it is moved to suspend a rule, the reason must be stated and the suspension cannot be used for any other purpose. As soon as the matter for which the rule was suspended is accomplished the rule goes back into effect. The proper form of the motion is: "I move to suspend the rule which interferes with . . . ." When a question is pending, the motion to suspend the rules cannot be made unless it has to do with the pending question. The motion to suspend the rules is undebatable and unamendable and requires either a two-thirds or a majority vote depending upon the rule to be suspended.

It yields to all privileged motions except orders of the day and to all incidental motions which are concerned with it. Also it yeilds to the motion to lay on the table.

T

408. TABLE, MOTION TO LAY ON THE. The motion to lay on the table is the highest ranking of all the secondary motions. It is a method of postponing business. The proper form is: "I move to lay the motion on the table." A tabled motion cannot be considered again until a motion is passed "to take from the table." A motion laid on the table may be taken up again at any time when no business is pending either during the same session or the next session in a society meeting as frequently as quarterly. The motion to lay on the table cannot be amended and is undebatable. It may not be reconsidered, but may be renewed after progress. It requires a majority vote.

409. TABLE, MOTION TO TAKE FROM THE. To take from the table is a special main motion because it reintroduces a piece of business which has previously been before the assembly. It cannot be made while any motion is pending, but if it is made at the same session or the next session (in organizations meeting as frequently as quarterly) and at a time when business of the class being taken from the table is in order or unfinished or new business is in order it has the right of way in preference to any other main motion. Thus, if a member rises to make a main motion and another member rises to take from the table and so states, the floor should be given to the member wishing to take from the table even though the other motion has been made and seconded as long as it has not been stated by the chair. If it has been stated by the chair, it is the pending business and cannot be interrupted by the motion to take from the table which must then wait until it is disposed of.

The motion to lay on the table is intended to be used for the purpose of laying aside temporarily a piece of business in order to make way for some other matter with the full intention of taking if from the table as soon as the interrupting business is disposed of. When a matter is laid on the table, all motions adhering to it go with it and when it is taken from the table, it and its adhering motions have exactly the same status as when set aside. There are two exceptions to this rule. (1) If the motion to postpone to a certain time was adhering to the motion when it was laid on the table and it is not taken from the table until after the time stated in the motion to postpone, then this motion is exhausted and does not apply. (2) If the previous question is adhering to the motion when laid on the table, it still adheres if the motion is taken from the table at the same session. If it is not taken from the table until the next session, the previous question is exhausted and does not adhere. If, at the time a motion is laid on the table, a member has exhausted his right of debate and the motion to take from the table is passed on the same day, the member has no further right to debate, but if it is taken from the table on another day, previous speeches are ignored.

The motion to take from the table is undebatable, cannot be reconsidered or amended and can have no secondary motions applied to it. It may be renewed and requires a majority vote. It takes precedence over secondary motions and yields to privileged and incidental motions.

410. TAKE UP A QUESTION OUT OF ITS PROPER ORDER. If an agenda or program or order of business has been adopted, it has the same status as any rule of the society and cannot be set aside except by a motion which, in effect, suspends the rules. Therefore, a motion to take up a question out of its proper order or assigned place in the agenda has the same status as a motion to suspend the rules. It requires a second, is neither debatable nor amendable and requires a two-thirds vote. The same rule applies if it is desired to take up a matter that has been postponed to a certain time or which has been made a special order of business before the time to which it was postponed arrives. Any question may be taken up out of its proper order by the above method. The proper form of the motion is: "I move to take up such and such a matter out of its proper order."

411. TELLERS, DUTIES OF. Tellers are used in a ballot vote and are usually appointed by the presiding officer. In the ordinary society, it is the duty of the tellers to distribute ballots, to collect the ballots when the vote is completed, and to count the ballots and to report the result of the vote to the presiding officer. The tellers are allowed some discretionary power in deciding the legality of a ballot, but in case of doubt, the matter should be brought to the attention of the chairman. The responsibility of the tellers is ended when the result of the vote is announced by the chairman unless the vote is challenged in which case a recount may be necessary. Ballots should not be destroyed until all possibility of a challenge is past.

412. TELLER'S REPORT ON BALLOT VOTE. When the tellers have counted the ballots and compiled the results, they must report. This report should contain, in tabulated form, all important information. Blank ballots are not counted and do not affect the number necessary for election. On the other hand, illegal ballots are included in the number of votes cast and therefore do affect the number necessary for election. For example, if one hundred votes are cast and there are two candidates, the number necessary for election is fifty-one. In this case, if there were two blank ballots, the number necessary for election would be reduced to fifty or one over one-half of ninety-eight. However, if one hundred votes are cast and ten are marked, but are illegal and two are blank, the number necessary for election would still be fifty or one over one-half of ninety-eight.

In the above example, the teller's report would be as follows:

Number of votes cast 98
Number necessary for election 50
Number cast for Mr. X 61
Number cast for Mr. Y 27

Illegal Votes

One ballot containing two for Mr. X
folded together 1
One ballot for Mr. Z, not a member
of the society 1
Number cast for Mr. A who is
ineligible 8

Notice this report includes the ten illegal ballots, but does not mention the two blanks.

413. TEMPORARY OFFICERS. The term pro tem or pro tempore means "for the time being" and is used to designate officers who are filling the post temporarily. The term is not applied, however, to an officer who is filling the post of another officer because it is his duty to do so. For example, one of the duties of the vice-president is to take the place of the president. When he fulfills this responsibility, he is not called president pro tem. There are three situations when temporary officers are used. (1) The officers of a temporary organization are officers pro tem. (2) In the formation of a permanent society, temporary officers, usually only a chairman and secretary, conduct the business until a constitution has been adopted and permanent officers elected. (3) When a regular officer is absent or wishes to abandon his office temporarily and there is no official substitute, an officer pro tem is appointed. For example, a secretary pro tem may be appointed in the absence of the regular secretary. Or if the president wishes to speak or make a motion and the vice-president is absent, the president may appoint another member to preside, He is president pro tem.

If an officer knows in advance that he is going to be absent from a meeting, he does not have the right to appoint a substitute. Such substitute must be elected by the body and his office is terminated by adjournment of the meeting or by the entrance of the regular officer.

414. TEMPORARY ORGANIZATION, FORMATION OF. The organizational procedure in setting up an occasional or mass meeting and in forming a temporary organization is the same. The steps are as follows:

1. When a group of persons decides to form a temporary organization or hold a mass meeting, they must decide on a time and place for the meeting, who shall be invited to the meeting, who shall call the meeting to order and who shall explain the purpose of the meeting. Sometimes they also decide who shall be nominated as temporary chairman and who shall do the nominating.

2. When those interested or those who have been invited come together, the person chosen to do so takes the chair and calls the meeting to order.

3. When the meeting has been called to order, the first business is that of securing a temporary chairman. This may be done in either of two ways:

A. The presiding officer may call for nominations and then declare the person whose name was first heard by him nominated and call for a vote on that name. If the name secures a majority vote, he is declared elected and he takes the chair as temporary chairman.

B. Or the presiding officer may call for nominations and when a number of names have been nominated and the nominations closed in the usual manner, the names are voted on and the name receiving the most votes is declared elected.

4. The temporary chairman, having taken the chair, then proceeds to secure a temporary secretary in the same manner.

5. The necessary officers now having been elected, the organization is complete and it proceeds to conduct whatever business it may wish.

6. When the business has been completed, the organization adjourns sine die.

415. TIE VOTE, EFFECT OF. Since most motions require a majority vote to pass, a tie vote defeats the motion. In a vote other than by ballot, the chairman has the right to vote only if his vote will change the result. If the question has an affirmative vote by one over a tie, the chair may vote "no" to create a tie and thus defeat the motion or measure. If the vote is a tie, the chair may vote "yes" to break the tie by giving the measure a majority.

416. TIME, METHOD OF FIXING, IN FILLING BLANKS. When an amendment is proposed for the purpose of filling blanks, the one least likely to be accepted is put first. In filling a blank with a date or a time, the most distant date or longest time is the first to be considered. For example, suppose it is proposed to allow a painter *blank* time to paint the meeting hall and suppose three times have been proposed — ten days, two weeks, and three weeks. The chair would take a vote on three weeks first. If a majority are willing to wait three weeks, that is the time with which the blank is filled. If this does not receive a majority vote, the chair moves to the next time (two weeks) and so on until a time does get a majority. In filling the blank with a date, it is wise to start the most distant and proceed toward the present.

417. TREASURER, DUTIES OF. The major function of the treasurer is to serve as custodian of the funds of the society. This includes receiving monies from various sources of income, keeping a record of receipts, banking, disbursement of monies upon order of the society and keeping a record of disbursements. The method of ordering disbursement of monies is determined by the society in its rules. Sometimes it is by order of the society, sometimes by a warrant signed by the president or by the president and the secretary. Sometimes the treasurer is authorized to pay out monies upon his personal recognition of the legitimacy of the claim. The treasurer should be prepared to report on the state of the treasury at all meetings. An annual report is always required and frequently an official quarterly report is a part of his responsibility. He is custodian of and should keep on file all receipts, cancelled checks, bills, warrants for the payment of bills, bank statements and all other papers pertaining to the funds of the society. He issues receipts for monies received. He is frequently a member of, and sometimes chairman of, the standing committee on ways and means.

418 TREASURER, REPORT OF. The treasurer should be prepared to report on the state of the treasury at any meeting of the society. Such reports are for information only and are not official, therefore, they usually contain only a statement of the balance on hand at the time of the last report, the total amounts received and paid out in the interim and the balance on hand at the time of the current report. Sometimes the report also contains a statement of anticipated income and unpaid obligations. Details in these reports are unnecessary and would only serve to confuse. Treasurer's reports are not accepted and no action is necessary, if the books are to be examined by an auditing committee; the report of the auditors is accepted instead. If the society does not have its books audited, the quarterly and/or annual reports of the treasurer are accepted.

419. TRIAL BY MEMBERS OF THE ASSEMBLY. Every assembly, society or organization has the right to require its members to live within the legal and moral code set up by the society. Therefore, the organization has the right to investigate the character and actions of its members. The society can request its members to testify and can punish them by expulsion if they refuse. When a charge is brought against the character of a member, it is usually referred to an investigating or disciplinary committee. Some organizations have a regular standing committee on discipline which reports any cases brought to its attention.

When a case is brought to the attention of a committee, whether standing or special, it investigates and reports. The committee report, while it need not go into complete detail, should make a recommendation of action and should contain resolutions to cover the case so it is unnecessary to make any additional resolutions from the floor. When it is recommended that a member be expelled from the society, the committee usually offers two resolutions. One fixes the time to which to adjourn and the second instructs the secretary to order the accused to appear before the assembly at the adjourned meeting to show cause why he should not be expelled.

As soon as charges have been preferred and the member notified to appear for trial, he is technically under arrest. He is deprived of all his rights as a member of the society until the trial is completed. A member should not be tried at the same meeting that he is accused unless he wishes it or unless the charge is something he has done at that meeting.

The secretary should notify the member in writing to appear at the appointed time and should include with this notice a copy of the charges against him. If the member fails to appear, it is usually sufficient reason for immediate expulsion.

If the member appears at the appointed time, he is given a form of trial with the membership of the society sitting in judgement. The committee again reports and frequently this is the only evidence necessary. However, the committee may offer additional evidence if it wishes. The accused member has the right to make any explination he wishes and introduce evidence and witnesses. Both parties have the right to cross-examine opposing witnesses and refute opposing testimony. If the accused wishes, he may be represented by counsel as long as the counsel is a member of the organization in good standing.

When all the evidence for both sides has been presented, the accused member should leave the room and the membership should consider the evidence and finally vote on the proposed punishment. The vote should be by ballot unless the evidence, one way or the other, is so overwhelming that the decision is reached by general consent. Expulsion should require a two-thirds vote with no less than a quorum voting including the members of the investigating committee.

There is considerable difference between a trial in a court of law and one in a society, organization or assembly. In court of law concrete evidence is necessary to convict. Common knowledge is not enough. In a society where the greatest punishment possible is expulsion, common knowledge or moral conviction is sufficient for a verdict of guilty.

Sometimes if the nature of the accusation is very delicate or it appears that the trial will be long and complicated, the accused appears before a committee instead of before the whole assembly. When this is done, the committee hears the evidence and reports its recommendations to the society. The committee offers resolutions to cover the punishment and the society acts on these resolutions. When the report of the committee is submitted, the accused is permitted to reply and then leaves the room while the society votes. All members of the society, except the accused, are permitted to vote.

420. TRUSTEES, BOARD OF. A board of trustees is one of the names given to a small deliberative group which represents a larger parent organization from which it derives its authority. (see also **BOARD OF MANAGERS.**)

421. TWO-THIRDS VOTE DEFINED. The term two-thirds vote is defined as two-thirds of the legal votes cast, not counting blanks in case of a ballot vote. If any other meaning is to be attached, such as two-thirds of the total membership or two-thirds of those present, it must be so specified.

422. TWO-THIRDS VOTE, DIFFERENT USES OF. A two-thirds vote is required for any motion which:
1. prevents consideration of a matter or prevents or restricts or extends debate.
2. interferes with the fundamanetal rights of members.
3. sets aside any rule of the society.
4. amends the fundamental laws of the society.
5. sets aside any vote previously taken unless previous notice has been given.

423. TWO-THIRDS VOTE, MOTIONS REQUIRING. In accordance with the basic principles regulating the use of the two-thirds vote, the following motions require a two-thirds vote to pass:
1. amend constitution, by-laws and rules of order.
2. amend standing rules unless previous notice has been given.
3. close debate (previous question)
4. limit or extend limits of debate.
5. close nominations
6. objection to consideration.
7. to make a special order of business.
8. postpone orders of the day.
9. rescind, repeal or annul unless previous notice has been given.
10. suspend the rules.
11. call up an order of the day before its alloted time.
12. take up a matter out of its proper order.
13. extend the time set for adjournment or taking a recess.
14. close the polls.
15. limit the number of candidates to be nominated for office.
16. expel from membership.
17. depose from office unless previous notice has been given.

424. TWO-THIRDS VOTE, PRINCIPLE REGULATING. It frequently happens that a conflict occurs between the rights of the individual and the rights of the society of which he is a member. For example, a conflict could occur between the right of the individual to make any motion he wishes and the right of the society to prevent the consideration of a question which is distastful or detrimental to it. The two-thirds vote has been established as a compromise between these opposing interests on the theory that if two-thirds of those voting wish to restrict the rights of the individual, he should agree to that restriction, but that his rights should not be restricted by a bare majority of those voting.

425. UNANIMOUS BALLOT. A vote cannot be made unanimous without the unanimous vote of the assembly. The motion to cast an unanimous ballot is defeated if it receives one negative vote. In an election, the motion to make the vote unanimous for the winning candidate should be made only by the candidate receiving the second highest number of votes or one of his friends. Even this cannot be done except by secret ballot if the election was by ballot. Even so, the unanimous vote is only complimentary and not legal. If the election is not by secret ballot and there is only one candidate, it is common practice to move to instruct the secretary to cast an unanimous ballot for the candidate. One negative vote defeats this motion. Frequently this motion is made in conjunction with the motion to close nominations, when only one name has been nominated. The motion is stated thus: "I move that nominations be closed and an unanimous ballot be cast for the candidate."

426. UNANIMOUS CONSENT. Unanimous consent (more frequently called "general consent" and less frequently "silent consent") is a device by which the chairman can expedite the conducting of business by avoiding the formality of making motions and/or voting by assuming that everyone agrees. Much of the business handled in meetings is routine or of little importance and may be handled in this way unless there is an objection. Perhaps the best example of the use of unanimous or general consent is the approval of the minutes of the last meeting. They are read and the chair says, "Are there any corrections?" He pauses and then says, "Hearing none, the minutes stand approved as read." This assumes that since no one spoke up, there were no corrections to be made. Secondly, it assumes that since there were no corrections, the assembly will approve the minutes as read and therefore there is no need to waste time by putting the matter to a vote.

This device may be used by the chairman at any time when he believes that there will be no objection. For example, when a committee announces that it is ready to report, the chair may say, "If there is no objection, we will receive the report of the committee on (naming the subject)."

Objection on the part of any member of the society will prevent the use of this device. If there is an objection, the chair simply reverts to the usual method of deciding the matter by putting it to a vote. Even though no objection is made, it does not necessarily mean that every

U

member is in favor of the motion. The opposed member may simply realize that it is useless to object since the matter would be passed anyway and so in the interest of facilitating business he does not object.

427. UNANIMOUS, DECLARING, WHEN VOTE IS NOT. It is a common practice, when an election is not held by ballot, for some member to move to make the vote unanimous for the winning candidate. This should never be done except by the runner-up or one of his supporters and even then it is a dubious compliment and only that. A motion to make the vote unanimous is defeated by one negative vote.

428. UNDEBATABLE MOTIONS. The following motions are not open to debate and are put by the chair as soon as they are seconded if a second is required or as soon as they are made if no second is required:
1. fix the time to which to adjourn (when priviliged).
2. adjourn (when unqualified and made in an assembly that has provided for future meetings).
3. take a recess (when privileged).
4. call for the orders of the day.
5. any motion relating to the priority of business.
6. appeal from the decision of the chair.
7. suspension of the rules.
8. objection to consideration of the question.
9. point of order.
10. parliamentary inquiry.
11. leave to withdraw a motion.
12. division of the question.
13. division of the house.
14. lay on the table.
15. previous question.
16. limit debate.
17. extend limits of debate.
18. amend an undebatable motion.
19. reconsider an undebatable motion.
20. dispense with the reading of the minutes.

429. UNFINISHED BUSINESS, EFFECT OF ADJOURNMENT UPON. The effect of an adjournment upon unfinished business is as follows, unless the organization has adopted rules of its own to the contrary:

1. If the adjournment does not end the session (see **SESSION AND MEETING, DISTINCTION BETWEEN**) the interrupted business becomes the first in order at the next meeting after the reading of the minutes. It is treated exactly the same as if no adjournment had taken place because an adjourned meeting which does not end a session is legally the continuation of the previous meeting of which it is an adjournment.

2. If an organization has regular sessions as often as quarterly, when the last meeting of a session is adjorned and thus the adjournment closed the session (such as the last meeting of a session of Congress), the same situation as (1) pertains. That is, the interrupted business is taken up at the first meeting of the next session exactly where it was broken off by the adjournment. The exception to this rule is in elected bodies where either all or part of the membership is elected for a definite term. In this case, the unfinished business which was interrupted by the adjournment becomes dead with the expiration of the term for which all or part of the organization was elected. For example, if a piece of business is interrupted by adjournment of the last meeting of a session and if there is an election of membership in the interval between that session and the next session, then the interrupted business does not hold over and must be introduced as new business just as though it had not previously been brought up. Thus members of an organization who have been defeated for reelection, but who are continuing to meet while finishing their term cannot force their successors to consider a piece of business, because they cannot postpone it nor make it a special order of business if either an election or a change of membership intervenes.

3. If the organization does not meet as often as quarterly and business is interrupted by adjournment which closes a session, the interrupted business is also dead at the end of the session. As in the case of elected bodies as stated above, the interrupted business may be introduced at the next session just as though it had never been considered before.

430. UNFINISHED BUSINESS, ITS PLACE IN THE ORDER OF BUSINESS. Unfinished business is any matter which has been before the assembly previously and was not disposed of or any business which was pending when the previous meeting was adjourned. This includes business "postponed to the next meeting" or "general postponement" which means the same thing. In the order of business, unfinished business follows "special orders" and precedes "new business."

431. VACANCIES IN OFFICE, FILLING. Vacancies in office may occur as the result of a number of contingencies. The officer may become incapacitated through illness, injury or death, he may be forced to vacate the office by the necessity of moving away, he may resign from the society, or he may simply be disinclined to continue and resign from the office. Also an office may become vacant as the result of the removal of an officer. Regardless of the reason for the occurance of the vacancy, it is filled in one of three ways.

1. The office may be filled automatically by the officer next in line. This is true of the succession of the vice-president to the presidency. Of course, this leaves a vacancy in the office of the vice-president which is filled in another manner. In the case of a first, second, third, etc. vice-president, if a vacancy occurs in the presidency, the first vice-president succeeds him and each vice-president moves up, leaving a vacancy in the last vice-presidency only.

2. If no succession of officers is provided for, the vacancy may be filled by appointment of a successor by the president or the board of director.

3. Or an election may be held, at the call of the president, to fill the vacancy.

A method for filling vacancies should always be provided in the rules of the society.

432. VICE-PRESIDENT, DUTIES OF. The vice-president has two basic responsibilities in the ordinary society. He takes the place of the president when the president is absent or wishes to vacate the chair for purposes of debate or to make a motion. The vice-president succeeds to the presidency in case of the resignation, removal or incapacity of the president. In addition, he is a member of the executive committee (or its equivalent) if there is one. Other duties may be specifically assigned to him by the by-laws of the society. In some organizations such as corporations, various vice-presidents have charge of different departments of work such as, vice-president in charge of production.

433. VICE-PRESIDENT, SUCCESSION TO OFFICE OF PRESIDENT. If the vice-president takes the place of the president temporarily to enable the president to make a motion or to debate or because of the absence of the president, this is not considered as succession to the office. On the other hand, if the vice-president takes over the presidency to complete the unexpired term of the president, he has

272

succeeded to the office. This distinction is important because it may have a bearing on the number of terms an officer has served when the rules of the society place a limit on the number of successive terms an individual may hold the same office.

434. VIVA VOCE OR VOICE VOTE. The most common method of voting is by voice or viva voce. Although it is the least accurate, it is the easiest and quickest and is entirely adequate in most instances because most questions will either pass or fail by a large majority so the difference in the number of voices is easily determined. In taking a vote by voice, the chairman says, "All those in favor of the motion make it known by saying 'aye'. Those opposed say 'no'." By the volume of sound, he determines whether the motion has passed or failed.

435. VOTE. Voting is the democratic method of settling issues and determining policy. Since it is an integral part of Democracy, people are properly jealous of their right to vote. For this reason, the chairman should exercise great care in conducting a vote, to prevent any stigma from becoming attached to the process. The procedure in handling most issues is as follows; a motion is made, seconded and stated by the chair. It is then ready for debate. During the process of debating the motion, it may be changed by amendment, if desired. When debate is completed, the chair restates the motion and puts it to a vote. The result of the vote is announced and the issue is settled.

436. VOTE, ABSENTEE. An absent member of a strictly deliberative body cannot vote. This is especially true in governmental bodies, the state legislatures and the United States Congress. In such organizations as these, the members must be present when the vote is called for. Many organizations such as national societies, however, have a membership which is so scattered that it is virtually impossible to get them all together at any one time.

When it is desirable to secure as nearly a total vote as possible, two methods of absentee voting are available. These are by mail and by proxy. Voting by mail is allowed in governmental elections, but proxy voting is prohibited. However, absentee voting must be provided for in the rules.

Absentee voting by mail is used in elections in societies which are widely scattered and in organizations which seldom or never meet. It may be used also if a member must be absent, but wishes to express his opinion on an issue which he knows is to be decided.

Proxy voting is permitted only if provision for it is made in the rules of the society and if the proxy is given in writing. In this case a member may give his proxy to another member who then votes for both on all issues or on such issues as are specified in the proxy. In proxy voting, it should be noted that governmental law is above the rules of the club, society or organization. Thus if the laws of the state allow members of corporations to appoint proxies the only recourse for such a secret lodge or society is not to incorporate.

437. VOTE, ANNOUNCING THE RESULT OF. When a motion has been properly made, seconded, debated, put and voted on, it becomes the duty of the chair to announce the result of the vote. When a voice vote is used, the chair says, "All those in favor of the motion to . . . . make it known by saying 'aye'. Those opposed 'no'. The ayes (or noes) have it and the motion is carried (or lost)" depending on which side has the majority. If the vote is close and the chair cannot decide which side has won, it is wise for him to change the method of voting. He should say: "The chair is in doubt. All those in favor of the motion to . . . . make it known by raising the right hand. Down hands (after count). Those opposed raise their right hands. The ayes (or noes) have it and the motion is carried (or lost)." The chair has the right to ask the secretary to assist him in the count and to consult with him to determine the accuracy of the count. If the vote is a tie and the chair does not wish to vote in the affirmative, he announces the tie and declares the vote lost. If it is a tie and he wishes to vote in the affirmative, he announces that it is a tie vote, announces his vote for the affirmative and declares the motion passed.

438. VOTE BY AUTHORIZING CASTING OF UNANIMOUS BALLOT. A vote cannot be made unanimous without the unanimous vote of the assembly. The motion to cast an unanimous ballot is defeated if it receives one negative vote. In an election, the motion to make the vote unanimous for the winning candidate should be made only by the candidate receiving the second highest number of votes or one of his friends. Even this cannot be done except by secret ballot if the election was by ballot. Even so, the unanimous vote is only complimentary and not legal. If the election is not by secret ballot and there is only one candidate, it is common practice to move to instruct the secretary to cast an unanimous ballot for the candidate. One negative vote defeats this motion. Frequently this motion is made in conjunction with the motion to close nominations; when only one name has been nominated. The motion is stated thus: "I move that nominations be closed and an unanimous ballot be cast for the candidate."

439. VOTE BY BALLOT. Voting by ballot is the most secret method of voting and this is its main attribute. It is the most time-consuming and therefore should be used in the ordinary society only when secrecy is desired.

When the vote is by ballot, the chair should allow a reasonable amount of time to vote and then should ask if all have voted. If no one objects, he should instruct the tellers to collect the ballots. Tellers are usually appointed on the spot by the chairman. Sometimes in larger groups the motion is made to close the polls. The chair should not entertain such a motion until he is certain that all have voted who wish to do so. This motion requires a two-thirds vote. If it is desired to reopen the polls, it may be done by a motion to that effect which requires only a majority vote. Neither the motion to close the polls nor the motion to reopen them is debatable.

Because of its secrecy, voting by ballot is used whenever there is a possibility that members might hesitate to express their preference publicly. Most organizations use it in elections and in taking in and expelling members.

If two ballots are folded together and both are marked, both should be rejected and counted as one fraudulent vote, but if a blank piece of paper is folded with an otherwise legal ballot, the ballot is considered legal. Persons not wishing to cast a vote and not wishing to reveal the fact may turn in a blank piece of paper. Such blanks are merely discarded and are not counted as fraudulent ballots. Misspellings and other slight errors do not invalidate a ballot as long as the meaning is clear.

When the rules of an organization require that a vote be taken by ballot, it is out of order to make any motion which cannot be opposed by members without exposing their views on the pending motion. For example, if the rules require that the vote on motion "X" be by secret ballot and the result of such vote is not unanimous, it cannot be moved that a unanimous ballot be cast because opposition to this motion would reveal that the member had not voted in favor of motion "X".

Secret ballot may be required by the passage of a motion to this effect. Such a motion requires a majority vote.

440. VOTE BY GENERAL CONSENT. Vote by general consent (sometimes called "silent consent" or erroneously "unanimous consent") is a device by which the chairman can expedite the conducting of business by avoiding the formality of making motions and/or voting by assuming the fact that everyone agrees. Much of the business handled in meetings is routine or of little importance and may be handled in this way providing that there is no objection. Perhaps the best example of the use of general consent is the approval of the minutes of the last meeting. They are read and the chair says, "Are there any corrections?" He then pauses and says, "Hearing none, the minutes stand approved as read." This assumes two things: First, it assumes that since there were no corrections to be made, the assembly will approve the minutes as read. Secondly, there is no need to waste time by putting the matter to vote.

This device may be used by the chairman at any time when he believes that there will be no objection. For example, when a committee announces that it is ready to report, the chair may say, "If there is no objection, we will receive the report of the committee on (naming the subject)."

Objection on the part of any member of the society will prevent the use of this device. If there is an objection, the chair simply reverts to the usual method of deciding the matter by putting it to a vote. Even though no objection is made, it does not necessarily mean that every member is in favor of the motion. The opposed member may simply realize that it is useless to object since the matter would be passed anyway and so in the interest of facilitating business, he does not object.

441. VOTE BY MAIL. When the membership of an organization is so scattered that it is virtually impossible to get them to a meeting or when it is desired to get as nearly an unanimous vote as possible, vote by mail is the only solution; also, this method is used even when the membership is not scattered, but when it would be waste of valuable time to call a meeting merely for the purpose of voting on a single issue. Some organizations, such as the faculty of a large university, use this method almost exclusively. It has the advantage of being convenient, but there is the disadvantage of not being able to hold open debate on the issue before the vote is cast.

When an amendment to the constitution or by-laws or a proposal is to be voted on, the proposed amendment or proposal should be printed on the ballot or on a separate sheet enclosed with the ballot. Also it is sometimes permitted to include the arguments for and against the proposal. A return, self-addressed envelope should be enclosed, one marked, "Ballot for . . . . (state the issue)," to be placed inside the self-addressed one. The voter should place his signature on the inner envelope. In order for the tellers to prevent fraudulent voting, it is necessary for them to check the envelopes against a list of the names of the membership. For this reason, vote by mail cannot be a secret ballot.

442. VOTE BY PROXY. Proxy voting is a method by which a member is granted permission, in writing, to vote in the place of another member. An absent member may request another member to vote for him on all questions that come up at a given meeting or he may restrict the proxy to a certain matter or matters. If a member holds one proxy, it means that he may vote twice, once for himself and once for the person whose proxy he holds. In corporations, where the right to vote is determined by the possession of transferable stock, state law often permits proxy voting. In the ordinary society, proxy voting is not a good practice. It is never allowed or permitted unless specifically provided for in the rules of the society and unless the proxy is given in writing by the absent member.

443. VOTE BY RISING. Standing or rising vote is one of the common methods of voting. Because it is more accurate than voting by voice or even a show of hands, it is used if the vote is likely to be close or when it is desired to record the exact number of votes on each side. This frequently happens when a motion requires a two-thirds vote. If the chair has taken a vote by voice and he is in doubt concerning the outcome, he says, "The chair is in doubt," and then orders a vote either by standing or by a show of hands. When division of the assembly is demanded, the vote is by rising. The proper procedure in taking a standing vote is as follows; the chair says, "All those in favor of the motion make it known by rising." He then counts those standing and says, "Be seated. All those opposed please rise." After counting the negative vote, he says, "Be seated," and announces the result.

444. VOTE BY ROLL CALL. Voting by yeas and nays or roll call as it is more commonly called, is one of the most time consuming and least used methods of voting. Since it is not common practice, it is customary to use it only upon demand. The motion to vote by roll call requires a second and majority vote. Roll call vote is used more frequently in representative bodies because the members represent a constituency which has the right to know how their representative voted on issues directly concerning them.

When a roll call vote has been ordered, the chair says, "When your name is called, those in favor of the motion will answer 'yes' (or yea) and those opposed will answer 'no' (nay)." He then orders the secretary to call the roll. The names are called in alphabetical order except the chair whose name is called last (provided he has the right to vote). A member may vote yes or no or he may answer "present" if he does not wish to vote. The secretary records the vote beside each name, usually in a separate column for each possible answer. In order to eliminate any possible error, when the vote is completed, the secretary re-reads the roll and repeats the vote recorded beside each name. The result is given to the chair who announces the outcome of the vote. The roll sheet upon which the vote was recorded becomes a part of the minutes of the meeting.

Roll call vote cannot be ordered in committee of the whole.

445. VOTE BY SHOW OF HANDS. Of the several methods of voting, the "show of hands" is one of the most common. When an issue is put by the chairman, he says, "All those in favor make it known by raising your right hand." The hands are raised and counted by the chairman or secretary or both if it is desired to double check. The chairman then says, "Down hands; all those opposed raise your right hand." The negative vote is counted and the vote announced. This method of voting is more accurate than a voice vote, but less accurate, especially in large assemblies, than a standing vote or a vote by ballot. One difficulty is that people do not raise their hands high enough to be certain that they are voting. Also hands are frequently lowered before they are counted.

446. VOTE, CHAIRMAN ENTITLED TO, WHEN IT AFFECTS RESULT. The chairman always has the right to vote if the vote is cast by written ballot, however, his ballot must be cast with the rest of the membership and not after the polls are closed or the tellers have

278

commenced to count the ballots. In all other methods of voting, the presiding officer may vote if his vote will change the result. There are four conditions under which this is the case.

1. When the issue requires a majority vote to pass and the actual vote is a tie, the chairman may vote in the affirmative, but not in the negative. A tie vote does not give a majority to the issue and therefore the motion is lost. An affirmative vote by the chairman will cause the issue to be passed and thus change the decision.

2. When the issue requires a majority vote to pass and the affirmative has one more vote than the negative (yes - 16 . . . .no -15, for example), the chair may cast a negative vote, but not affirmative. An affirmative vote will not change the result because the issue has passed anyway, but a negative vote will create a tie and cause the issue to be lost.

3. When the issue requires a two-thirds vote to pass and it lacks one (yes - 15 . . . .no - 8, for example), the chair may vote yes, but may not vote no. A no vote would not change the decision since the issue is lost anyway, but a yes vote would give the affirmative two-thirds and thus cause it to pass.

4. When the issue requires a two-thirds vote to pass and has exactly that (yes - 16 . . . .no - 8, for example), the chair may vote no, but may not vote yes because since the issue already has two-thrids, it has passed anyway, but a no vote would prevent a two-thirds majority and thus change the decision.

447. VOTE, CHANGE OF, PERMITTED BEFORE RESULT IS ANNOUNCED. Unless the vote is by ballot, a member has the right to change his vote at any time before the result of the vote is finally announced. After the result of the vote is announced, a member may change his vote only by permission of the assembly which may be granted by general consent or by means of a motion which is undebatable, unamendable and requires a majority vote.

448. VOTE, DECLARING UNANIMOUS WHEN IT IS NOT. It is a common practice, when an election is not held by ballot, for some member to move to make the vote unanimous for the winning candidate. This should never be done except by the runner-up or one of his supporters and even then it is a dubious compliment and only that. A motion to make the vote unanimous is defeated by one negative vote.

279

449. VOTE, EFFECT OF A TIE. Since most motions require a majority vote to pass, a tie vote defeats the motion; in a vote other than by ballot, the chairman has the right to vote only if his vote will change the result. If the question has an affirmative vote of one over a tie, the chair may vote "no" and create a tie and thus defeat the the measure. If the vote is a tie, the chair may vote "yes" to break the tie by giving the measure a majority.

450. VOTE, MAJORITY. In voting, a majority is defined as more than half of the votes cast. Blank votes or ballots are not counted as a vote cast, but illegally marked ballots are counted.

451. VOTE, NOT IN ORDER TO ADJOURN DURING. The motion to adjourn enjoys a very high rank in the precedence of motions. For this reason, it is sometimes misused to disrupt business or prevent the conducting of business. The chairman has the right to refuse to recognize the motion if it is proposed for this purpose. The motion to adjourn is never in order (except in case of emergency or disaster) while a vote is being taken. If a vote is taken and a division of the house is called for, the motion to adjourn is out of order until the vote has been retaken since this is still a part of the process of taking the original vote. When the vote is by ballot, it is in order to adjourn before the ballots have been counted and the result announced, if the actual voting is completed.

452. VOTE, PLURALITY. The term plurality vote is used only in elections. When there are more than two candidates, the candidate who receives the highest number of votes is said to have a plurality and wins the election even though he has not received a majority of the votes.

453. VOTE, PUTTING THE QUESTION TO. The process of putting the question or motion to a vote involves several steps which are:
1. the chair asks; "Are you ready for the question?" or "Is there any further discussion?"
2. the chair restates the motion.
3. the chair takes the affirmative vote.
4. the chair takes the negative vote.
5. the chair announces the result of the vote.

When it appears to the chair that the discussion on a motion is finished he asks, "Are you ready for the question?" or "Is there any further discussion?" If no one claims the floor to speak, he restates the motion and puts it to a vote by saying, "The motion is that we should do thus and so. All those in favor of the motion make it known by saying, 'aye'. (or whatever method of voting is to be used). Those opposed say, 'nay'." He then announces the result by saying, "The motion is carried" or "The motion is lost." This whole process is called putting the question because it puts the motion to a vote.

454. VOTE, TWO-THIRDS, DIFFERENT USES OF. A two-thirds vote is required for any motion which:
1. prevents consideration of a matter or prevents or restricts or extends debate.
2. interferes with the fundamental rights of members.
3. sets aside any rule of the society.
4. amends the fundamental laws of the society.
5. sets aside any vote previously taken unless previous notice has been given.

455. VOTE, TWO-THIRDS, MEANING OF. The term two-thirds vote is defined as two-thirds of the legal votes cast, not counting blanks in case of a ballot vote. If any other meaning is to be attached, such as two-thirds of the total membership or two-thirds of those present, it must be so specified.

456. VOTE, WHEN NULL AND VOID. Strictly speaking, from the legal point of view, an illegal vote is one cast by a person who is not eligible to vote. In the ordinary society, any vote by ballot is null and void if it is not intelligible or it is cast for an ineligible candidate. Misspellings do not invalidate a ballot if the intent is clear. Blank ballots are not null and void, they simply are not counted nor listed in the total votes cast. The only time a blank ballot is counted is in determining a quorum.

457. VOTING, PERSONAL INTERESTS DEBAR ONE FROM. It is a generally accepted rule that a member should refrain from voting on matters which concern him directly, either personally or financially. If a member is on trial, he is theoretically under arrest and so is deprived of his rights of membership. Even if he is not under arrest, a sense of propriety prevents him from voting on matters concerning himself. There are so many exceptions, however, that the right to vote in such matters is not prohibited, but merely established by the delicacy of the situation. For example, a member has the right to vote for himself when he is a candidate for office or membership on a committee. Also he has the right to vote when his vote will affect the decision. A member has the right to vote when others are involved with him. If this were not the case, a small minority could bring charges against the rest of the membership, since the majority could not vote, they could even be deprived of membership. If a member could never vote on any matter involving himself, the society could never vote to do anything which would benefit its members. The members could not vote to decrease the dues, for example, because each member would benefit financially from such decrease.

458. WITHDRAWAL OF A MOTION. Before a motion has been stated by the chair, the maker of the motion may withdraw or modify it without permission. After it has been stated it is the property of the assembly and the maker must be granted leave or permission to withdraw or modify it. If a motion has been made and seconded and the maker modifies it before it has been stated by the chair, the seconder may withdraw his second if he does not favor the motion as modified. After the motion has been stated, if permission is granted the maker to modify the motion, the second may be withdrawn.

If the maker wishes to withdraw his motion after it has been stated by the chair he says, "Mr, Chairman, I ask leave to withdraw the motion." The chair asks whether there is any objection and if there is none, the permission is granted. If there is objection, the request is put to a vote and can be granted by a majority vote. Also another member can move to grant leave to withdraw a motion. This motion does not require a second because it is presumed that the maker favors the withdrawal and this constitutes a second. Leave to withdraw a motion can be granted any time up to the taking of a vote and may be made even while incidental and secondary motions are pending. If the main motion is withdrawn, all secondary and incidental motions connected with it are also withdrawn. The motion to withdraw cannot be amended or have any secondary motions applied to it. It is undebatable. If a motion has been divided, one part may be withdrawn without affecting the rest of the motion.

459. WITHOUT DAY, ADJOURN. There is no such motion "to adjourn sine die (without day)." Sine die is a Latin term meaning "without day" and refers to the effect of adjournment on the future status of the society. If the simple, unqualified motion to adjourn is passed and if the organization has not made provision for a future meeting, then it is said to have adjourned without day and the effect is to dissolve the organization since a society which adjourns without any provision for another meeting has actually adjourned itself out of existence.

460. "WRITE-IN CANDIDATES," BLANK FOR. When elections are held by secret ballot and printed ballots with the names of the nominees on them are used, it is necessary to provide space for "write-in" candidates. Unless it is prohibited by the rule of the organization, members may vote for any eligible person whether or not he has been officially nominated.

Y

461. YEAS AND NAYS, VOTE BY. Voting by yeas and nays or roll call as it is more commonly called, is one of the most time-consuming and least used methods of voting. Since it is not common practice, it is usual to use it only upon demand. The motion to vote by roll call requires a second and majority vote. Roll call vote is used more frequently is representative bodies because the members represent a constituency which has the right to know how their representative voted especially on issues directly concerning them.

When a roll call vote has been ordered, the chair says, "When your name is called, those in favor of the motion will answer 'yes' (or yea) and those opposed will answer 'no' (nay)." He then orders the secretary to call the roll. The names are called in alphabetical order except the chair whose name is called last (provided he has the right to vote). A member may vote yes or no or he may answer "present" if he does not wish to vote. The secretary records the vote beside each name, usually in a separate column for each possible answer. In order to eliminate any possible error, when the vote is completed, the secretary re-reads the roll and repeats the vote recorded beside each name. The result is given to the chair who announces the outcome of the vote. The roll sheet upon which the vote was recorded becomes a part of the minutes of the meeting.

Roll call vote cannot be ordered in committee of the whole.

462. YIELDING THE FLOOR. When a member addresses the chair and is recognized by him, he is said to have the floor and is entitled to it for the purpose of debate or to make a motion for any other legal purpose. If another member wishes to interrupt the one who has the floor, he asks him to yield the floor. He addresses the chair and says, "Will the member yield the floor?" The chair relays the request and if the member yields the floor, it is turned over to the one requesting it. If a member wishes to ask a question of the speaker, he says, "Mr. Chairman, will the speaker yield to a question?" If the request is granted, the question is asked, answered and the speaker continues as if no interruption had taken place. The time consumed in asking and answering the question is deducted from speaking time of the speaker.

463. YIELDS. In the precedence of motions, if one motion takes precedence over a second motion, the second motion yields to the first.

For example, the motion to adjourn yields to the motion to fix the time of the next meeting because the latter takes precedence over the former.

APPENDIX

OUTLINE GUIDE
FOR A COURSE IN
PARLIAMENTARY PROCEDURE

The problem of developing a well organized course in parliamentary law is a difficult one because there is much over-lapping and it is practically impossible to consider one area of the subject without becoming involved with other areas. For this reason, it would seem wise to keep the organization of the course simple. The task is made somewhat easier by the fact that there is a basically logical approach. For example, it seems sensible to deal with the problems of organizing a society before considering such questions as conducting business and order of business. With this logical approach in mind, the following outline guide has been developed. The authors have used this outline in teaching both college and adult classes in parliamentary law for twenty years with only minor changes.

The numbers under the heading, "Reading assignment" refer to the article numbers in the text of this book. They are listed in numbered order and not with reference to any sub-area of this outline.

I.   Methods of organization.
  A. Temporary organizations.
  B. Semi-permanent organizations.
  C. Permanent organizations.
  D. Mass meetings.
  E. Conventions.
  F. Reading assignment.
      41 - 42 - 82 - 92 - 185 - 210 - 211 - 226 - 275 - 276 - 277 - 338
      - 366 - 387 - 414.

II. Rules.
  A. The constitution.
  B. The by-laws.
  C. The standing rules.
  D. The rules of order.
  E. The parliamentary authority.

F. Reading assignment.
    30 - 62 - 73 - 74 - 88 - 124 - 125 - 126 - 130 - 151 - 161 -
    162 - 163 - 177 - 178 - 179 - 259 - 260 - 261 - 282 - 283 - 292 -
    296 - 318 - 322 - 335 - 370 - 371 - 380 - 383 - 397 - 398 - 417 -
    432 - 433.

III. Order of business.
    A. Call to order.
    B. Roll call.
    C. Reading the minutes.
    D. Treasurer's report.
    E. Reports of standing committees.
    F. Reports of special committees.
    G. Correspondence.
    H. Special orders.
    I. Old business.
    J. New business.
    K. Announcements.
    L. Adjournment.
    M. Reading assignment.
        16 - 64 - 69 - 70 - 71 - 72 - 109 - 128 - 129 - 132 - 232 - 263 -
        264 - 268 - 269 - 270 - 271 - 272 - 273 - 274 - 295 - 410.

IV. Conducting business.
    A. Obtaining the floor.
    B. Making motions.
    C. Stating the motion.
    D. Discussing the motion.
    E. Putting the motion.
    F. Methods of voting.
    G. Committees and committee reports.
    H. Reading assignment.
        1 - 2 - 3 - 15 - 35 - 37 - 47 - 48 - 49 - 50 - 55 - 56 - 57 - 58 - 60 -
        61 - 65 - 66 - 67 - 77 - 78 - 79 - 80 - 81 - 84 - 85 - 87 - 91 - 96 -
        97 - 98 - 99 - 104 - 106 - 107 - 110 - 112 - 113 - 114 - 115 -
        116 - 117 - 118 - 119 - 121 - 123 - 127 - 131 - 133 - 134 - 135 -
        136 - 137 - 138 - 139 - 140 - 141 - 142 - 143 - 147 - 148 - 149 -
        152 - 157 - 159 - 160 - 166 - 168 - 169 - 170 - 171 - 172 - 173 -
        174 - 175 - 176 - 181 - 186 - 188 - 190 - 191 - 195 - 196 - 197 -

202 - 204 - 208 - 213 - 214 - 215 - 216 - 218 - 219 - 220 - 221 -
222 - 223 - 224 - 225 - 231 - 235 - 236 - 243 - 250 - 255 - 258 -
278 - 279 - 281 - 285 - 287 - 289 - 297 - 303 - 304 - 305 - 306 -
307 - 308 - 309 - 310 - 311 - 313 - 314 - 319 - 320 - 323 - 325 -
327 - 328 - 332 - 336 - 337 - 343 - 344 - 352 - 355 - 356 - 361 -
362 - 367 - 368 - 369 - 377 - 378 - 384 - 385 - 388 - 389 - 390 -
394 - 395 - 396 - 400 - 406 - 411 - 412 - 415 - 418 - 419 - 420 -
421 - 422 - 423 - 424 - 425 - 426 - 427 - 428 - 429 - 430 - 431 -
434 - 435 - 437 - 438 - 440 - 445 - 446 - 447 - 448 - 450 - 451 -
453 - 454 - 455 - 457 - 460 - 461 - 462.

V. Motions.

A. Forms of motions.
B. Purpose of motions.
C. Precedence of motions.
D. Reading assignment.

4 - 5 - 6 - 7 - 8 - 9 - 10 - 11 - 12 - 13 - 17 - 18 - 19 - 20 - 21 - 22
23 - 24 - 25 - 26 - 27 - 28 - 29 - 31 - 32 - 36 - 38 - 39 - 40 - 43 -
76 - 90 - 93 - 94 - 95 - 146 - 154 - 155 - 164 - 165 - 184 - 198 -
199 - 200 - 201 - 206 - 207 - 209 - 228 - 233- 234 - 239- 241 -
247 - 248 - 249 - 251 - 252 - 253 - 256 - 280 - 284 - 288 - 290 -
291 - 294 - 298 - 300 - 301 - 302 - 315 - 316 - 317 - 321 - 326 -
329 - 330 - 333 - 334 - 339 - 340 - 342 - 346 - 347 - 348 - 349 -
350 - 351 - 353 - 354 - 357 - 358 - 359 - 360 - 373 - 374 - 375 -
376 - 391 - 392 - 393 - 407 - 409 - 416 - 458 - 463.

A
B
C
D
E
F
G
H
I
J
L
M
N
O
P
Q
R
S
T
U
V
W
Y

DIRECTIONS
FOR USE OF
THUMB INDEX

- Place thumb on desired letter.
- Flip pages until the letter appears under thumb in the body of the book.
- Turn pages to the desired article.